LOOKING
AT GOD'S

IMPACT

ON YOU
& OTHERS

Devotional book

GW00362984

© Copyright 2013 Colin Tinsley

ISBN 978-1-909751-07-1 Impact On You And Others

Published by

Colin Tinsley
6 Hawthorn Hill, Kinallen, Dromore,
Co. Down, BT25 2HY, Northern Ireland.

www.hopeforyouthministries.org

Printed by JC Print Ltd Email: info@jcprint.net

Foreword

When you come to the end of your life and look back, will you be able to say you made an impact in someone's life? As you think upon the day of your conversion would you say God made an impact upon your life? Now then, is your opportunity to make an impact for God upon someone else's life. In this devotional, I have sought to encourage you how to do this. Every one of these devotions are fresh as the Lord challenged and inspired me to live for Him. Many of these were written as I journeyed around the world on mission trips from China to Poland, Israel to Lithuania. Life is a journey, don't waste your life, endeavour to start now desiring to make an impact for God in everything you do and everywhere you go.

Colin Tinsley   September 2013

Dedication

I would like to dedicate this book to all the volunteers within 'Hope for Youth Ministries' who encourage us along the Christian life. Your willingness to help out and do what needs done have impacted us more than you'll ever know. You have helped to make up teams on camps and trips where it would be impossible for Joanna and me to do the job. While you came to be a help and a blessing, like me you went away helped and blessed. That's what the Christian life is all about. May God bless you all as you seek to live for Him and serve Him. May your lives continue to impact many people along life's journey. Impact them for God to such a degree that irresistibly, they too will want to serve the Lord with all their heart, body, mind and soul. Keep going on for God!

Make an IMPACT

Psalm 69:1-9

"The zeal of thine house hath eaten me up." Psalm 69:9

As we begin a new year, there are many things we can be zealous about, many things that take up our time. Some of these are good and necessary. Others, if we are honest are not so important yet we can be so zealous about them. This brings us to focus on what is now important in our lives. Even in church work and being involved in our local church we can be so zealous and involved with running to meetings that it actually eats us up and we can starve spiritually.

In order to make an impact for God we must be sharp, focused and in touch with the Lord. Pray that the Lord will make you a zealous Christian. The zeal you had when you first got saved, ask the Lord to give it back to you. Whatever it is that is eating you up, needs to be sorted out before it overcomes you. Learn to say 'no', if you have to. It is better to do less, well, than to take on a lot and lose heart and do the job half hearted. Sometimes we can be so caught up with being busy that we can miss out on the blessing. This year, have aims and objectives as to what you want to do for the Lord. Keep focused and let nothing come between you and the Lord. Don't lose your zeal, maybe you have already lost it, ask the Lord to give it back to you, He will restore unto the years the locusts have eaten.

I will do a new thing

Isaiah 43:18-28

"Behold, I will do a new thing; now it shall spring forth; shall ye not know it? I will even make a way in the wilderness, and rivers in the desert." Isaiah 43:19

These verses certainly come with freshness to our souls. Maybe you are stuck in a rut and there doesn't seem to be any way out with you in your present situation. Well my friend take courage as from today. Sometimes we can continue to talk about the old days and how good they were because there doesn't seem to be anything happening today. We are told here in verse 18 to "Remember ye not the former things, neither consider the things of old." We are not to continually lament about how good the old days were. We are to think about the present and start looking to the future.

The Lord said to Isaiah, "Behold, I will do a new thing; now it shall spring forth; shall ye not know it? Maybe the time has come for the Lord to do a new thing in your life. Whatever it is that has been on your mind, the Lord is maybe just about to make it happen. He will do a new thing for you. The question is are you ready for change? Are you willing to let the Lord turn your life inside out and upside down for His glory? Are we willing to shut the gate of the past behind us and move on without looking back with regret? Sometimes our past needs to be left behind and completely forgotten. Are you willing to do that? God will not move in your life until you are fully surrendered to His will and not yours!

Being thankful

Psalm 136

"O give thanks unto the LORD; for he is good: for his mercy endureth for ever."

Psalm 136:1

Two things the Lord mentions many times in His Word are prayer and thanksgiving. Every time one thousand prayers are offered to the Lord, I would imagine there are very few thanksgiving petitions offered to the Lord. We tend to be very good at asking and expecting and yet when an answer comes our way in our favour sometimes better than we even imagined, why is it that we are not very thankful when the Lord has done so much for us. Ministers and Pastors come to my mind right now. All year round they do so much good to people, and the moment they slip up, people seem to be very ungrateful and unthankful.

On the other hand so many times we read of the Psalmist returning thanks unto the Lord. No matter what he has got or whatever situation he finds himself in, he continually thanks the Lord. This is one thing Joanna and I have tried to do since we got married, we wanted to be thankful for everything the Lord brings to us or takes away from us. We were born with nothing and we will leave with nothing. When we first got married we had very little of material wealth, so anything we have as a result belongeth to the Lord. Anything we lose was never ours to start with so we give the Lord thanks for that too. Challenging at times, but the blessing that comes after from the Lord is indescribable. In everything and in every situation give thanks unto the Lord.

IMPACT *Daily readings*

The ministry of women!

Judges 4:1-21

"Deborah, a prophetess......judged Israel at that time." Judges 4:4

Sometimes we can be prone to thinking that the only work that is to be done for the Lord is by men. This is so far from the truth. Of course the scriptures have laid down specific guide lines for the role of women within the church. But there are so many aspects of the Lords work and so many areas where everyone can get involved.

Deborah was raised up as a prophetess and in so many ways did a wonderful work for the Lord. Through her bravery to go with Barak to battle, against Sisera, the Lord gave them a wonderful victory. Deborah was not afraid of the battles; she went straight into them guided by the Lord. She was prepared to do what she would expect others to do.

It all culminated in the terrible death of Sisera, at the hands of Deborah, a woman. When running away from the battle, he took shelter in the tent of Heber, whose wife was Jael. While Sisera slept, through sheer exhaustion, Jael took a large tent nail and with a hammer, drove it right through his skull into the ground. At Sisera's home, his mother looked out the window, watching for the son who would never come back (Judges 5:28)

Are you a female? God has a great work for you to do, so don't allow any prejudice or opinions of men stop you from serving. In the work we do, we have lots of volunteers and most of them, in fact the best and often the most useful ones are the girls. Many a girl has put many a man to shame. Be like Deborah, the judge of Israel, and do what you can to advance the cause of Christ.

Every Christian's responsibility

Ezekiel 3:15-27

"Son of man, I have made thee a watchman....... hear the word at my mouth, and give them warning from me." Ezekiel 3:17

This is one of the passages in the Bible that needs to be read carefully. It is extremely challenging as we ponder what it really means and of what our duty and responsibility is in being a Christian. From reading this portion, I understand that every person we come into contact with needs to hear the Gospel. We will give account before the Lord on that great day of why we failed to warn the people we met of their need of Christ. What they do after you tell them is no longer your problem, but we must warn them by telling them.

Your friends will die and go to hell if they are not saved. Their blood will be our responsibility; the Lord requires it from us. We must stand before the Lord and tell Him why we were ashamed of Him, why we never took the opportunity when the Lord gave it to us, why we shied away from the opportunity of telling our friends about the love of Christ.

"Whosoever therefore shall be ashamed of me and of my words in this adulterous and sinful generation; of him also shall the Son of man be ashamed, when he cometh in the glory of his Father with the holy angels." Mark 8:38

When the Lord sends you to warn a sinner of their sinful condition before God, then it is best to go immediately and tell them. The Lord has opened the door, He has prepared the way. Go and take the opportunity. Your very action might be the very means of rescuing your friends from an eternity without God.

Pray about everything

Zechariah 8:1-23

"Yea, many people and strong nations shall come to seek the LORD of hosts in Jerusalem, and to pray before the LORD." Zechariah 8:22

Praying is simply talking to the Lord. God loves it when we talk to Him. Imagine how a parent would feel if their child got up in the morning and never spoke to them. Then after a whole day at school still never spoke to them but rather just ignored them, talked and laughed with everyone else but them. Then the next day the same thing happened and the day after that the same thing happened. Eventually the parent would feel deeply saddened that their child had chosen to go through life without them.

Or in a relationship, I can imagine how Joanna would feel if I never made a fuss over her, and talked to her from morning till night, even calling her when I'm away for a certain length of time. She would feel sad, although sometimes when I come home late and she is already sleeping and I begin to tell her about my day, sometimes then it can be a different story. That goes without saying as I'm normally fully alert at night and want to chat although at the same time I also tend to be a morning person.

Yet in a similar way the Lord tells us to pray without ceasing about everything. God already knows everything, but He is pleased none the less when we come before Him and pray. No matter what is on your heart, good or bad, glad or sad bring it before the Lord in prayer. He promises to answer our prayers, but how can the Lord help us if we choose not to ask Him in the first place. The Psalmist was often in great trouble and in his trouble he called upon the Lord, what an example he sets before us to follow.

Those who envy us

Genesis 26:1-14

"For he had possession of flocks, and possession of herds, and great store of servants: and the Philistines envied him." Genesis 26:14

God had blessed Abraham and now He continued to bless Isaac, Abraham's son. All seemed to go well with Isaac. Even though he was far from perfect, he was a child of God. It seemed to be that everything he turned his hand to the Lord seemed to bless him. He had become rich with his farming; he had lots of servants, flocks of sheep and herds of cattle.

It is true with life, the more we seem to be blessed there are those who will envy us. Jealousy is a terrible thing, wives get jealous of wives, husbands of husbands, farmers of other farmers and the list goes on. Sadly in the Christian life, the same problem seems to occur. The more active you are in the Lord's work, sadly the more other Christians will envy you and become jealous of you. They may even start to gossip and spread rumours about you, making up lies and allegations about you, your life and even your very motive for serving God. Sadly a lot of good Christian workers have thrown in the towel and given in to the pressure from the Philistines out there who seek to destroy the work of God. Don't give up in the battle, it may become intense but don't give up. Keep battling on and don't let those who envy you conquer you.

The silent missionary!

Ecclesiastes 11:1-6

"Cast thy bread upon the waters; for thou shalt find it after many days." Ecclesiastes 11:1

Sometimes we are afraid to speak to someone about the Lord Jesus because we assume they are not interested in the Lord. If the person who first spoke to you thought that, where would you be today? There is another way of reaching people with the gospel without speaking to them; it is the gospel in print. This can be a very dependable missionary! It never flinches or shows cowardice, is never tempted to compromise, tires or becomes discouraged.

It can travel cheaply, it doesn't require a hired building, It works while others are sleeping, never loses its temper, it can continue to minister from generation to generation. It can reach those who, otherwise, might never be reached. It points the way to eternal life through Jesus Christ. A pamphlet written by Martin Luther fell into the hands of John Bunyan, through which he was eventually converted. The outcome was the immortal "Pilgrim's Progress."

Some people think you have to be gifted to give out tracts, this is nonsense. You can post them; leave them here and there at convenient places for someone to pick up. I know a man called Billy who walked the streets of Lisburn for years; people looked upon him as a beggar and a tramp. Little did they realise that he loved the Lord, his pockets were always full of tracts, every day he walked the streets, dropping off tracts in the shops, telephone boxes, wherever people's hands would be, they would find a tract, and I often wonder did they ever wonder who kept putting them there.

This is one way of reaching people with the Gospel. Let the printed page speak of itself, all you have got to do, is get it into someone's hand. Who is on your mind right now? Then send the silent missionary to them and let the Lord do His work.

IMPACT *Daily readings*

The fourth man

Daniel 3:13-30

"Our God, whom we serve, is able to deliver us." Daniel 3:7

Can you imagine for one moment the test that these three young men were about to go through? Shadrach, Meshach, and Abednego, the close friends of Daniel, refused to bow down to the ugly idol which Nebuchadnezzar had set up. The penalty for such refusal was to be burned to death in the flames of the furnace. Their love for God was very great. Nothing was going to come between them and their love for God. They were willing to die rather than re-cant their faith. Their love for God was real and very strong.

How would you have re-acted if you were placed in a similar situation? Most of us will never go through having to make such a serious decision, but imagine for a moment if you did, what would you do? There are many idols all around you today, to which idol are you bowing down to today? Anything that takes the place of God in our conversation, action or even general living without God, is a form of idol.

The wonderful part of the story is when the king looked in and when he was expecting to see three men, he saw four. "Did not we cast three men bound into the midst of the fire? Lo, I see four men....and the form of the fourth is like the Son of God." Indeed it was! Jesus, the blessed Son of God, was walking with his faithful servants through the fire. Not even a hair of their head was singed! Remember as you walk through the fires of this life, affliction, persecution, or misunderstanding; remember that you do not walk alone. You may not escape the fire, but Jesus will deliver you in the fire!

Let the Lord have His way!

1 Kings 12:21-24

"....this thing is from me." 1 Kings 12:24

King Rehoboam, the son of Solomon, had gathered around him an army of soldiers, one hundred and eighty thousand warriors. His intention was to fight against the house of Israel. Suddenly the word came to Shemaiah, a man of God, to command the vast army to withdraw. Part of his message contained these words, "this thing is from me." Although the king and his troops probably could not understand at the time, we read that, "they hearkened unto the word of the Lord."

Are your present circumstances confusing and, at times, you just don't know where to turn, or what to do? Something has happened recently which has completely mystified you. You try to explain it but cannot, you try to understand it, but you cannot. You try to work it out, but it just cannot be worked out. Maybe what is going on in your life right now is what you need. The secret is to let the Lord have His way in your life every day. God brings things and people into your life at times when you least expect them. Sometimes the Lord says advance, wait or withdraw. Take this word to heart, "this thing is from me."

The Lord is full of love and compassion; He never makes mistakes and is never wrong in His judgement of you. Sometimes one of the secrets in life is to trust where you cannot see, it then becomes exciting, wondering what the Lord has in store for your life. We all make mistakes, but they are not always mistakes, God has a plan in all things. Let Him have our plans, then we can let the Lord have His way, whatever way that will be, may it truly be from the Lord!

Discouraged because of the way

Numbers 21:1-5
"And the soul of the people was much discouraged
because of the way." Numbers 21:4

Discouragement is a hateful thing that often leads to bitterness, disappointment, murmuring and gossip. It is not God's will for you to be discouraged all the time, therefore if you are continually discouraged and find yourself doing all of the above, not only are you missing out on God's best for your life, but in effect could be out of God's will and plan for your life.

Israel's desire was to walk through Edom to get to the Promised Land, but Edom refused them entry. As a result they had to walk much further than they had anticipated. Due to the length and way of the journey, discouragement set in. They were now taking the same journey, same rocks, same sand, same old route that they had come to despise.

Is this like you? Have you come to despise life's journey, same old thing day after day? Have you become discouraged because of the way of life? Maybe by now you thought you would have gained what all others around you seem to have got and it hasn't worked out, job, marriage, children or something about your life or your health that discourages you greatly. The lesson is simple, we all need to get a fresh vision of the Promised land, the land that is promised to us. One day all will be revealed as to the reason why it is this way, for now that is, don't give up, don't be discouraged because of the way.

The Lord doesn't change!

Malachi 3:1-6

"For I am the Lord; I change not." Malachi 3:6

A little boy was saying his prayers one night and his mummy was listening in. The next day the whole family were moving house to a different town. He said this, "Well, now, good bye God, tomorrow we are leaving and it was really nice knowing you in this house, if you want to come with us, mummy says we are leaving just after breakfast."

Little did that little boy realise that the Lord was already there waiting for him before he even woke up the next morning. It is such a wonderful, humbling thing listening to children pray.

Have your circumstances changed recently? Maybe you find yourself in new surroundings, in an entirely different environment, college, work, home, church. It can be exciting, yet daunting at the same time. Isn't it lovely to know, whatever changes may come, Jesus remains the same? People come and people go all the time, things are always changing, time is swiftly passing, yet the Lord doesn't change. Methods, ways and means for living are always changing. We feel we must jump on the wagon to keep up with the fast speed of life. God doesn't change. In fact the faster life becomes for us, in some ways the more difficult it often is to keep in regular touch with God.

We should never let the speed of life distract us from a loving relationship with God. Always keep your focus on Him. He will not let you down. He won't push or rush you. Rather the Lord says "calm down"! Always keep in mind the words of Hebrews 13:8 "Jesus Christ, the same yesterday, and today, and forever."

IMPACT *Daily readings*

The hidden secret!

Job 15:1-11

"Is there any secret thing with thee?" Job 15:11

Job had three friends, the eldest and wisest of these friends was Eliphaz. He was of a noble and dignified character, firm in his opinions of plain, common sense. He gave Job wise advice, which also contained a word of warning. He asked Job "Is there any secret thing with thee?" This a very deep searching question. Would such a question bring conviction to you? Is there anything in your life, secret to you, but not, of course to God?

Remember the words in Genesis 16:13 "Thou, God, seest me" If there should be any secret sin in your life, be wise and have it dealt with. If you continue to try and conceal it, it will grow and fester within you. It will drive you further and further from God. No matter who may be offended, or what may be your loss, expose it before God, and have it put under the power of the precious Blood of Christ. Take this warning seriously, do it today. The Lord will forgive you and even forget all about it, but you must come clean before Him.

Job's friend could have become an enemy, but that is why he was a true friend, he helped Job with something, many would be afraid to touch. A true friend is an honest friend, one you could trust with even your deepest secrets.

IMPACT *Daily readings*

The rising generation!

Deuteronomy 6:1-9
"And thou shalt teach them diligently unto thy children." Deuteronomy 6:7

A father, who was a professing believer, was having a personal chat with his young son, explaining what a Christian should be and how he should act. After he finished, the boy looked enquiringly into his face and asked the pointed question: "But, Daddy, have I ever seen a Christian?" What a rebuke! The father was both dumbfounded, and humiliated, realising, in those moments, how much he had failed.

In the Scripture passage we have today, Moses was being very definite about how God's law should be displayed in the homes of the people. He was especially concerned that the children should be taught the commandments of the Lord from their early years.

Now, in our present age, instead of scripture texts in the rooms of the children, there are television sets, computers, play stations and smart phones. The challenge today is great to teach the rising generation the things of God. The devil is having such a field day in the minds and hearts of the children when we think of the hours of worldly entertainment they receive compared to the few minutes of Bible teaching they may receive.

Read verse seven again and think of the challenge that lies before every Christian parent to teach and instruct their children in the things and ways of God, not just parents but those who have any influence in instructing children in the ways of God.

IMPACT *Daily readings*

Where have you gleaned today?

Ruth 2:17-23

"Where hast thou gleaned today?" Ruth 2:19

I n this lovely story of Ruth, we read here how that Boaz, who was to be Ruth's future husband, gave her permission to glean or gather up what she was able, after the reapers had done their work. "She gleaned in the field until even, about an ephah of barley" Ruth 2:7. This was a considerable amount for Ruth to carry, so she must have worked hard all day. When she arrived home, Naomi, her mother-in-law, asked the question: "Where hast thou gleaned today?"

Where have you gleaned today? In other words, what have you done for God today? You are probably working hard in your own job or profession. You may have saved up quite a lot of money with your job or in your business or profession; but what have you done for eternity. As Ruth arrived home in the evening, after gleaning, so the evening of our time on earth is fast approaching.

When we meet the Lord Jesus Christ one day, as we will, to give account of our time here on earth, the question will be asked, what have you done, what have you to show, where hast thou gleaned? What will your answer be? What will your excuses be? How many regrets will you have? Always keep in mind the value of eternity. How true the saying is, it's only what's done for Jesus will last. Your savings, investments, career, good living will mean nothing in the eyes of the Lord.

John Ellerton wrote that immortal hymn: "The day thou gavest, Lord, is ended." When it does, where will you have gleaned and what will be your reward. That day is coming! What a day that will be when my Jesus I shall see!

The family altar

Proverbs 22:1-15

"Train up a child in the way he should go: and when he is old,
he will not depart from it." Proverbs 22:6

I remember as a child every night we would all sit as a family and read the Bible together, we would all take it in turns. As children we were taught early in life the importance of the family altar. Both my parents were believers in the Lord Jesus Christ. They knew and realised that their responsibility was not only to raise their children, but to raise them in the fear and admonition of the Lord.

When a couple come together and form a relationship, it is a good thing to start praying and reading the Word of God together. It is vitally important to make God part of your lives together. It shouldn't be a chore but rather a joy to include the Lord. As I look back upon my life, many of the instructions and challenges remain with me and have helped to mould and make me out to be the person I am today. Every opportunity we get to teach children the Word of God should be taken. Children need the Lord; they love to hear about the Lord Jesus and what He has done for us. Why should children not be instructed and trained in the ways of the Lord? If you don't have a regular family altar, don't lament and regret over it, rather start afresh in your walk with God and begin today. He will bless you for putting Him first. Bible before breakfast and Bible before bed is a good day well spent.

IMPACT *Daily readings*

Keeping in touch

Lamentations 3:20-25

"The LORD is my portion, saith my soul; therefore will I
hope in him." Lamentations 3:24

One of the things I love to do is travel. No matter where in the world we travel, my parents love us to keep in touch! It's a natural thing to do. Parents always want to know what their children are up to and if everything is ok. Sometimes we agree to stay in touch more often with friends we haven't seen in a while.

There is a similar lesson here for us today and that is keeping in touch with the Lord. We don't need to text, email or call the Lord! We just have to think about Him and speak. How often do we forget? If we are honest, hours roll into days and become weeks before we realise again we are not keeping in touch with the Lord.

There is a promise here, in that the Lord is good to us when we keep in touch with Him. When we seek Him every day, He is good to us. How can we really expect Him to bless us, help us and encourage us every day if we leave Him out of our lives and plans like a far out relation? Like visiting our relations, we want to and we know we should but for some reason it just doesn't happen very often. Is this not the same with our relationship with the Lord? Then surely the time has come to revisit and come afresh to the Lord. He is waiting to strengthen you afresh, but you must seek and find Him.

Who do we go to the most often, our closest relatives or the Lord?

Watch out for the Lord today!

Leviticus 9:1-7

"To day the LORD will appear unto you." Leviticus 9:4

Moses instructed Aaron to prepare a sacrifice unto the Lord. It was to be a bullock and a ram. The ram had to be without blemish with no marks on it at all. When the Lord wants to use us for His glory, He wants us to be without blemish with no marks of sin upon us. It all must be put under the blood and we must be as pure as possible.

The Lord was going to appear before them, but not before the sacrifice was made. Sometimes we have to make a sacrifice in the spiritual sense before the Lord will come bless us. This can be anything else from giving up a meal so someone can have one, buying a less expensive car and giving the difference in value to someone in need etc. Sometimes things have to be burnt or put away that hinder the Lord from coming before us, only you know what is stopping the Lord from blessing! Whatever it is, it must go and must go now.

When all is put on the altar for God, then you are ready for His appearance. He may come in different forms, but He will come. God works and moves in mysterious ways, His wonders to perform. When God has a message for you, He will deliver it either through His Word, written or spoken, or through an incident or accident. But we must be ready, waiting and expecting to hear from God today. Don't miss your appointment with the Lord! Remember your disappointment could be God's appointment.

IMPACT *Daily readings*

God knew me before I was even born!

Jeremiah 1:1-5

"Before I formed thee in the belly I knew thee." Jeremiah 1:5

This is a wonderful verse whenever we think how powerful and wonderful God really is. Before the foundation of the world, God knew exactly when, where and how I would be born. This is an amazing thought as we think about God and who He really is. Sometimes we tend to keep God in a wee box in our homes or maybe even confine Him to a particular room in the home or work place. One thing we must not forget is that God cannot be confined or locked up. He is the all powerful, all seeing God. He is absolutely everything and when I think about that, what a privilege it is for me to be one of His children, a child, follower and servant of the King of Kings.

God had a plan for the life of Jeremiah even before he was born. I love that thought, that God has all things worked out and planned for our good. This is why in my opinion it is wrong and an insult to God to continually worry about things in life. God has it all perfectly planned out and yet we tend to be the ones wondering all the time, is this the way it's meant to be? Jeremiah was ordained a prophet unto the nations, a follower and servant of the Lord, what a privilege to be in the perfect plan of God as we journey through this life. Do you ever ask the question, "Am I in the perfect plan of God?"

Have you ever asked the question WHY?

Haggai 1:1-9

"Ye looked for much, and, lo, it came to little; and when ye brought it home, I did blow upon it. Why? saith the LORD of hosts." Haggai 1:9

Everyone at some stage in their lives has asked the question why? Especially when something goes wrong or not the way we would expect. Sometimes we expect something great to happen and it doesn't. Sometimes we may expect something to go our way and it doesn't then we ask the question why? We get so confused and discouraged and can hardly believe what has happened and is going on that we ask the question why? There is nothing new about this question and there is not always an answer.

God is sovereign and knows all things. He knows all about you, your needs and your desires. There is not always an answer for your situation and God does not have to tell you. The question and real challenge is can you accept the situation you are in without asking why? God brings us through many struggles and challenges along life's way. Sometimes we are at wits' end and have no second plan or nowhere to go or turn to. We are about to ask why again? But wait a moment, are you at the stage in life when you can say I am in the good, acceptable and perfect will of God right now? Maybe you are where you are right now to make sure you are. Instead of saying why, try saying why not, after all Christ never questioned why He had to die for you. He willingly did it.

IMPACT *Daily readings*

The Lord heals people

Exodus 15:20-26

"I am the LORD that healeth thee." Exodus 15:26

Most people enjoy good health, yet at the same time most people have some sort of complaint about their health. Sometimes we are almost afraid to ask someone how they are because we know we are going to hear all about their pains and woes. There is a major difference between someone going through genuine pain and sorrow and someone who moans about everything under the sun. Such company is not good to keep as you will soon become negative like these people.

In the Bible there are often conditions placed upon God's promises. This part of scripture tells us that we must comply with the conditions God makes. In verse 26 the Lord said: "If thou wilt diligently hearken to the voice of the LORD thy God, and wilt do that which is right in his sight, and wilt give ear to his commandments, and keep all his statutes, I will put none of these diseases upon thee, which I have brought upon the Egyptians: for I am the LORD that healeth thee."

We are challenged to listen to what the Lord is telling us so we can carry out and follow His commandments. Maybe we have hatred in our hearts towards someone, maybe we are jealous of someone or maybe we are doing something deep down in our hearts which is just not right. Now is the time to search our hearts afresh and come clean before the Lord. Let's plead for the Lord to heal our body, our pain, our head, our heart. Wherever that pain has come from we can come boldly before the Lord because He has said, "I am the LORD that healeth thee."

Have you ever asked the Lord to help with your sickness?

IMPACT *Daily readings*

Should we fight back?

Deuteronomy 32:29-35

"To me belongeth vengeance." Deuteronomy 32:35

A natural tendency is to fight back when someone does us wrong; retaliation seems to be the only way to sort things out. Some people say, "an eye for an eye and a tooth for a tooth." However when we look at the teaching of the Lord Jesus in this matter, it would appear that the teaching of Christ is different than the way we would think naturally.

In His Sermon on the Mount, the Lord Jesus taught us that we are to love our enemies; to pray for those who spitefully use us and persecute us. It is not an easy thing to do I'm sure you would agree. Of course like many things and situations in the Christian life, it is to be filled with the Holy Spirit. He will help you forgive your enemies. Even though the natural man wants to fight back, the supernatural new man tells you to hold your peace, to forgive and move on.

The Lord in His own way will deal with those who seek to harm you, take advantage and even use you. Remember as a child of God, He promises to be with us and to look after us. He is very much aware of your situation. You are not alone; you are not a fool for obeying scripture. Vengeance alone belongeth to God; the time will come when He will execute judgement upon wrongdoers. There is a blessing and a wonderful peace that comes upon us whenever we take the high ground in a situation that may seem unbearable and very frustrating at the time. Bring it to the Lord and leave it with Him. He will take care of your situation and your enemies.

Time for the test

Amos 7:1-15

"The Lord stood upon a wall........with a plumb line in His hand." Amos 7:7

One of the essential tools a builder will use is a spirit level and a simple piece of string. This string is stretched out and used as a line to make sure the wall is plumb or straight and level, otherwise known as a plumb line. If a wall is built without this then it is in great risk of being unlevel which could lead to eventual disaster the higher the wall gets built. The essential time to fix a wall is before the mortar hardens; once it does the only way it can be mended is to break the wall.

In this vision given to Amos long ago, he could see the Lord standing on a wall with a plumb line in His hand. He was about to test the spiritual condition of the people. If the Lord were to lay a plumbline upon your life what would He find? Are there things that are still soft and tender which need to be quickly worked on, fixed and put right before they harden? Maybe there are things there for a long time and need to be broken, to be put right. The only way to bring a wall down is to use pressure, with a big sledge hammer or even a big digger.

What pressure must the Lord apply to our lives to fix the wall of our lives? If the Lord was to test how level we are in our Christian lives what would He find? Every area of our Christian life needs to have God's plumb line upon it. He is the builder; every area in our life must pass His test. When the master builder looks down upon you as his creation, is He well pleased with how you have turned out, or has there been a time when things started to look the way they shouldn't have turned out? Before it gets worse like the pruning of the roses, let the Lord take a big hammer to areas of your life that need a good hammering in order to make things right again.

The double portion

2 Kings 2:9-15

"Let a double portion of thy spirit be upon me." 2 Kings 2:9

I find this to be one of the most amazing requests ever made. Elisha could have asked for anything from Elijah but instead of something like money, health or a long life, he simply asked for a double portion of God's Spirit. What a request! It is totally amazing and so encouraging to think that Elisha would ask for such a thing. Imagine if we all had a double portion of God's Spirit upon us! We would live a life so in touch with God. Even for others to look at us and say, "I would like to be twice the Christian they are," is such a challenging thought.

Sometimes we can drift through the Christian life and forget it is a spiritual journey. When we get saved we receive the Holy Spirit as a gift. It comes with Salvation. But in order to live in the strength of the Lord we must be filled with the Holy Spirit every day of our lives just like a watering can pouring out all the time will eventually run out of water. It will still be a watering can, still looks like a watering can but is totally useless without the water. Likewise we will be totally useless if we try to live the Christian life in the energy of the flesh. "Be filled with the Spirit." (Ephesians 5:18)

Elijah told Elisha that he had asked for a hard thing and so he had. Likewise to really live out for God, to go the extra mile and to live the Spirit filled life is a hard thing. It takes prayer, dedication, stamina and stickability. The question is twofold. Do you want it? and are you ready for it? Often it is the hard and difficult thing which brings the blessing. It's easy to go with the flow! Instead try the hard thing for God and see what happens!

Don't let anyone stop you

1 Samuel 14:1-7

"Do all that is in thine heart...behold, I am with thee
according to thy heart." 1 Samuel 14:7

Sometimes we have got to go where our conscience tells us to go and do what our conscience tells us to do. Jonathan here was like that, deep in his heart he knew he must act and as he did the Lord blessed him and gave him victory. To others, he was mad and a fool. But his armour bearer who went with him, told him to do all that was in his heart and he supported Jonathan.

Sometimes we can be afraid to act because of what others might say; even when we know it is the right thing to do. We will be told to be silent and wait for a more convenient time but that time will never come. I urge you that if the Lord has put something irresistibly on your heart, then act upon it because He has promised to be with us!

Don't waste your life wishing you had done something for God, now is your opportunity. So many things and people will put us off, but remember all things are possible with God. Go in Jesus name and do that thing for Him. Will you be like Jonathan and be courageous? Sometimes we've got to go against the tide, against the crowds, family and even friends. If it is God's will then you and only you must do it. Remember there is no restraint with God, in the verse found before our text we are told that "there is no restraint to the LORD to save by many or by few."

When God lays something on your heart, follow it through to completion and don't let anyone stop you.

Praise ye the Lord

2 Chronicles 20:14-22

"When they began to sing and to praise, the Lord set ambushments....
and they (the enemies) were smitten." 2 Chronicles 20:22

Many Christians will tell you that when they are at their lowest, one of the ways they will often get back on their feet is by praising the Lord. There is something about praising the Lord that brings joy to your heart. Purchase a hymn book or some good praise songs and listen to them. Ones with good meaningful songs in them, not just noise without a message. Praise is a wonderful thing and there is no better way to prepare you for prayer or the preaching of the Word of God. If you are at a crisis moment in your life now with all sorts of problems and difficulties coming your way, then you have got to praise the Lord with all your heart. Once you get your focus back on the Lord, then the Lord will put His focus back on you.

Here in this story, we read about King Jehoshaphat doing this when his enemies were approaching. By faith he appointed singers to go in front of the trained soldiers! When the Lord God was glorified through the praise of the singers, He intervened and scattered the tribes that were arrayed against the people. Here it seemed that they were going to be defeated as the enemy was so powerful. Yet when they tried praise, it gained them a great victory.

For King Jehoshaphat there seemed to be no hope at all, that was until they tried praise. Many today look at themselves and sigh, I would suggest we begin to look to the Lord and sing.

Giving your best for God

Leviticus 22:17-25

"Blind, or broken, or maimed...ye shall not offer these
unto the LORD." Leviticus 22:22

Sometimes when something becomes broken or no longer useful, we tend to think of someone who could make use of it. We would no longer use it ourselves but yet think of someone else who might benefit from it. Reality is there are some people who don't like to throw things out. I used to be like that, felt bad for throwing something out so I would collect it all together and take to my Dad; he seemed to find it useful for something. Then I no longer felt bad or guilty.

Is this like the Lord and His work? Do we tend to give away the clothes and toys we no longer use? Do we tend to give Him the money we think we can do without? Really when we weigh it all up there is often no real sacrifice in our giving to the Lord in His name. Have you ever been tempted to give something really good away to someone who might have need of it? Like give away something good instead of something broken, sometimes something broken can be mended and made like new. There are lots of broken people out there, Christ can mend them and make them into new creatures, will you help find them?

In this verse the people were told not to give away something blind, broken or maimed. It had to be the best of what they had. Like our service to the Lord. God expects the best years of our lives, the best of our talents and abilities to be used for His glory. He gave His best for you, why should you in turn not give your best to Him? It is more blessed to give than to receive the Bible tells us, try helping someone in need today, there is an indescribable feeling that comes with helping someone in Jesus name.

IMPACT *Daily readings*

Modern day chariots

Nahum 2:1-4

"The chariots shall rage in the streets, they shall justle one against another in the broad ways: they shall seem like torches, they shall run like the lightnings." Nahum 2:4

If you imagine the traffic we see in many of our streets, the way people drive, always in a rush (myself included) then you will see this verse as a prophetic picture of what is talked about here in this verse. Especially in major cities around the world, with the constant sound of horns because of impatient drivers you will hear the rage of the traffic and the roar of engines. Then at night time around the cities, along the highways and motorways is the constant stream of lights, moving traffic continually moving like torches. When a car drives past at a very fast pace, many use the expression "it was like lightning" referring to the speed of the car. Do you drive with a good testimony? Are you guilty of road rage? Would you put a sticker on the back of the car that says, "I'm a Christian?" Maybe you wouldn't because the way you drive is not within the law.

This seems to be the way life is going now, faster and faster. We all are in the same race of life. The real challenge is how fast we run this race and how careful we are running it. When we think about the cars we drive, some people buy the best cars for their own enjoyment. Would you pour the same money into the Lord's work? Some people would seldom let anyone else into their car. Have you ever considered using your car for the Lord. Maybe there is someone you can take to a gospel meeting or to church. There are many ways in which we can make less do and do more with what we have for the glory and honour of the Lord.

IMPACT *Daily readings*

Humility verses pride

Proverbs 15:25-33
"Before honour is humility." Proverbs 15:33

In every one of us there is an element of pride within us. How we control our pride determines the type of person we really are. There are some things God specifically hates and one of them is pride. In James 4:6, it tells us that, "God resisteth the proud, but giveth grace to the humble." When thinking of the Lord Jesus, "He made himself of no reputation, and took upon him the form of a servant and became obedient unto death." This is very challenging for me as pride is a thing within us that we are continually battling with. The fact that God hates it and resists it makes me think then if I want God's approval upon my life then I have got to think of humility.

I remember while in Israel leading a small team of nine people. While arranging to make our way back to the airport, we had arranged for two cars to take us back. Some of the group were continually concerned that we could not get all the cases into the two cars. After a short time, I raised my voice to one in the group and told them it will work and stop complaining. It hurt the person and I felt bad about it. After a little while it was becoming uncomfortable, so I got up shook his hand and told him I was sorry for reacting like this, I felt he was undermining my judgement. He now felt good and I felt bad. The next morning all nine people as well as all the cases fitted in the cars and off we went to the airport. Sometimes it pays to be sorry, it brings humility within the soul and God is glorified. Now I felt good and my friend felt bad!

Wise behaviour

Psalm 101:1-8

"I will behave myself wisely in a perfect way. O when wilt thou come unto me? I
will walk within my house with a perfect heart." Psalm 101:2

The real challenge for the Christian today is maintaining a good
testimony. There are many out there just waiting for the opportunity
to trip you up and find fault with you. This is why we have to be like
Joseph and David and behave ourselves wisely in everything we do and
everywhere we go. In the Christian life the old man must die, we are new
creatures in Christ Jesus. This is such an honour and privilege to be a child
of the King, to be a son of the living God.

Saying or doing the wrong thing at the wrong time could set us back years
in our Christian walk. While the Lord forgives us when we are wrong,
human beings sadly do not. This is why we must keep our focus on Christ,
looking unto Jesus the author and finisher of our faith. The Psalmist talks
about walking around his own house with a perfect heart. How many of us
grumble and complain, yap and gossip about everyone else and sometimes
our conversation or our conduct is anything but Christlike. Very often we
expect God to be with us and help us, how often do we forget He is always
there, as He has promised never to leave us. When we remember this then
perhaps we will behave more wisely and watch our walk and our talk while
out and about and at home in the house.

Under the shadow of the Almighty

Song of Solomon 2:1-17

"I sat down under his shadow with great delight." Song of Solomon 2:3

There is no greater delight in this life than to sit in the presence of the Lord Jesus and to know that all is well with our soul. Equally important is to know that all is well in our relationship with God and that we enjoy that personal and intimate communion with Him. It is so important that we maintain this blessed relationship with the Lord. In everything we say and do, may it never be hindered, harmed or spoiled.

Maybe we are too busy running around, living life and yet missing out being under His shadow. Sometimes we need to slow down, take time to reflect, relax and enjoy sweet communion with Him once again. Living the Christian life, going to church etc, should not be a duty but rather a happy privilege. If it becomes a duty then something is wrong. Be careful or your fire could burn very, very low. Do we delight to sit in His presence, even with great delight?

Once we have the joy and presence of Jesus upon us, then we will have the joy and the heart to see others won for Him. Someone has put it like this: "A vision without a task makes a visionary. A task without a vision makes drudgery. But a vision and a task make the missionary." Oh to be a soul on fire for God, constantly under the shadow of the Almighty!

Do I delight to be in the presence of the Almighty? Lord Jesus give me this delight today!

IMPACT Daily readings

Early morning

1 Samuel 7:9-17

"And as Samuel was offering up the burnt offering,
the Philistines drew near to battle." 1 Samuel 7:10

One thing the devil hates is earnest prayer before God. The more intense we are in prayer, the more opposition from the enemy of souls we can expect. That is why it is so important to pray together with your spouse, in your relationship, with your friends, whatever Christian company you have. Satan is not so much bothered by activity in Christian circles, but once you start going for souls and especially prevailing in prayer then he fears this the most. The Philistines will always be around preparing to attack when you get alone with God.

It is always wise to arrange your time to be alone with God in the early morning, before the day starts. The longer you leave it, the more distracted you will be and the more difficult it will be to find that time to be alone with God. Once you start meeting people and begin to take care of the challenges and problems of the day, you probably will not have time for the Lord that day.

Time after time, we read, "Joshua rose early in the morning." It was then he received his instructions from the Lord and faithfully carried them out. The same could be said of many men and women of God, rising up early to meet with God. Maybe we cannot rise up early because we are going to bed too late at night. Even as the Philistines were drawing close to battle, Samuel did not cease praying to God. As he continued to pray, God sent a thunderstorm which discomforted them. Afterwards they were defeated by the men of Israel.

If you get to bed at night without opening the Word of God or praying all day, then the Philistines have won. Make sure that you put God first in the day; then leave Him to deal with the Philistines.

IMPACT *Daily readings*

The angel of the Lord

Exodus 23:20-25

"Behold, I send an Angel before thee, to keep thee in the way,
and to bring thee into the place which I have prepared." Exodus 23:20

God had made a promise to Moses and the children of Israel that He would be their guide and keeper. The Angel of the Lord watched over them and preserved them from danger as they listened, obeyed His voice and followed Him.

It is so encouraging to know that just as the Angel of the Lord (who was in fact the Lord Jesus Christ in the Old Testament) was with Moses and the Children of Israel, so He can be with us. We must watch for the leading of the Angel of the Lord in our lives. It is important to listen to His voice as He leads and directs us, so we won't go astray and as a result grieve the Holy Spirit.

We naturally have an inclination to follow our own way in life. But this is in direct contradiction to God's plan for the Christian because God wants to lead you in life, He wants to guide you. He has a perfect will and plan for your life. In order to have that perfect peace, we must stop trying to live in our own humanistic way and be totally sold over to letting God have His way in our lives. So whatever crisis, problems, failures or challenges that come our way, bring the Lord into the situation and watch Him work everything out for your good. He can and He will!

The years are passing by

Psalm 90

"We spend our years as a tale that is told," Psalm 90:9

Sometimes it is good to reflect upon the years as they pass by. The reality is that they are passing by so very quickly. Don't linger too long about this as it could lead you into depression. What we need to do is realise that we cannot turn back time. We are at the stage in life where we are presently at. We cannot do anything about it. Everything in the past becomes memories. Eternity will claim all of us one day, so one day soon we will be gone from this scene of time.

If the Lord spares you to grow old, do you look back upon your life as one with wasted years? Up until now if you have lived with regret about wasted years, then if you are earnest about living the rest of your life for the Lord, then the Lord gives us a wonderful promise, "I will restore to you the years that the locust hath eaten." (Joel 2:25) By now the 'Locusts' will have done their deadly work through carelessness, bitterness and worldliness. The Lord can and will restore these years for you. Sometimes we can be so caught up in life at home or work as if we can never be replaced. We can be and we will be replaced and you will be forgotten sooner than you care to think. Someone who will never forget you is the Lord, so why not start living your life for him now and stop wasting more years of your life?

IMPACT *Daily readings*

God always keeps His promise

Numbers 11:16-29

"And the LORD said unto Moses, Is the LORD'S hand waxed short? Thou shalt see now whether my word shall come to pass unto thee or not." Numbers 11:23

As Moses led the children of Israel through the wilderness, there were no shops or filling stations along the way for coke and a packet of crisps. In fact there was no food at all; they had to completely trust the Lord for their daily provision. When they got hungry, their faith was really put to the test.

God always performs His promises. The word of God is sure, it cannot be broken. Feeding the people in the wilderness seemed like an impossible task, but God said He would do it so, it would be done. This brings into reality the all sufficiency of an invisible God. The Lord directs our attention to His word. He calls it "My Word." The word of God cannot lie and will never die. What God was promising them was not a probability or a possibility but rather an actuality. How we need to take God at His word, I love to hear people talking about reading the word. There is a promise and a plan in the word for you today. Get into it and start digging. Start searching and discover God's will and plan for your life, it's not too late yet.

Get into the Word until the Word gets into you!

IMPACT *Daily readings*

Power and strength

Isaiah 40:28-31

"He giveth power to the faint, and to them that
have no might He increaseth strength." Isaiah 40:29

Trying to live the Christian life in your own strength is like starving yourself. Yes, you will still be a human being but as the days go on, eventually you will feel empty and begin to look worse and worse. This is similar to the Christian life, if we neglect prayer, reading of the Word, the infilling of God's Spirit, then yes, we are a saved soul with a wasted and useless life.

Andrew Murray was renowned for his godly life. His writings are still a blessing to many today. He gave this advice regarding prayer and Bible study; "Little of the Word, with little Prayer, is death to the spiritual life. Much of the Word, with little Prayer, gives a sickly life. Much prayer, with little of the Word gives an emotional life. But a full measure of both the Word and Prayer, each day, gives a healthy and powerful life."

When you feel so weak that you are ready to faint, remember this verse that the Lord does give power to the faint. When you have no might and you are at your weakest then remember that is when the Lord gives you strength. It is there for the taking if only we will ask Him for it. There is no excuse for continually being down in the dumps, it's a battle and we need to keep fighting until we get our strength back.

IMPACT *Daily readings*

Time to stop praying

Joshua 7:1-10

"Get thee up, wherefore liest thou upon thy face." Joshua 7:10

The men of Israel, who had gone out with such confidence to conquer Ai, were defeated, humiliated and chased. This was immediately following the great victory of conquering Jericho. The Lord had promised Joshua that He would be with him and would grant him great victories. Joshua was soon on his face, before God, to find out the reason why everything had gone wrong.

Within a short time, God ordered him to stop praying and to get up and deal with the sin that had come into the camp after the defeat of Jericho. It was discovered that Achan had 'taken of the accursed thing' during the battle and as a result had brought God's anger upon the people. They were told specifically not to touch or take anything from Jericho; it alone belonged to the Lord. Achan stole and hid the money and garments in his tent thinking no one saw him, not realising that God see's everything. As a result drastic judgement fell on Achan and his whole family as they were stoned to death in the valley of Achor.

Joshua could have still continued in prayer, but Israel would still have been defeated. Of course it was right for him to pray, but what was needed now was action. When there is sin and wrong doing in the camp, there will be no blessing. Joshua needed to find out where it came from and he did. It was not covered up, it was dealt with. Joshua longed for God's help, presence and blessing and one man's selfish greed was not going to take it away from him.

We may not be popular if we challenge someone about wrong doing, but sometimes for their best and the best of everyone it has to be confronted, it's not about being popular, it's all about doing good and being faithful to the Lord.

IMPACT *Daily readings*

The dream of a bald man

Judges 16:22-31

"The hair of his head began to grow again after he was shaven." Judges 16:22

Samson was a judge for 20 years when he was taken captive by the Philistines. He was a strong man, a man of God whom the Philistines feared. Eventually his secret was discovered when he was tricked by Delilah the woman he loved. Once his hair was shaven he became weak as any other man. He held to the Nazarite vow that no razor would come upon his head. God gave Samson unusual, extraordinary strength. But once he was shaven he no longer had that God given strength.

Samson then had his eyes put out by the enemy, he was blinded and jailed as a criminal. He came out before all the Philistine Lords and up to 3,000 people and there they laughed at him as if he were a dog. The Bible then tells us how his hair began to grow again. The Spirit of the Lord revived within him, he asked the lad who guided him to put his hands on the pillars of the huge building. He pushed with all his might, causing the building to collapse, killing himself along with 3000 of the enemy. Samson was blind therefore he could no longer see the enemy, how we need to guard our eyes. His problem first started because of his love for women, he loved the flesh, this is one of the worst enemies of the Christian and many have fallen snare to this trap. Losing his hair was like losing God's infilling Spirit, therefore, he no longer had the strength to fight the battle. His hair then began to grow, teaching us the importance of being filled with the Spirit of the living God to fight against the world, flesh and the devil. When his hair grew, he regained his strength from God.

Obedience

Numbers 32:1-31

"As the LORD hath said unto thy servants, so will we do." Numbers 32:31

The children of Reuben and Gad were cattlemen. Here on the east of Jordan they had found the cattle country and the best ground for grazing. They requested the land and Moses gave it to them on the condition that every man armed for battle would go with him to the land of Cannan, the Promised Land.

Their response was amazing; "as the Lord has said, we will do." The Lord honoured them with possessing the land because of their immediate obedience to His word. The goodness of the Lord in a ready answer to prayer should motivate us to further obey the word of God who daily loadeth us with benefits. God continued to help them further by protecting their families at home and the men while at war. All that God promised He fulfilled. His promises should encourage us into full obedience as the little chorus goes, 'trust and obey, trust and obey for there is no other way to be happy in Jesus but to trust and obey.'

"But we never can prove the delights of His love, until all on the altar we lay, for the favour He shows and the joy He bestows, are for them who will trust and obey."

IMPACT *Daily readings*

Be still and know

Psalm 23

"He leadeth me beside the still waters." Psalm 23:2

The 23rd Psalm is probably the best known of all the Psalms and without doubt the most quoted throughout the world. It is the verse two that I want to focus on for a moment. The Psalmist here was led by the Lord beside still waters. There are times in our lives when we need to come beside the still waters. Still waters picture peace and quietness. Often there can be anything but peace and quietness in our lives. The Lord tells us to come aside and rest a while. We need to spend that quiet time alone with the Lord.

The Lord was the Shepherd for the Psalmist. Once he had the Lord with him; he had need for nothing else. Sometimes we seem to be discontented with the Lord. The reason I say this is because we are searching for help and answers in so many other sources. When we really have the Lord we should be in want of nothing else, in other words we should be totally contented with the Lord. Notice the shepherd led the sheep to the still waters, where it was safe and peaceful, not the fast flowing waters where the sheep might fall in and be in great trouble. There is something tremendously peaceful about a still river. Maybe the Lord is challenging us about quietness, our quiet time, that time alone with him. A time of peace, a time of not being lonely, but being alone with God. When is the last time we switched off completely and waited on the Lord till His presence filled the room? This is a real experience and one we should long and pray for.

I will do a new thing

Isaiah 43:18-28

"Behold, I will do a new thing; now it shall spring forth; shall ye not know it? I will even make a way in the wilderness, and rivers in the desert." Isaiah 43:19

These verses certainly come with freshness to our souls. Maybe you are stuck in a rut and there doesn't seem to be any way out with you in your present situation. Well my friend take courage as from today. Sometimes we can continue to talk about the old days and how good they were because there doesn't seem to be anything happening today. We are told here in verse 18 to "Remember ye not the former things, neither consider the things of old." We are not to continually lament about how good the old days were. We are to think about the present and start looking to the future.

The Lord said to Isaiah, "Behold, I will do a new thing; now it shall spring forth; shall ye not know it?" Maybe the time has come for the Lord to do a new thing in your life. Whatever it is that has been on your mind, the Lord is maybe just about to make it happen. He will do a new thing for you. The question is are you ready for change? Are you willing to let the Lord turn your life inside out and upside down for His glory? Are we willing to shut the gate of the past behind us and move on without looking back with regret? Sometimes our past needs to be left behind and completely forgotten. Are you willing to do that? God will not move in your life until you are fully surrendered to His will and not yours!

Gossiping

Proverbs 26:1-20

"Where there is no talebearer, the strife ceaseth." Proverbs 26:20

Gossiping is a terrible thing to be involved in; it is so unhealthy and so negative. Human nature often enjoys this type of conversation. But the Bible teaches us much about telling tales and talking about someone in a negative and unpleasant way. The next time you are listening to a talebearer, ask yourself would you like to be the person they are talking about? Reality is that you could be the next person.

The story is told about a wealthy old grandfather who was very hard of hearing. One day he decided to buy himself a hearing aid without telling anyone, especially his close relatives. Unaware that he could now hear, one day the whole family was round, at times saying some unpleasant things, even about him and how tight he was.

One day he was telling the story to a close friend and with a little laugh told his friend about the things that were said in general and especially about him. Then with a chuckle, he told his friend, "and you know what, I've changed my will twice already!!"

There is an old saying that "walls have ears" it would amaze you what people hear when you are talking. If you find yourself continually gossiping, try to stop it, it's not good for a Christian. Likewise if you find yourself in the company of those who continue to gossip a lot, it may be good to distance your friendship with them. A talebearer brings strife and division and can cause family feuds. When there is no tale bearing, there will be peace in the family, try it and see. God's Word is true.

IMPACT *Daily readings*

Give me this mountain

Joshua 14:6-15

"Now, therefore, give me this mountain." Joshua 14:12

From all the characters in the Bible, Caleb is surely one of the most inspiring. His tremendous courage is an incredible example to all believers. We first learn about Caleb when Joshua and the others entered into the Promised Land. They were spies who brought back a good report that they could conquer the Promised Land. Even at eighty five years old, Caleb was as determined as ever to claim Hebron as his own, and he did so, in the power of God.

Caleb was a soldier for the Lord fighting on until the last, claiming what he could for God. All Christians should have the same courage to succeed in the Christian life. Not so much as what we can do for ourselves in this life, but rather for glory and the life to come. Sometimes we focus on retiring when we reach a certain age. Many of us need to focus on starting to do something for God before we reach a certain age. There was no quitting with these great men of God and so there should be no quitting with us. When it's time to quit, God will take us home to glory. We must take every opportunity the Lord lays before us to speak a word for Jesus or do something in His name. Ask the Lord for the courage and determination that Caleb had and He will surely give it to you.

Nothing beats a good hammering!

Isaiah 54:1-17

"Lengthen thy cords, and strengthen thy stakes." Isaiah 54:2

If the Lord desires to lengthen the place of our tent and to lengthen our cords, the stakes will have to be strengthened. The greater the responsibility in His work the more it will require a deeper spiritual life; otherwise we may not pass the test the Lord is taking us through. This may mean we may have to take a good hammering in God's school. If the stakes are going to take hold, they have got to be hammered into the ground, really beat into the ground, so no matter what wind will blow the stakes will hold the tent. I remember one of our camps in Tollymore Forest Park, at 4am we encountered a huge storm of wind and rain as never seen before. We had to evacuate the entire camp to another safe camp site. The big marquee had to be tied to five vehicles as the stakes were lifting, most of the equipment and smaller tents were destroyed or torn to pieces. Thankfully everyone was safe. In the morning the sun came out and we wondered was there really a storm last night, although there was enough evidence to prove it.

Maybe you are being hammered at the moment. If so, God in love is working out His own purpose. There is a greater work ahead for you and your life will be deeper in Him because of it. I have had my days of hammering too; I know what it is like. It can be lonely, painful and even nights of tears wondering why. Your faith will be rocked and tried to the core. But once you empty yourself of me and rely completely on Him, then the hammering will be a pleasure because it is all part of God's plan as you seek to find that good, acceptable and perfect will of God for your life. So as I look back on my life I can honestly say, though painful at the time as the blows were coming, nothing beats a good hammering when you can look back and see where it can really take you with God.

IMPACT *Daily readings*

Adam was afraid

Genesis 3:8-21

"I heard thy voice....and I was afraid." Genesis 3:10

This is the first time in the Word of God where we read of man being afraid. Where did this come from and why was Adam afraid? The answer is simple, because of sin. Adam disobeyed God and as a result of both Adam and Eve eating the forbidden fruit, sin came into the world. They were now conscious and very much aware of it. Adam was now hiding in the garden because he was aware now that he was naked and when he heard God calling his name he was afraid. If God came by and called your name, would you be afraid? Are there a few things you would have to straighten out first before the Lord? One day the Lord will come back and He will call us by our name, how will we stand on the judgement day? Will we run to meet Him or will we be hiding in the crowd hoping to slip in with the rest?

Sin still brings fear; the devil implants fear in the heart and a guilty conscience fills the life with fear. Fear is a terrible thing and many today are living in fear. There is a difference though in fear and being afraid. Having a fear of God is having utmost respect for God so we don't want to offend Him. There are at least three hundred and sixty five 'fear nots' in the Bible. We could have one for every day of the year to help us keep looking to and trusting in the Lord. Don't be afraid any more, keep trusting in Him and learn to fear none but God.

MPACT *Daily readings*

Help someone today!

Exodus 2:11-17

"Moses stood up and helped them." Exodus 2:17

A man was driving along in his car when in the distance he noticed a lady standing beside her car in some sort of bother. As he approached he realised she had a flat wheel. The man naturally asked her if she needed some help. She was delighted at this and he proceeded after some time to change the wheel. Just as he was about to lower the jack, the woman asked him to lower it slowly. Slightly confused and wondering why, she went on to say her husband was asleep in the back seat and didn't want to be disturbed. Can you imagine what went through the man's mind? I know what I would have done! Cold water has a cure for a lot of things!

Sometimes we can go through life being very self-centred and think about no one else but ourselves and our own families. The Bible tells us that it is more blessed to give than receive and there is a blessing that comes with helping other people. It is a good rule in life to do unto others as you would have others do unto you.

In the case here with Moses, there were seven daughters drawing water for their father's sheep and were chased away by the shepherds. There was an immediate need for Moses to stand up or lie down. He stood up and helped them; as a result the father of the girls gave one of his daughters to Moses for his wife. So helping out that day, without any personal benefit or agenda turned out to be a wonderful blessing for Moses.

When the need comes for you to help or encourage someone today, will you rise to that need?

Be careful of too much study

Ecclesiastes 12:1-12
"....much study *is* a weariness of the flesh." Ecclesiasties 12:12

Three times in the Bible do we find the word study and in this verse it makes an interesting read. For many to succeed in university life or in their work, many hours of study and research is necessary. The verse does not say it is wrong, of course not, but it does say our bodies can become weary. It is vital then if possible to exercise and eat as healthily as possible as we can become sluggish with constantly sitting down all the time.

When our bodies are healthy, our minds can stay active longer. Along with this is good ventilation, drinking enough water etc. The Word of God tells us that our bodies are the temple of the Lord; therefore we should try to take care of them as well as possible. After all, the Lord lives in our heart so we should endeavour to look after our heart as best we possibly can.

Little and often can be a fruitful method. Study until you start to become weary, then get up, go for a walk, fresh air, drink of water and then return and continue your study. You will find this efficient. Always start your day with the Lord, you will find you will accomplish much more in the day when you begin the day with the Lord.

IMPACT *Daily readings*

Soaring like an eagle

Deuteronomy 28:47-53

" ... as swift as the eagle flieth." Deuteronomy 28:49

I have always been amazed by the eagle, this great bird of prey! It is one of the most powerful birds of the air. With a wing span of more than seven feet, it can soar to great heights, crossing mountains and rivers constantly looking out for prey.

There are many lessons we can learn from the eagle. Firstly there is our prayer life. Here we should seek after God and reach new heights as we talk to Him in our prayer life. An eagle can reach heights which no other bird can reach; any one of us can reach that higher place with God which is only obtained in the place of prayer.

The life of an eagle is often a lonely one. Seldom do you see two eagles together. Very often you will spot an eagle gliding through the air all alone. In the Christian life, if we are to do anything for God and really mean business with the Lord it can become the beginning of a lonely journey. Maybe at school, work or even in your home you are the only Christian, a lonely Christian, but remember the eagle!

The eagle also has excellent eyesight and can see its prey at very long distances. It is constantly on the alert. We must always be on the look-out for souls, perishing without Christ. We must constantly be on our guard. The eagle will often sit for a long time and then off it goes, soaring into the sky. It has the strength for that great flight. Waiting on the Lord with a weary soul is the secret to getting your strength back again.

Are you now ready to walk and run and keep running for God? It is time to be up and doing!

IMPACT *Daily readings*

The den of lions

Daniel 6:10-24

"My God hath sent his angel, and hath shut the lions' mouths,
that they have not hurt me." Daniel 6:22

This without doubt is one of the most popular children's Bible stories. Why is that? I would say because Daniel was placed in a most impossible situation humanly speaking. Yet we can read the amazing account in the scriptures of how God shut the lion's mouths and protected Daniel from harm. With God all things are possible!

Daniel was thrown into the lions' den for simply praying to his God. Even when he was ordered not to, he still prayed. Contrast that to our lives today, that whenever we are encouraged to pray, we don't. Daniel honoured God, regardless of what others thought of him. Quite often today we are more concerned about what others will think of us at the expense of honouring God. As Daniel walked down the steps to meet the lions, I have no doubt in my mind that he was certain God would preserve him. How important it is for us to be faithful to God at all costs, even if it means becoming unpopular.

There are many enemies today for the Christian; we must be earnest and regular in our communication with God. Pray for the protecting hand of God to be with you as you seek to live the Christian life. Expect to have enemies; Daniel had them and they sought to put him to death, but they were destroyed in the end. Christ had enemies; they cried for His death and they crucified Him. So then surely to suffer in the name of Jesus is an honour!

If you were told to stop praying, or face the lions, what would you do?

IMPACT *Daily readings*

Discouraged

1 Kings 19:1-9

"What doest thou here Elijah?" 1 Kings 19:9

The story of Elijah is fascinating, full of adventure and excitement. It is hard to believe that he has come to the point in which he is at. He had just challenged the King to battle. He had just proven to Ahab that his God was the true God by sending the fire to light the sacrifice. It all happened on Mount Carmel, after challenging the 450 false prophets of Baal, he then slew them all with the sword. Not only this, as Ahab made his way home in his horse and chariot, Elijah ran past him on his bare feet. Then he ran over 100 miles, running in the opposite direction because Queen Jezebel said he would be dead in less than 24 hours.

Now we find Elijah sitting under a juniper tree, so discouraged that he wished to die. Why should this happen to a fiery servant like Elijah? How could it happen after he had been blessed so much? The answer, I don't know but it did. The reality is that it could happen to anyone of us. He thought he was the only servant of God. The angel told him there are seven thousand just like him. Discouragement is a terrible thing. Whether it is satanic, work related, chemical imbalance or from whatever source, I would urge you to shake yourself out of it. If you cannot seek medical help, Christian counselling, do whatever it takes before it takes you to your grave. Plead the blood of Christ to lift you up again, and once again do great exploits for the Lord.

I will restore wasted years!

Joel 2:18-25

"I will restore to you the years that the locust hath eaten." Joel 2:25

Through the prophet Joel, God said to Israel, I will restore to you the years that the locusts have eaten. Maybe as you sit here now, the years are passing you by and with regret you have wasted them. You wonder where they have gone to. Time waits for no man and stops for no-one. Unfortunately we cannot turn back time; we cannot change the time or even speed it up.

However the Lord says to His people 'I will restore unto you the years that have been wasted and destroyed.' Maybe you have wasted your years, doing little or nothing for God. There is little point in crying about it, you have wasted them. But the Lord is telling us to now change and do something about the present and the future. We can make up for lost time by endeavouring to serve God with all our hearts from today on. If we have failed the Lord by not reading and praying as we should, now is the time to make up for lost time. The Lord will give you your desire and earnestness back to Him when you ask Him too.

Make it your prayer that you will no longer waste your years searching, but rather start serving!

Behaving wisely

1 Samuel 18:1-14

"And David behaved himself wisely in all his ways; and the
LORD was with him." 1 Samuel 18:14

David was a man after God's own heart. He was greatly used and blessed of God. Like so many people who become great for God, they just start off in very humble circumstances. David was a shepherd boy; his father did not even think him eligible to be considered for king compared to his brothers.

Now the Lord had exalted David into a position of great authority and power. As a direct result of David's victory over Goliath, Saul placed him in command of the army. This was a position with great responsibility. David as a man of war, a leader, required great wisdom and discretion. God loved David and the people greatly loved him too. His position didn't go to his head as it can in so many cases and we don't read of him being unwise in his ways. Rather the Bible says, "He behaved himself wisely in all his ways; and the LORD was with him."

This is a wonderful thought, to be wise in all matters of life. The world is full of fools, so don't be another one. The Lord was with David and this was his secret. As a believer, the world, the flesh and the devil will seek to bring you down by making a fool out of you but like David, be wise in all your ways. Pray for wisdom, don't do anything rashly, seek to be discreet in all your ways. Constant vigilance can often be the price of freedom. To be careless, rash, foolish at any moment could lead to a disaster in your Christian walk. Walk wisely in all your ways before others; don't give them any opportunity to point the finger. The Christian is under constant observation and this is why it is so important to behave wisely.

IMPACT *Daily readings*

God hears your cry

2 Chronicles 18:29-34

"Jehoshaphat cried out, and the LORD helped him;
and God moved them to depart from him." 2 Chronicles 18:31

Often we can be in turmoil and agony of soul and nobody really cares or wants to know. Even when we try to talk to someone and explain, we often get the impression they don't really want to know. Most people today are so busy and caught up with their own problems they don't want to bother with others. Other times our enemies can be too big and powerful for us to fight. It can even be a loved one who grieves us to the core! Then we must take them to the Lord and cry out to Him to help us.

Jehoshaphat was in real danger, being surrounded by his enemies. All he could do was pray and in a most powerful way the Lord heard his cry and moved his enemies away. Sometimes our enemies are all around us. They seem to mount pressure upon us to test our Christian faith to the limit. If this is the case with you dear friend, then take courage like Jehoshaphat and cry unto God. Ask the Lord to deal with your enemies. Maybe it's not an enemy but it is something or someone that is beyond your strength to deal with. Then the same lesson applies; take it to the Lord in prayer and let the Lord fight your battles for you.

Who is it that really bothers you? It is not impossible for God to remove them from you.

IMPACT *Daily readings*

Think twice before you speak

Proverbs 11:1-14
"A talebearer revealeth secrets." Proverbs 11:13

There are few people in whom you can completely trust to keep a secret. One is almost afraid to tell someone something because before you know it they are telling half the world. Are you one of those people who love to gossip and tell tales? Do you find yourself continually talking about someone especially in a negative and criticising manner? Quite often some of these stories have no sure foundation, they may have an element of truth to them but for the most of it they are just gossip.

Always remember that a person's reputation could be ruined for life by a simple rumour that started somewhere and spread like wild fire. No matter how innocent that person is, they will always be talked about and viewed with suspicion. If you have a problem with spreading these tales about people and are a person who seems to gossip, try to stop it because it certainly is not God glorifying or Christ honouring. Imagine if a friend genuinely wanted to confide in you about something that was important to them and did not in case you could not be trusted to keep it to yourself, how would that make you feel? May we all be convicted about gossiping, it's not only old ladies who are guilty, we all tend to enjoy hearing the latest gossip, but it's not healthy. Learn to say, "not interested in hearing it" to your friends the next time they start gossiping. That will soon teach them!

IMPACT *Daily readings*

Sheltered in the storm

Isaiah 25:1-8
"Thou hast been...a refuge from the storm." Isaiah 25:4

All of us at some stage in our lives will find ourselves in a storm. Maybe you find yourself in one right now. You may feel the continual beat of the wind and rain with no sign of the storm calming down. Maybe it's a personal problem in your life, a person in your life, bringing everything into turmoil and you have no one to run to. Have you considered Jesus? He is our refuge and strength, a very present help in trouble.

Here in this fourth verse, Isaiah speaks of the Lord as being a strength to the poor. Sometimes the better off we are, the less we tend to rely on God for the simple things in life. Poor Christians, I believe, have a better and closer relationship with the Lord because they look to Him for absolutely everything. So whenever our wealth gets a blow and we find ourselves with a few less coins, use the opportunity to get closer to God and don't waste your time running after the wealth of this world.

He also talks about the Lord being a strength to the needy in distress; we all have needs in one form or another. Many today experience stress from various sources. Others are suffering from depression and their moods can swing from one extreme to another. There are multiple cures and all sorts of medicine one can take to overcome stress and depression. Can I suggest that you stay close to the Lord in this storm of life? He is your refuge and your shelter. When the heat is on, He is the shadow. In the great and terrible storms of life, flee to the arms of our loving Saviour.

IMPACT *Daily readings*

Give me a blessing

Joshua 15:10-19
"Give me a blessing." Joshua 15:19

Achsah, the daughter of the faithful Caleb, had received a husband and a great inheritance-a south land. Interestingly she was not content with this, she wanted more. When you receive a blessing it always creates a thirst for more. When I do a mission, I want to do another one, when I see souls saved, I want to see even more souls saved.

When God blesses us there is nothing wrong with wanting more blessing providing our motives are right. It is always good to have a thankful heart and not to forget how the Lord has blessed you in the past. Achsah also asked for springs of water, without the water the land would be useless and barren; with the water the land would become fruitful. When she asked for this she got springs in the upper part and the lower part of the land. When our hearts are right and our motives are pure, then the Lord often gives us more than we could ever ask or think. Acknowledge how the Lord has blessed you in the past, put your case to Him now and then wait to see how it happens, such is the life of faith.

Stillness

Job 37:1-14

"Hearken unto this, O Job: stand still, and consider the
wondrous works of God." Job 37:14

If ever you are to be strong in the Lord and desire to live and do well
in the Christian life then there is a simple lesson to learn. The lesson is
one called stillness, 'Be still and know that I am God', the scriptures tell
us. We live in a very busy age, a generation that is driven by advancing
technology, time demands, living beyond our means and the list goes on.
My friend if ever we are to be strong in God, we need to learn the secret
of stillness.

With the constant rush, hustle and bustle of life continually upon us, no
matter how busy your life is, it is vital that if we fail to "come apart"
then we may come apart. People can be very demanding, especially
thoughtless, professing Christians. It is becoming more common for people
to suffer from physical and mental breakdown. Have the courage to know
your own limits; no one knows your body better than you. The danger of
going full on for God is that you can have no time for God.

One of the best cures for spending time alone with God is in the evenings,
turn off the television, computer and telephone and just sit alone and wait
for the Lord to come. Keep talking until He comes, then when He does you
won't want Him to leave; there is no sweeter presence than the presence
of the Lord. Just ponder over in your heart and mind the wondrous works
of God.

No turning back

Judges 11:19-40

"I have opened my mouth unto the LORD, and I cannot go back." Judges 11:35

I remember when I was a young Christian, I found myself in a very dangerous situation, hopeless and helpless with no way out. I remembered crying unto God for mercy. There and then I promised God that if He got me out of that situation, I would devote my life entirely to His service. How easy it is to make a promise! It is a serious thing when we vow unto the Lord. Sacrifice is required when paying your vows and going through with God but the blessing that comes with it is indescribable.

Jephthah had proved God in a most remarkable way to deliver Israel out of the hands of the Ammonites. He had made a sacred vow unto the Lord (verse 30-31) and he did not fail to keep it. There was no turning back on his part. How easy it is to sing "I have decided to follow Jesus, no turning back, no turning back." Many today are falling down and turning back. I say be strong in the Lord and go through with God! It's easy to turn back and go with the crowd. Be a real Christian and be strong in the Lord.

Maybe you have vowed to the Lord; are you paying your vows? Costly they may be, but they must be paid. Be a man or woman of your word. Many have vowed to go all the way with God; where He will lead me I will go. Is this you? We must obey the Lord at all costs; it is a serious thing to follow God. Go in the power of the Spirit of God! He will give you the strength and encouragement and He will enable you to go all the way, wherever life's journey leads you!

IMPACT *Daily readings*

A merry person makes good company

Proverbs 15:13-33
"A merry heart maketh a cheerful countenance:
but by sorrow of the heart the spirit is broken." Proverbs 15:13

This so true that a merry heart maketh a cheerful countenance. Many people love to talk about all the gloom and doom subjects. There is always someone sick, the rain is on its way and did you see whose death notice is in the paper? There are some and it gets to the stage you almost avoid them coming across your path as they are always moaning about something or someone. This type of lifestyle is not pleasing in the Lord's eyes. Try to optimise your conversation, be more positive on your outlook on life. Think of the Lord's beautiful creation, continue to be amazed at all the parts in your body that make you tick from day to day.

When you find yourself in a conversation that is always gloom and doom, throw in a sentence or a statement to turn the whole conversation around. Those bearing the sad tidings will soon realise the rest aren't interested in their negativity. The second part of the above verse tells us that by the sorrow of heart is the spirit broken. So it is in many ways, the spirit of fellowship can be strained, the spirit of the love of God will certainly be broken and there will no longer be good harmony in the room. People are living in times when things are doom and gloom enough without making it worse, especially in Christian conversations. We have been set free, focus your conversation on Christ and you will soon find it will be warm and enjoyable and once again you will have a cheerful countenance and a merry heart.

God knows all about us

Genesis 16:7-13
"Thou God seest me." Genesis 16:13

Probably one of the sweetest thoughts of the Christian is how the Almighty God of Heaven and earth sees them at all times. Not only does the Lord see us, but He knows how we feel, how we hurt, how we think and so much more.

Hagar was so lonely after being told to leave the home of Abraham and Sarah; and she had lost everything. She was hungry, thirsty and felt like giving up. When the angel came and gave her a message that all would be well with her, she could hardly believe it! She thought her life was over but the Lord knew He still had plans for her life.

Sometimes in life it can take a crisis of pain, suffering, loss or failure to make us realise that the Lord sees us and knows all about us. If this is what it takes to bring us back in touch with the Lord, then it needs to happen. Sometimes we can be guilty of terrible things in our lives, and things can start to go terribly wrong for us. Right now we have got to come clean before the Lord and also before man if it needs be. If you want the presence and blessing of God upon your life again then you have got to stop running. God sees you and maybe, like Hagar; you are scared and afraid of the future. Let the Lord see you as you are. Be honest with Him and accept what He has in store for you. Don't try to fool the Lord as He knows all about you. God is not harsh rather He is gentle and loving.

How does it make you feel, that out of all the millions of people in the world, God sees you?

IMPACT *Daily readings*

Sit still

Ruth 3:11-18

"Sit still, my daughter, until thou know how the matter will fall" Ruth 3:18

When I was young my mother often told me to stop fidgeting and sit still. Sometimes it is very difficult to sit still. We always feel that we must be on the move and doing something. Maybe one of the reasons we don't hear from God is because He wants to get our attention and all we seem to be doing is running around being busy all the time. Sometimes it is good just to sit still.

Here in this portion of scripture, Naomi had good advice for Ruth and that was to "sit still" until she would see what would happen. It was good advice for Ruth, because as she waited, the perfect plan of God was taking place in her life as the greatest love stories of all time was about to be revealed.

Maybe you are at a point in your life and you just don't know what to do. You may find yourself going here and there, talking to this one and that one, doing everything to find answers. Have you ever tried to "sit still" and wait on God doing His work in your life? His timing is perfect in every one of His children's lives. You are no exception! The Lord knows all about you and the decisions you have to make, the move you must make. Wait on the Lord; this is the time to wait.

The world rushes on so fast these days. With all the technology it just seems to get faster. There are few people who understand the valuable lesson of patience and waiting on the Lord. Take the time to be alone with God! Sit still until the Lord tells you to move on or tells you what to do.

IMPACT *Daily readings*

How God uses trouble!

Psalm 107:1-15

"Then they cried unto the Lord in their trouble." Psalm 107:13

As a boy growing up, every time I would find myself getting into trouble, I would often find myself praying, asking the Lord to help me and promising that if He could get me out of this mess, I would never do it again. Many times I would have found myself praying such a prayer, a natural thing when in trouble, run for help and who best to run to than the Lord.

Today, it is a similar thing for people, for Christians, when something goes wrong we tend to cry unto the Lord. Why not come to the Lord all the times, whether in trouble or not. Maybe it has been years since we have earnestly sought the Lord. Why wait until trouble comes. Start to talk with the Lord today, keep Him up to date with what is going on with you in your life. The Lord loves to be briefed. He specialises in guiding His children through this world on their way home to glory.

Maybe you are backslidden in heart and have wandered far away from the Lord. The Lord has tried to bring you back but in your stubbornness and rebellious nature you have dug in your heels and refused to come. Now trouble has come your way and you don't even see a way out. Maybe the Lord has allowed this trouble to come your way to bring you back to Him. If this has been the case then believe me, whatever the trouble is in your life, it has been worth it.

IMPACT *Daily readings*

The flowing waters

Proverbs 18:1-24

"The words of a man's mouth are as deep waters,
and the wellspring of wisdom as a flowing brook." Proverbs 18:4

One of the most peaceful places to be is by a riverside. I love water, not just water fights or soaking people but actually being beside a riverside. It is so peaceful and quiet. The world continues to move on and yet the river just flows by. This is a tremdeous lesson for us in the busy world in which we live. A river keeps flowing no matter what is around it. There can be cattle, tractors or people and still the river flows, nothing can stop a river flowing, unless the source itself is dried up.

Many Christians today are drying up, so caught up with the world around them, they cease to flow the way they once did. When a river stops flowing, it becomes stagnant and no good for people, fish or even to be around. This is like the dried up Christian, there is no longer sweet fellowship to be enjoyed. Being around a Christian flowing from God is wonderful. They are so in touch with the source of their Master, the Lord God.

God's man

Joshua 1:1-10

"Now after the death of Moses the servant of the LORD it came to pass, that the LORD spake unto Joshua the son of Nun, Moses' minister..." Joshua 1:1

Joshua was the servant of Jehovah God and also the servant of Moses, God's great prophet. As a servant he went up the holy mount with Moses and spent eighty days in the immediate presence of God. He is also noted for remaining in the tabernacle of the congregation. He tasted Heaven on earth, for in Heaven it is said His servants shall serve Him. He gained the highest title, the servant of Jehovah.

God always has His man in place throughout the generations, a man or woman who has stood in the gap as a Christian paving the way to God. What a challenge this is to all of us who are saved to make an influence for good and God while we are alive on this earth. Would you be classed as a servant of the Lord? Do people even know you are saved? Would they be shocked if you told them? Joshua spent time in the presence of God; God's presence is what we need, what we plead. Just to feel and know His presence makes all the difference.

Do not be afraid of them

Jeremiah 1:1-10

"Be not afraid of their faces: for I am with thee to deliver thee,
saith the LORD." Jeremiah 1:8

This surely is one of the most encouraging verses in the entire Bible. How often have we put off doing something for the Lord because of someone's face? Someone or a group of people can so easily hinder you from being effective for God. Maybe you have to meet someone today or tomorrow and your heart is so afraid because of the faces of the people you are meeting.

Take heart and take courage and don't be afraid any longer! The Lord says He will deliver you and He will! He will make the journey easy for you but you must trust in Him. Fear does not come from God. "For God hath not given us the spirit of fear; but of power, and of love, and of a sound mind." (2 Timothy 1:7) Why then should we be afraid of the person we have to meet when we can be sure the Lord is with us? Fear comes from a lack of trust.

Jeremiah had many enemies who opposed him; he really needed this promise from the Lord not to be afraid. Jeremiah was a faithful witness for God and if you are going to be a faithful ambassador for Jesus Christ then the devil will make sure he puts the fear of man into you. Do what you have to do! Do what you know is right and be not afraid of them. This verse has challenged, helped and blessed me so much, especially when I would have been afraid of their faces.

Are you afraid to do something for the Lord because of someone's face? Don't be afraid any longer.

Keep looking to the Lord

Isaiah 45:15-22

"Look unto me and be ye saved all the ends of the earth" Isaiah 45:22

This is one of the most beautiful gospel verses in the Bible. It has a universal application for all to come to Jesus, the Saviour of the world. It was in London, many years ago in a small church, when on a cold Sunday evening the visiting preacher did not turn up to take the service. One of the men who was there was neither a noted nor a gifted speaker. However as he read this text he shouted to a young man who was sitting in the back row who was looking very miserable, a young man of 16 years of age. "Young man" he shouted, "you look very miserable, you need to look to Jesus and live." Suddenly it dawned on him, why he was so miserable; he was a sinner in need of salvation. This young man become a world famous preacher and was called Charles Haddon Spurgeon.

Likewise, when we look to Jesus to save us, He does just that! In many ways however we need to keep looking to Him, not for salvation, but for continual guidance and help during our Christian lives. Christians from all over the world talk to and pray to God every day. He knows everyone by name, knows what they are saying and even knows what we want before we ask Him. Stay close to God throughout your Christian life. Life will be miserable without Him and ultimately you will be the one who will lose out. Be like young Charles and give your life over entirely to God.

Start the journey!

Genesis 29:1-14

"Then Jacob went on his journey,
and came into the land of the people of the east." Genesis 29:1

When Jacob went on his journey, he had no idea what would become of it. He wondered: where would he sleep, would he get a job, would he get married? He just simply trusted in the Lord to look after him. Sometimes we are afraid to start the real journey with God because we are too comfortable with where we are. Jacob would not have had his dream or felt the presence of the Lord as he did if he had never went on the journey. He wouldn't have fallen in love and married Rachel if he hadn't taken the journey. Jacob was blessed in so many ways because he went on the journey.

He didn't know what lay before him; he just went from day to day waiting to see what would happen, continuing to look to the Lord. Although, it was on the journey when the Lord really blessed him. Sometimes we want to be blessed before we do something for God. However, the Lord often blesses us after we serve Him. Maybe you have been blessed with a strong marriage, a nice home, a secure job...is that it? Is that your journey for this life? Is your journey for God complete with these things? What if there is another journey, something else, a different path for you to take? Would you be willing to take that journey? That's the real challenge for us; to take a journey with God, having nothing but His continual presence and guidance.

IMPACT *Daily readings*

The presence of the Lord!

Exodus 33:12-23

"If thy presence go not *with me*, carry us not up hence." Exodus 33:15

One of the most beautiful things we can enjoy and be sure of in the Christian life is the presence of the Lord. I remember hearing about a woman who was a widow and just lost her only daughter in an accident. She was terribly sad in a most understanding way. Her countenance seemed to be sadder by the day. She just longed for glory to be with her husband and daughter again one day.

Suddenly after some time a friend came by, one month since visiting the sad lady. The friend hardly recognised the sad woman this time around. Her countenance had completely changed. The friend could hardly believe the change in her friend and wondered what had happened. The sad lady began to tell her about the advice the same woman gave her one month before.

The friend advised her to speak to Jesus like He is real in your home because He is real in your home. When you put the key in the door, say aloud, "Jesus I know you are here and I'm coming in." When you light the fire, put the kettle on, everything you do, just as you would have talked to your daughter and husband, speak to the Lord because He is in your home, His presence is very real and you need to feel His presence once again. This is what made the difference in this woman's life.

Desire to be an encourager today, speak a word in season to some needy soul today. Maybe your life is one of constant loneliness; bring Jesus into your everyday life. Speak to Him; He is a guest, invisible, but there none the less.

"My presence shall go with thee...." Exodus 33:14

Let God take control of your life!

Psalm 37:1-11

"Commit thy way unto the LORD; trust also in Him; and
He shall bring it to pass." Psalm 37:5

Here is a simple challenge in the Christian life. We are instructed by the Psalmist to commit our way unto the Lord. This simply means to give our lives over to the Lord, so that He will look after us. Sometimes we can try to live our own lives in our own strength. This may be possible but if you want to live the Christian life, serve God and live for Him, it is essential that we commit our way unto the Lord!

Not only are we to commit our way to the Lord but we are also to trust in Him. This means to completely rely on God. Sometimes we can worry about lots of different things in life including school, work, relationships, family, personal health issues and many others. Maybe we worry excessively because we do not trust enough!

In this verse, the Psalmist seems to be concerned about something that is about to happen. He is encouraging us to commit it or give it over entirely into the Lord's hands, trusting completely in the Lord and we can be confident that the Lord will bring whatever it is to pass. Can we be encouraged today to commit our lives afresh into the Lord's hands, trusting in Him completely with our lives? Whatever it is you are worried about, trust God to look after you. He can and He will, providing you let Him take full and absolute control of your life in every single way.

Trouble may come your way

Nahum 1:1-8

"The LORD *is* good, a strong hold in the day of trouble;
and he knoweth them that trust in him." Nahum 1:7

What an encouraging verse we have before us today. This is a verse of strength to motivate us to keep going full on for God. The Lord is good. In every circumstance and situation in life the Lord is good and always will be good. Can you say that from the bottom of your heart that your situation in life right now can easily be blamed on others?

Whatever way you find yourself now, one day trouble may come your way. Trouble beyond your control, trouble that will be difficult to understand and even difficult for you to see the way out of it. Will you be able to say the Lord is still good to me? This is the real challenge of our strength and reliability in God. The verse goes on to tell us and remind us that the Lord 'knoweth them that trust in Him.' Isn't this wonderful to think that God knows us, the moment we put our trust in Him, He knows us as one of His children and will never leave us nor forsake us. When we trust in Him, He protects us, cares for us and loves us more than we will ever know, understand or appreciate. When we trust in Him, things change, we should tend to worry less; the more we trust the less we worry. Have you tried this?

Caution with promotion

Numbers 22:13-17

"For I will promote thee unto very great honour." Numbers 22:17

The devil will use whatever bait it takes to lure you into his trap. He will use the bait to catch, corrupt and captivate his victims; we read all about it in this chapter and how Balaam rose to the devil's bait. At first he said no, but eventually the bait became irresistible and he fell into the trap. At first the bait may seem normal and quite ordinary, like promotion in work, the ladder of ambition may seem like a step in the right direction but be careful the higher you climb, the harder may be the fall. It may mean more money and lots of benefits but be careful. Don't compromise on your principles just because of money.

History is full of those who were going well until they got promotion. When you start to love your money then it becomes a problem, it becomes the root of all evil. Sometimes you will have to make the choice, gold or God. The devil will tell you that you can have both and without realising it, the gold will become what you think about, dream about and ultimately live for, it becomes your God. Balaam was offered whatever it took to lure him. How strong are you to resist the devil when he comes at you? When promotion comes, think it right through to the very end and ask yourself is it worth the risk? Sometimes we have to choose to be humble with God or honoured by man.

IMPACT *Daily readings*

Something God hates

Proverbs 6:16-35
"The Lord doth hate...a proud look." Proverbs 6:16-17

We often hear people talk about God being a God of love which He is. But there are some things which the Lord cannot tolerate and one of them is pride. There is pride of race, there is pride of place and there is pride of face! The Lord hates all three of them. "God resisteth the proud but giveth grace unto the humble." James 4:6

God cannot tolerate pride in any shape or form, and let us always remember that "pride cometh before a fall." Sometimes we can easily fall into the trap of suddenly feeling very proud of ourselves. Money can become the root cause of this, suddenly when money comes our way we can start to look down at others; this can be pride when we think we are better than them. Have you ever thought where you would have been today, had the Saviour not have reached down and saved you from your sin? Never allow pride to mar your testimony and don't make the mistake of pandering up to and after people with lots of money. Stay in your own surroundings. Let the Jones' have their tea parties with their fancy china teacups. If keeping company with people causes you to be unnatural in your conduct you are not in the right company, especially if keeping company with some people causes you to look down at other people. This is called the beginning of pride and it will bring you down. God loves the humble but hates the proud heart.

Claiming our possessions

Deuteronomy 2:26-31

"Behold, I have begun to give...begin to possess." Deuteronomy 2:31

Finally after wandering in the wilderness for forty years, the children of Israel were about to enter the land which God had promised them, which was the land of Canaan. The word of the Lord came to His servant, saying: "Behold, I have begun to give...begin to possess."

Today God has so much for His people but, today many are in the wilderness still searching. We must go forward by faith and claim that which is rightfully ours. Just in front of the people lay the land "flowing with milk and honey" but they had to go in and possess it. This would mean fighting the battles in the land, remembering that the Lord was going before them, preparing the way.

Today, if we are to go anywhere in the Christian life, it may mean many battles; battling temptation, peer pressure, financial struggles, family feuds or even problems with people in your church. We must learn the secret of surviving and winning the battle. Many today are trying to fight the battle all alone in their own strength and if they admit it, they are being defeated. The secret is a life full of power in the fullness of the Holy Ghost, sanctified wholly and completely set apart for God. This is possible for you, my friend! It can be a lonely, lowly life and few will journey with you but it can be one of tremendous blessing. We must enter into God's will by faith and trust the Lord completely for this life. (Acts 1:8)

Now we must prepare for battles and with it severe temptation. Many difficulties may come your way but we know that in the name of Jesus we will be conquerors, claiming our possessions all the way.

Are you willing to be set apart, ready to do God's will? If not, what is it that is stopping or hindering you?

IMPACT *Daily readings*

Strength from above

Daniel 10:16-21

"O man greatly beloved, fear not: peace be unto thee, be strong, yea, be strong. And when he had spoken unto me, I was strengthened, and said, Let my lord speak; for thou hast strengthened me." Daniel 10:19

Like so many other great men of God Daniel suffered from sad and depressive moods. He was sometimes very sorrowful and in verse 16 he says, "Sorrows are turned upon me, and I have retained no strength." There are times when the Christian may feel like this. When it happens we must fight it or it will only become worse and we will become weaker.

When the voice of the Lord came upon Daniel again, then he was strengthened. We need to and must hear from God for our daily strength. Maybe you are weak at this moment; maybe you are not the spiritual giant you once were, well, you can be! Seek today to hear once again from God. We all need a touch from Almighty God to renew us again for the battle. We cannot fight in our weakness, but when we are weak, then through Christ can we be made strong.

We need to and we must hear His voice saying to us, "O man greatly beloved, fear not: peace be unto thee, be strong, yea, be strong." To live an effective Christian life here in the world we must be strong like Daniel of old. There are many enemies to bring us down in this life. That is why we must feed on God's Word and take the time to ask God for His strength. "Only be thou strong and very courageous!" Joshua 1:7

What is it in my life that makes me sorrowful and what can I do to overcome it?

IMPACT *Daily readings*

Where are the men?

Exodus 10:1-11

"Go now ye *that are* men, and serve the LORD." Exodus 10:11

Moses and Aaron were again before Pharaoh, requesting permission for him to let the people go. Moses was preparing the people to get ready to go. He always wanted to put the Lord first. This was a tremendous challenge for the men to serve the Lord. There is such a challenge and need for men today, real men willing and ready to take a stand for the Lord.

The mission field is crying for missionaries, pulpits are empty of men, real men with a real calling and conviction, not a career that pays the bills. Women are crying for men, real men who will love them, lead them, guide them and look after them the way it is supposed to be. Children are crying for the fathers to be real men, to spend the time, to instruct, train and guide them in the way they should go.

It doesn't take a special calling to serve the Lord; rather it is a special calling. When life comes to its end for you, can you honestly say, I served the Lord with my body, mind and soul? Can you say I took every opportunity and enjoyed every possibility that came my way? If there was ever a time when real men are needed it is today. There is no point in complaining about the state of the nation when there is nothing we are willing to do to make a difference, to stand in the gap, to be counted as one who is ready and willing to serve the Lord.

IMPACT *Daily readings*

Pour out your heart

Lamentations 2:13-19

"Pour out thine heart like water before the face of the Lord." Lamentations 2:19

The situation here was very serious, it appeared hopeless. Jerusalem's streets were littered with the bodies of victims slain by the invading Babylonians. No food was available for the people who remained. But the few survivors heeded the prophet's call to repentance and prayer (v19). We know from history that conditions improved and the exile came to an end.

Sometimes in life we can find ourselves in circumstances beyond our control. Often when we face serious and sad situations, we may find ourselves against the wall with nothing or no-one to turn to. Even when you feel you have nothing left, you still have prayer. Very often that's enough to change things. In parts of the world where people are suffering, they have little practical help or even proper medical attention, very often all they have as believers is prayer. They lean so much on God for everything. This surely is a vital lesson for us, to be reminded that there is power in prayer. On other occasions we find we just have to be frank and honest with the Lord about every situation and decision in our lives. The Lord wants and expects us to hold nothing back from Him. Just simply get alone with the Lord and earnestly pour out your heart to Him. He knows your heart and He wants to help you more than you will ever know.

IMPACT *Daily readings*

So annoying!

Job 29:1-15

"Oh, that I were as in months past, as in the days when
God preserved me." Job 29:2

The longings of Job continue in this chapter. "As I was in the days of my youth, when the secret of God was upon my tabernacle." The ancient patriarch was certainly passing through a severe time of sorrow, as he remembered former days of peace and happiness, when he walked with God.

Do you ever go through life and wish things could be a little different? When there is just something you would love to do, but cannot. Somewhere you would love to be, but it just isn't possible? It becomes so annoying! There are times in our lives when we try to work things out, when we cannot it becomes frustrating and so annoying! Whenever someone comes into our lives for a season and we try to work out why they came at that time, why they said that, why they did that and we cannot work out the reason why, even though there may be no explanation, it still becomes so annoying!

Sometimes we can look at the past, with pleasure or regret. The past is behind us now, the old year has gone. Job looked back with fondness and what beautiful thoughts they were. He realised the time for Him to live for God was now, this is the same for us, to make every day count, every day is not a dream, it is real, make it real, enjoy today. It has been given to you by God! When you look back, maybe everything was not so annoying after all.

Are you easily annoyed with little things? God has a wonderful sense of humour and I have no doubt He laughs when he sees you getting so annoyed.

Watch what you say

Proverbs 21:23-31

"Whoso keepeth his mouth and his tongue keepeth his soul from troubles." Proverbs 21:23

How many of us have been hurt by someone saying something to us or about us? There is a saying "Sticks and stones may break your bones but words will never harm you." Sadly this is not true; we have all been hurt and deeply offended by words that people say. Worse than that, have we ever hurt anyone by our words? The tongue in our mouths is a very dangerous weapon and can get us into a lot of trouble.

James, the Apostle, used very strong words in condemning the tongue when he said, "The tongue is a fire, a world of iniquity: so is the tongue among our members, that it defileth the whole body, and setteth on fire the course of nature; and it is set on fire of hell" (James 3:6). If we are living the Christian life in the flesh then our tongue will be a continual problem! How our tongue needs to be cleansed and purified in the precious blood of Jesus Christ, so that we will not have this problem.

Maybe you have a problem with your tongue and you are always complaining, moaning, going on about something or someone which often leads to contention and makes everyone depressed. Having a complaining spirit and a gossiping tongue is not good company. Try not to be around such people or you will become like them. Maybe you are this person. Have you ever wondered why you don't have many friends? Maybe they don't come around you because they are scared you will talk about them.

Pray that God will help you control your tongue so that it can be used more for His glory.

Are you like a horse?

Psalm 32

"Be ye not as the horse, or as the mule, which have no understanding." Psalm 32:9

All of us at some stage in our lives need guidance, guidance from people and guidance from the Lord. Although quite often we tend to take guidance from our friends before we take guidance from the Lord. We tend to make up our own mind about something and then seek the Lord's approval for it. A horse or certainly a mule can be a very stubborn animal. No matter what direction you want to take they will still be determined to go their own way.

I remember doing a summer camp in Ohio, America, working as a camp counsellor in a children's camp. Part of my job was looking after the horses and riding them each day. One particular day while riding my horse through the forest something spooked it and it took off at top speed. It would not turn right or left and I had such bother getting it stopped. What was worse, I was riding it bare back and I jumped up and down like a kangaroo until I nearly fainted with pain. When it eventually stopped I jumped off and thought to myself that is one stubborn animal. All it wanted to do was do its own thing and run its own way.

There is no point in asking the Lord for guidance if we are deliberately going to do our own thing anyway. When we come before the Lord with a clean pure heart, empty of self, pride and stubbornness then the Lord says, "follow me and I will show you the way in which you shall go."

Rest

Zephaniah 3:10-17

"The LORD thy God in the midst of thee is mighty; he will save, he will rejoice over thee with joy; he will rest in his love, he will joy over thee with singing."

Zephaniah 3:17

During the autumn, together with four friends we headed off to Lithuania on a fact finding mission to see what potential there would be in possible evangelism within the country. While we went to try and help the local Christians, encourage them in their faith and walk with God we found the trip was more effective in different ways.

The team was made up of five individuals, all married men, with different jobs, different churches yet with one common purpose in life. This purpose was to live for God and serve Him with our lives. We found that the Christian life had many challenges and restraints put upon it. Often the focus was on the church and not Christ, on others and not God. We found as the hours and days went by we began to get strangely warmed again in our love for Christ and fellow man. The rest in Christ we enjoyed in sweet fellowship was wonderful. The fellowship of brothers and sisters in Christ is essential in maintaining your focus in the Lord.

Get to know the book

Joshua 1:1-9
"This book of the law shall not depart out of thy mouth;
but thou shalt meditate therein day and night...." Joshua 1:8

Here the Lord was giving specific instruction to Joshua. He was to be the newly appointed leader of the people, to lead them out of Egypt. This was going to be an enormous task for Joshua. He had enemies on every side. He soon realised that in order to be a strong leader he needed to keep close to God. He needed to listen to daily instructions from the Lord as to how to eat and how to live. What a challenge this is for us today, to stay close to the Lord and to be strong in the Lord. The Lord gave great promises to Joshua as He does to every one of His children. Joshua was encouraged to be strong and very courageous in His walk and service for the Lord.

We find the secret of Joshua's strength was the law of God. The Lord instructed Joshua that the Word of God should not depart from his mouth. Isn't it wonderful when the Word of the living God just flows from our lips as we have a normal conversation? Every time you have a conversation, seek to bring the Lord into it. He will bless you for it, not just once a day was Joshua encouraged to seek the Lord, but rather continually day and night. How easy it is for us to read about the book, but rather spend your time getting into the book. I remember while in Bible College being overwhelmed with all the different books to study about the Bible when a wise old minister told me to get to know the English Bible, rather than books about God, get to know the God of the book.

IMPACT *Daily readings*

The enemy will attack!

Isaiah 59:16-21

"When the enemy shall come in like a flood,
the Spirit of the Lord shall lift up a standard against him." Isaiah 59:16

Have you ever noticed when a flood comes how it takes everything with it, everything that is before it? That is what the old devil; the enemy of the gospel seeks to do. If you are serious about the Lord and His work then you can expect opposition. When I was going with the flow in my life, everybody seemed to love me, but when I got serious about the ministry, opposition came from everywhere, even my closest friends in the gospel I lost. This is often what happens when you become serious with God, your faith will be tested to the core, you may have to walk a lonely journey but what great comfort I got knowing the Lord was with me.

Whatever forms the flood of the enemy comes in, remember the Spirit of the Lord will lift up a standard against him. Pray that your enemies can even be at peace with you so that the gospel can flourish and have free course. Just like Hezekiah did, long ago, stand back and let the Lord deal with all the opposition that comes your way. Be careful not to get caught up with all the unnecessary affairs, you will often find you cannot beat the enemy, therefore from my experience don't fight them, ask the Lord to sort them out!

At last

Genesis 26:15-22

"And he removed from thence, and digged another well; and for that they strove not: and he called the name of it Rehoboth; and he said, For now the LORD hath made room for us, and we shall be fruitful in the land." Genesis 26:22

Every time Isaac started building wells of water he seemed to come across fierce opposition from many sources, especially the Philistines. This is a lesson for those involved in the work of the Gospel that opposition will come from many sides, even those most unexpected. Isaac moved from the well of Esek and Sitnah and now finds himself at Rehoboth. The enemy moved him on but finally he found a place where he could dig freely without opposition.

The work of the Gospel will have its obstacles and hindrances, but the time will come when you can enjoy much freedom and liberty. This is the time to dig hard and work for the souls of the people. The enemy had stopped striving with them. Notice in the verse, "now the Lord had made room for us". This is the difference, make sure the Lord is in all your plans because you can then enjoy His protection and His guidance. Even though Isaac was in enemy territory, the land of the Philistines, the Lord still made room for him. Don't be afraid to advance into enemy territory, go and go with the Lord. You may have to keep moving but the Lord will have a place for you to stop and start digging.

Hold steady

Exodus 17:8-16

"And his hands were steady until the going down of the sun." Exodus 17:12

Israel was winning the battle while Moses held his hands up in prayer, but when he let his hands down and lowered them, the enemy Amalek prevailed. Aaron and Hur rushed to his aid and helped to hold up his hands. When his hands were up again, Israel once again took control and won the battle.

More than ever before our hands need to be steady. Steady in prayer, steady in reading the Bible, steady in witnessing, steady in living the Christian life and steady when we are under attack from temptation.

The enemy is ever on the look-out to see us slipping. When we begin to slip and are at our weakest the enemy satan makes his move with temptation. Often when we think we are strong, we are really weak. Just like Aaron looked out for his brother Moses when he was weak, look out for your brothers and sisters as the time may come when they will need your help. Look out for signs that they are weak and be ready to encourage and lift them up.

We need to be continually watching and praying all the time as sometimes we can be sailing along just fine, and so can be tempted to take our eyes off the Lord, relying on our own strength. Eventually, an Aaron or Hur may come to help you. Don't despise them or reject them as they could be servants sent from God.

Is there someone I know who needs a little help from a friend? "Lord, help me help them."

IMPACT *Daily readings*

Overcoming anger

Ecclesiastes 7:1-29

"Be not hasty in thy spirit to be angry: for anger resteth in the bosom of fools."

Ecclesiastes 7:9

In my teenage years I had an awful problem with frustration and anger. Sometimes at the smallest thing I would find myself boiling inside, then to get it out of my system I would curse and shout, not at people but believe it or not, at cows! In my teenage years I grew up on a farm and really enjoyed looking after the cattle every morning and evening, before and after school. Looking back now I realise God was taking a dealing with my life. Every time He would try to get my attention and speak to me I would go off in a rage. I remember my mum wondering and asking what was wrong with me. Little did she realise, God was answering her prayers of seeing her son give up his sinful life. It was a terrible time and I really hated it! Many times it would cause me to weep uncontrollably, and I just didn't know how to control it.

Finally at the age of 17 on 25th June 1989, I found the answer. God called me one final time. I was about to go completely wild and throw the towel in on my Christian upbringing, but, as I walked the plank and was about to jump into the sea of this world, Jesus called one final time. I held out my hand and He took it and saved me. Suddenly my anger was now controllable. Christ was the answer! He saved me and now He helps me overcome sin, anger and frustration and all the other problems that come with it. I am by no means sinless, but with His help I try to sin less every day.

How do you control your frustration and anger?

Be strong and courageous

Deuteronomy 31:1-6

"Be strong and of a good courage.....He will not fail thee
nor forsake thee." Deuteronomy 31:6

It is very important that we read and memorise such portions of scripture that we have before us today. The Lord was with Moses and Joshua as they fought the battles for Him. We live in a very dangerous and discouraging world. It is changing every day. In many parts of the world children of God are being persecuted.

I remember being on a mission team to China and then on to Laos where we helped to smuggle Bibles to those dear Christians. On one occasion we got to go to their church in Laos. As the sermon was preached it was so real how much these people looked to the Lord for protection. Any day they could be arrested and put in jail or death. Many of them were and still are today taken from their home and are never heard of again. Bibles are so few in these countries that many of them have to share the Word with maybe six other believers.

When the Lord promised He would not fail them nor forsake them, they believed it. Many of us today are full of fear and doubt. We worry about the least little thing. Yet these believers are not in the least bit worried, they live and serve the Lord as if it was their last day on earth. If we knew today was going to be our last day on earth, maybe we would live it differently. Take courage in the Word of God my friend, the Lord is with you every step of the way. Ask the Lord to make you a strong Christian in these days in which we live.

IMPACT *Daily readings*

The soul winner

Daniel 12:1-4

"And they that be wise shall shine as the brightness of the firmament; and they that turn many to righteousness as the stars forever and ever." Daniel 12:3

For me this is a beautiful verse as it is so full of eternal richness and encouragement. Sometimes we labour away down here on earth for souls and there isn't much reward. Maybe you have been labouring for souls for years and haven't seen much fruit. We must remember that the Lord sees your heart; He knows the efforts you have made in the gospel to reach the lost.

Maybe you are a successful soul winner and other Christians don't seem to care much. Quite often you must realise they are jealous of your labours and success. While it is hard to understand why they don't rejoice with you, we must at all times keep our eyes on the prize and the eternal goal. Christ acknowledges and records everything we do for Him. He has a special love for the soul winner.

There are wise people in this world, but how much more special it is to have wisdom from God? What an honour it is to be used by God to turn many to righteousness and to turn away from the world and all its sin. The scriptures also tell us that "he that winneth souls is wise." This is the real battle today to rescue dying souls from hell. Many are so entangled with the cares of this world that they no longer have the passion and zeal for souls.

When is the last time you spoke to someone about salvation?

IMPACT *Daily readings*

The need for fellowship

Nehemiah 4:13-23

"The work is great and large, and we are separated upon the wall,
one far from another." Nehemiah 4:19

Nehemiah's task was great as he had the responsibility of re-building the great wall of Jerusalem. He was greatly concerned that as the people were working, the wall was now dividing the people as they were being separated upon the wall, far from one another. These were days of crisis when Nehemiah was seeking to re-build the walls of Jerusalem.

At the beginning of 2012, together with Joanna we were in Mexico for two weeks, it is there that most of this devotional was written. I remember seeing someone's deck chair with their towel on it and on top of it was a Christian book. My heart jumped with excitement at the thought of possibly meeting another Christian in the far side of the world. Suddenly denominations, Bible versions were broken down as the one thing that connected us was personal faith in Jesus Christ.

I know people who sit in the same church, read from the same Bible, have exactly the same convictions about all Biblical matters and yet they don't speak to each other, in fact cannot stand each other and we wonder why there is no blessing in the church. My friend, don't spend your life arguing and fighting over little things. Agree to disagree and focus on the bigger picture. Souls are perishing and few there seem to be who care. Make good friends with those you can enjoy fellowship with and protect those precious times together.

IMPACT *Daily readings*

What is the point?

Job 27:11-23

"Though he heap up silver as the dust." Job 27:16

Many people are fixed and focused on pensions and financial supply to see them into old age. Some have an endless supply of valuable assets like furniture, paintings, land, houses and the list could go on. But what will this really gain you in eternity. While many missionary organisations are struggling, some are sitting with large amounts of valuable assets. Although Job is talking about the wicked man with God, the lesson is equally challenging to Christians. What have we really sacrificed for the Lord when so many are struggling and we are so well off? There is a blessing in sacrifice and we will never know the blessing until we sacrifice, as the scriptures puts it, it is more blessed to give than to receive. When we give something to the Lord it should be done quietly expecting nothing in return.

Imagine your life at the very end; you are old and lying in bed very close to death's door. You have gathered and gained all your possessions worth a great deal of money, what next? I am often challenged with the parable of the rich fool who kept getting bigger and bigger with no thought of his eternal security. Again the real challenge is, how much are we really focused on things here on earth? Are we building God's kingdom on earth, or our own little kingdom with only our own selfish desires at heart? God could remove the whole lot over night and any one of us could be gone by the morning. Dust we are made and to the dust we shall return taking nothing of human wealth or possessions with us. So really and truthfully, what is the point?

Strengthen one another

1 Samuel 23:16-18

"And Jonathan...went to David into the wood, and strengthened his hand in God."

1 Samuel 23:16

Jonathan is certainly someone who we could learn so much from. He had so many characteristics for us to learn from and is a great role model. He was strong and courageous in battle, showing no jealousy or envy towards David. He was pleased to take second place and sacrifice everything for David, a friend whom he had come to love. At the cost of being misunderstood himself, he stood by David when his own father, King Saul, was persecuting him and seeking to kill him.

David was on the run and spent many years running for his life. Not only was David a shepherd boy who became a King after God's own heart, David spend many years hiding from the King and all his soldiers who sought after his life. Here in this portion we find David hiding all alone in the woods. Jonathan went looking for him, probably risking his own life, found him and began to encourage him in the Lord. Everyone else seemed to turn against David but there was Jonathan who went out of his way to encourage him in the Lord.

Maybe there is someone out there just like David who needs you, patiently waiting for someone like you. Someone who is lonely, discouraged, or depressed and they could be encouraged, helped back onto the road today if you would just make that call or make that journey. Whoever comes to your mind right now is waiting for you and your visit will do them more good than you will ever realise. They need strengthened in the Lord and you are the one to do it.

The battle is not yours

2 Chronicles 20:14-19

"Thus saith the LORD unto you, Be not afraid nor dismayed by reason
of this great multitude; for the battle is not yours, but God's." 2 Chronicles 20:15

King Jehoshaphat was a man of prayer. Sometimes he entered into
very serious and dangerous battles. Many of these battles looked
impossible to win, yet he took his battle to the Lord in prayer as he
realised he needed God's help and strength to win.

Jehoshaphat and his men didn't know what to do in this day of trouble.
They were greatly discouraged and dismayed. Yet the Lord told them not
to be afraid of the great multitude that was coming before them, because
the battle was His and not theirs.

Sometimes we can be in danger of fighting our battles in our own strength.
How we all need to learn the simple lesson of seeking the face of God in
every situation of our lives, especially during the battles. God always has
a plan and a way out of every difficult situation. Take your battle to Him,
leave it with Him and watch the Lord work it out. The Lord said in (v17)
"Ye shall not need to fight in this battle, stand still and see the salvation of
the LORD." He reminded them not to be worried or afraid as He was with
them. It is the same with us today. Why fight alone when the Lord is with
us every step of the way?

IMPACT *Daily readings*

Take it as from the Lord

1 Kings 12:16-24
"The word of God came..." 1 Kings 12:22

This reading is a tragic affair during some of the most troublesome times in David's life. Rehoboam the son of Solomon could not fully understand why the Lord sent the message but when he realised it was from the Lord, "...this thing is from me," he and his people accepted it. Have you ever blamed someone else on your circumstances or condition you find yourself in? It's always easy to blame someone else for something. This seems to be human nature. Or even blaming yourself for something is nearly even worse as it drives you to self pity.

Have you ever thought for a moment that the trying circumstance that you currently find yourself in may be sent from God? He does these things now and again, we may never know why, ultimately for our good and His glory. Take a moment and talk to the Lord and ask Him is your present circumstance sent to you from Him, He will confirm it in His Word. Then the real challenge is if it is from the Lord are you prepared to accept it? Obedience is one of the greatest challenges we all have to face, full obedience to the Lord and His will for our lives. Interesting walk this Christian life isn't it, I love it!

IMPACT *Daily readings*

God loves a cheerful giver

Deuteronomy 16:13-17
"Every man shall give as he is able."
Deuteronomy 16:17

Whenever we talk about tithing our money, the common belief is that ten percent of your income goes into the Lord's house or your local church and that is what your tithe is. Some would disagree and believe it should be given to the Lord's work where there is a need. In fact if ten people tithed to the local church that would be enough to pay a ministers salary. The lesson here is not so much that we give that matters but rather how we give it.

The Lord often watches, as He did long ago when, "He sat over against the treasury," how we give, and our attitude to giving. Some people give to the work of God and it is no real sacrifice to them even if the amount they give is quite large. The Lord looks for love and sacrifice in giving and He rewards accordingly. We are not to look at what others give, but rather what we are able to give ourselves; certainly there must be an element of sacrifice on our behalf. Some people give to the Lord what is left out of their wages, rather, I think we should give to the Lord first and then spend as we need to spend. You will find by putting the Lord first, by honouring Him that He in turn will honour you and in fact you may find your money going further than it previously did.

Watch God move

Exodus 14:13-29

"The LORD shall fight for you, and ye shall hold your peace."

Exodus 14:14

After the ten plagues in Egypt, Pharaoh finally told Moses to take the Children of Israel out of Egypt. They left immediately and made their way to the Red Sea. In the mean time Pharaoh was raging that they had gone and he and his mighty army followed them to bring them back. The journey was a long one through the wilderness.

When they came to the Red Sea, the people began to complain against Moses because they now saw the soldiers of Pharaoh coming after them and the Red Sea in front of them, there seemed to be no way out of the situation. They began to complain and wish they had stayed in Egypt as slaves than to die in the wilderness. Then Moses said these astonishing words, "Fear ye not, stand still and see the salvation of the Lord." Suddenly before their eyes the Red Sea began to part, and a pathway was formed for the Children of Israel to make their way to the other side. They quickly did so with the army of Pharaoh on their heels. Once the last Israelite crossed over, God closed the sea over again and Pharaoh and his army were destroyed. The Lord fought the battle for them that day and what a victory it was.

The situation seemed hopeless yet with God nothing is impossible. Never say a person or a situation is hopeless because God can save the most unexpected person in your eyes to be a great trophy of grace in his eyes and can turn any situation around for His own glory. Are you prepared to watch God move?

IMPACT *Daily readings*

I feel so tired!

Daniel 7:18-25

"He shall wear out the saints of the Most High." Daniel 7:25

I have a friend called Geoff and every time he would come to Poland with us on a mission trip he would soon suffer from a lack of sleep and the words he would continually say would be, "I am so tired". This can be one of the greatest problems in life, let alone the Christian life, being worn out and continually tired. Especially today with modern day entertainment in the home, it is so easy to sit up late and still rise up early but eventually your body won't be able to stick the pace and will cry for sleep.

The devil, on the other hand, wants you to be so busy in your Christian life that he manages to keep you away from growing in the Lord. He will want to wear you out mentally, physically and frustrate you spiritually that you will become useless as a Christian. He cannot steal your soul, but he can certainly disarm you as a soldier. He will want you involved in as many activities as possible, making sure you have no time for church or the Lord's work.

In Psalm 37, God exhorts His people to "Rest in the Lord" (verse 7). Sometimes we need to go slow, move at a different pace and accomplish more in the long run. Satan wants to wear you out, to bring you down. This could come as a warning to you, to get priorities right, to do something with your life that will last for all eternity. Are you so busy in your life right now that your head is completely turned to the degree that you don't know whether you are coming or going? Then come apart and rest a while before you do come apart. Wear on for Jesus, don't wear out.

IMPACT *Daily readings*

No turning back

Deuteronomy 17:14-20

"Ye shall henceforth return no more that way." Deuteronomy 17:16

Time after time as Moses sought to lead the Children of Israel, their hearts had that secret longing to be back in Egypt again, out of which the Lord had miraculously delivered them. Here is what they said: "We remember the fish, which we did eat in Egypt freely; the cucumbers, and the melons, and the leeks, and the onions, and the garlick: But now our soul is dried away: there is nothing at all, beside this manna, before our eyes." Numbers 11:5-6

It is not surprising that the anger of the Lord was kindled against them. How quickly these people forgot the goodness of the Lord in bringing them out of the terrible bondage of Egypt, the amazement of the Red Sea opening up before them as they passed through, and the destruction of Pharaoh and his army!

Human nature has not changed. There are often secret longings in the heart for 'the old haunts' and even the company of Godless friends who were dragging you down to hell. The fact that we are saved does not make us immune to temptation, and the devil is ever so busy, in his own subtle way, of enticing you to return.

Maybe you are presently being challenged to return to your old ways, be careful; or else it could bring you down. Keep in mind the command of the Lord: "Ye shall henceforth return no more that way." It is easy to give up, easy to go back; the real challenge for the Christian today is to keep moving forward, keep going on, never giving in and never giving up!

IMPACT *Daily readings*

A mother's love

Exodus 2:1-10

"And when she could not longer hide him, she took for him an ark of bulrushes, and daubed it with slime and with pitch, and put the child therein; and she laid it in the flags by the river's brink." Exodus 2:3

Think of the circumstances surrounding the story of baby Moses. He would have been slain but out of love, his mother made him a little ark of bulrushes and let it sail down the river resting by the rivers brink. Her only hope of this child's survival was the baby being found by the princess, whose natural love for an infant so young would cause the survival of baby Moses.

The story is almost unbelievable, as to how the mother of Moses was sent for and paid wages to look after her own son. It is a remarkable story. The focus is then on Moses, the chosen man of God to lead the children of Israel. However sometimes we can overlook the mother and all her hard work in the young and tender years of his early life. This is a lesson for us to focus and reflect upon the lives of our own mother, all the precious times in our early years of learning and development, our first walk, school and the list is endless. I am sure you will agree there is no one who has loved you, cared for you and wanted the best for you than your dear mother, truly a gift from God.

Put God first

Genesis 1:1-10
"In the beginning God created the heaven and the earth." Genesis 1:1

Notice here from the very first verse in the Bible God is put first. In the beginning God! What a challenge this is for us to put the Lord first in our lives every day in everything. It is one thing talking about it and another thing actually putting the Lord first in our lives every day, in our relationships, friendships, social gatherings and everyday living.

To put God first is to have our priorities right. I find in my own life it is essential to put the Lord first, before man, before church, before all things. To put the Lord second is rebellion and this often comes from a selfish heart. The very first thing God created was time; it had a beginning and an ending. In contrast eternity has no beginning and no ending. I will spend eternity with the Lord. This is a wonderful thought. Time is something we all have, it has begun and someday it will end. How we spend or waste our times depends on us. I would suggest spend the best time with God, early in the day and early in your life. There is a blessing that comes with starting the day and putting the Lord first in all that you do.

MPACT *Daily readings*

Consider your ways!

Haggai 1:1-5

"Now therefore thus saith the LORD of hosts; Consider your ways." Haggai 1:5

Twice in this chapter the Lord urges the people to consider their ways, in verse 5 & 7. Sometimes we need to be reminded, encouraged and even told to consider our ways. Especially when the Lord is speaking to us, we need to take heed and consider our ways. Maybe we are at a stage in our lives and we are being forced to make a rash decision, it is not always good to make a rash decision. Sometimes it can be the wrong decision to make.

More importantly, maybe you are at the stage in your life when you are growing cold in your heart. It is essential that you take time to realise where a cold heart will eventually lead you. The most miserable person in the world is a back slidden Christian. The time is here when the Lord's people must stand up and be counted, the Lord's work must go on. Consider your ways, that what you are doing does not hinder the work of God or lead others astray. The work of God needs to go on; people need to be reached with the Gospel. Maybe you are not involved in the Lord's work. Consider your ways and try getting involved in God's work and do something for the Lord. This is where the blessing is!

Breaking comes before blessing

Hosea 10:9-15

"Sow to yourselves in righteousness, reap in mercy; break up your fallow ground:
for it is time to seek the LORD, till he come and rain righteousness upon you."

Hosea 10:12

Breaking up uncultivated and fallow ground is not an easy task and takes a lot of work. In many ways so it is spiritually. It is not easy to earnestly seek after God. Whenever the farmer takes to the fields with the plough, it is set to cut deep into the earth so that all the soil can be reached if he is going to have any sort of harvest. This preparation time is vital for the farmer and will pay dividends later on for him. For us to expect and desire this blessing from God then the preparation to meet God is necessary. In the same way as the farmer spends time in the fields so we must spend time with God.

Surely, "it is time to seek the Lord;" this verse tells us God promises to always draw near to those who draw near to Him. "Draw nigh to God, and he will draw nigh to you." (James 4:8) Now is the time! Today is the day for you to get alone with God and to seek His face. He will be found of you when you seek and search for Him with all your heart. The "breaking" process may not be easy but allow God to work and allow His Spirit to search your heart. Any old stones, rubbish, idols, habits, people or anything found needs to be got rid of. Dump it and have it washed in His precious blood. Then you can wait and watch the showers of blessing that follow! Just like the cultivated ground needs the rain, so we need the showers of God's blessing upon us.

Smooth talkers

Jeremiah 37:16-21

"Is there any word from the LORD?" Jeremiah 37:17

King Zedekiah had a lot of advisers around him to help him in times of crisis when serious decisions had to be made. The King however didn't really trust them and had very little confidence in them. During this time the prophet Jeremiah was a prisoner and the king called for him to seek his counsel. He knew him to be a man of God, one who would speak his mind and tell him the truth.

The king asked Jeremiah if there was any word from the Lord in a very anxious manner. "There is," replied the prophet, "for thou shalt be delivered into the hand of the King of Babylon." As a result of his honesty and faithfulness, Jeremiah was allowed certain privileges in the court of the prison.

This is what is missing today, honest, faithful Jeremiahs. Pulpits are full of smooth talkers, in some ways false prophets for failing to tell their congregations the way to heaven, afraid of offending their people. Others are afraid to touch certain subjects in the Bible in case there is a fall out. Others fail to rebuke sin in case it offends someone, often someone wealthy in case they decide to leave the church.

That is why we must focus on the Lord. His children are genuinely looking for a word from the Lord and the Lord's servants often fail to bring the true word of the Lord to the people. Be like Jeremiah and speak the truth at all times, even if it hurts, even if it is difficult to do, speak the truth.

Time to praise the Lord

Joel 2:18-26

"And ye shall eat in plenty, and be satisfied, and praise the name of the LORD
your God, that hath dealt wondrously with you:
and my people shall never be ashamed." Joel 2:26

Sometimes life can go rolling by so quickly, like a child's roundabout, going so fast we can hardly stop it! As a result, our spiritual life and our relationship with God is affected. We find on the Lord's day that it is no different as we rush into church and rush home again to get the spuds and without realising that something has happened! We missed out and forgot to really take time to thank God and to praise His name the way we should have. Every time we have food we should thank and praise the Lord for His provision. What a lesson in this verse that we are never to be ashamed of the Lord.

As we think of the numerous blessings He has given us, is it not selfish of us not to take time to be thankful unto the Lord for absolutely everything we have and are? It is a good habit to thank the Lord every day for something. Even in the bad times in your life, thank God for them. No matter how difficult a situation you may find yourself in, give God thanks and work it out together. Look back to see everything He has done for you in the past and look around you to see everything He is doing for you at present. Why then should we worry about the future? Entrust your future entirely into His care and keeping. The more we praise and focus on the Lord, the less we'll worry about ourselves.

The beauty of childhood

Lamentations 2:10-21

"The children and the sucklings swoon in the streets of the city." Lamentations 2:11

As we read this very sad portion, we tend to believe that with children there is very little hope for them when they are young as far as seeking for and living for God. It is important to note that children can equally be saved as well as an adult. From my experience children can pray and be obedient to the will of God in their lives. Children can live godly and holy lives before the Lord. Children can be very receptive to the word of God as well as easily influenced to trusting and serving God.

Children can respond to the word of God, they can trust Him; they can be and are part of God's great plan. When children face problems in life they can easily trust the Lord to sort their problems out. I have noticed something else, and that is that children can take their stand for the Lord, they can be a tremendous witness for Him when they are young. They can also do what is right in the sight of the Lord. Children can also become cold at heart towards the Lord, they too can become discouraged, but they very quickly get over disagreements and discouragements. Children also love to praise God, they understand more than we think and remember more from a sermon than most adults do.

These are just some of the things I have mentioned about children. Read over them again slowly and ask yourself the question; do I have the faith and Christ likeness of a little child? Maybe this is what is wrong, when we doubt, have disbelief, continue to be discouraged, maybe it is when we need to have the faith and live the Christian life just like a little child again.

The purified life

Malachi 3:1-12

"He shall sit as a refiner and purifier of silver:
and he shall purify the sons of Levi." Malachi 3:3

When a silversmith or craftsman can see his own face in the silver, then he is satisfied with his work. When we come to Christ, He is forever doing a work of refining and purifying in the hearts of His own people. One thing we need to be aware of is that if Christ is going to use us, then we must be purified until all the filthiness of sin is brought to the surface and removed. Whatever it is that lingers underneath and within has got to go. All those impure thoughts, words and actions, they all must go! God will keep working until it's done. The longer it takes the more painful it may become. The colder the silver, the harder the hammer blows. The colder we become and further we go, then the harder the refining process may become.

Both the refining and purifying can be a long, drawn out and painful procedure. But it is the only way, if the blessed face of the Lord Jesus is to be reflected in your life and mine. Will you allow the Heavenly Silversmith to refine and purify you today? It is not too late to put your life afresh into His hands, with all your sin, failures and weaknesses. Ask the Lord to purge away all the sin and impurity that lies within by the power of His Spirit and the cleansing of His precious blood. Only then can we expect to, and will shine for God!

Be like the horse!

Proverbs 21:21-31

"The horse *is* prepared against the day of battle: but safety *is* of the LORD."

Proverbs 21:31

Quite often we can live in the Spirit of defeat and pessimism. This is the way the devil wants you to live. He doesn't want you to have the joy of the Lord in your heart, your life and your everyday living. Just like the horse is prepared and ready to go, we must be constantly ready for the battle, it is not a physical battle but rather a Spiritual warfare. We must always be ready to speak up for Jesus, to tell others what He means to us, what He has done for us and what He can do for them. The devil hates active Christians, therefore he will get you at your weakest point, whatever area of your life that is. Be careful, he is going to try to get you at this point, be on your guard.

Of course the great comfort of the Christian life is the sure knowledge that Christ is with us, the Lord had promised to be with us and to look after us. Therefore run to Christ for safety and shelter, especially when under attack in the heat of the battle, He will fight your fights for you. If you must fight them, then take the Lord with you. Don't lock Him outside the door of the battle of temptation. Don't refine the Lord to one room of the house or one day of the week. If you do then that's all He will get and take and a life of defeat awaits you if this is the case. Flee to Christ before the battle comes and He will give you victory in the battle.

IMPACT *Daily readings*

Put the hand brake on

Psalm 46

"Be still, and know that I am God." Psalm 46:10

Sometimes amongst the business of life we need to just 'take time out', be still, and simply wait on God. We live in a day when technology is at its best, pretty much everywhere in the world we can gain access to the internet. People have their phones on them 24/7. Try to ask them to do without their phone for one day and it's like taking a dummy out of a baby's mouth. The immediate access we have with communication is wonderful. However when we become addicted to this form of communication, it can seriously affect our communication with God.

You might wonder how this is so. Well years ago, when a Christian got up in the morning they went straight to God in prayer and read the Word of God in a paper paged Bible. Nowadays younger Christians, lift their phone and while they read the word on their phones, all the social networking sites and at the touch of a button and without realising it our time is spent wondering rather than worshipping.

The Lord says "Be Still", take the time away from all these things, however hard it may be and wait on the Lord. When He comes, the presence is very sweet to say the least, then you will know He is God.

The power of love

Song of Solomon 5:1-17

"I rose up to my beloved." Song of Solomon 5:5

The Song of Solomon is a beautiful book about love. It can be used as to how we express our love one to another. It can be used as Christ's love for you, or help us to realise how much we love Christ. Another challenge we find coming up in the scriptures is the challenge of rising up early to pray and spend time alone with God.

If we truly love the Lord Jesus in our hearts then we will wish to be alone with Him in the mornings. We too, shall rise up to open to our Beloved. This without doubt is the best time to be alone with God, any time of course is good, but there is something special about the early morning. This is not something we need to pray about, just do it. Some people think we need to specifically ask God for everything. The Lord has given us intelligence, brains and a will. We don't need to ask Him for the things we already need to do. Just do it. When wondering should you talk to a particular person about the Lord, just do it. The Lord has already put that person on your heart. The Lord doesn't need to do something for us that we can do ourselves.

Do you struggle with the mornings, then this is a challenge. We would do almost anything for our earthly loved ones. If Joanna asked me to walk two miles for a Chinese meal, I would do it. Just as we like to spend time with the ones we love here on earth, how much more should we be challenged to rise up early, for our Beloved Lord and Saviour Jesus Christ, just to spend time alone with Him.

No complaining

Numbers 11:1-15

"And when the people complained, it displeased the Lord." Numbers 11:1

There is nothing more grieving and displeasing to the Lord than grumbling and complaining on the part of His people. We have been given so much yet we tend to complain so much as well. Deep in the heart of Africa, the Christians there have nothing yet they praise the Lord for everything, sometimes for hours on end. We have everything and we praise the Lord for nothing, even listening to sound from some Christians' lips at church on Sunday is very difficult to hear.

We find it recorded here in Numbers that when complaining started, the Lord's anger was kindled and He sent fire amongst those who started it. Only when Moses prayed for the people was the fire quenched. Are you troubled with a complaining spirit, always finding fault with someone. This type of lifestyle is very grievous to the Lord. You cannot grow as a believer with a complaining attitude. If you are this type of person, ask God to deliver you from this sinful life. Maybe you are friends with someone who is always grumbling and complaining, tell them to stop it, that it grieves the Lord very much. You will find too by complaining less you will enjoy life much more because you will have more time to focus on the Lord, talk about Him and your heart then will be strangely warmed.

There is an old ancient Arab proverb which says: "I complained that I had no shoes until I met a man who had no feet!"

God's mountain

Isaiah 2:1-5
"Come ye, and let us go up to the mountain of the Lord." Isaiah 2:3

In March 2012 together with a team we went to Israel, this was such a special trip as we were able to see so much of this beautiful land. While we were there we travelled up several mountains. One of these mountains was Mount Carmel; this was the mountain that Elijah the prophet of fire slew all the false prophets of Baal. It was very inspiring as I sat and reflected upon all that happened on that mountain all those years ago. Mount Carmel was the very place where the fire of God came down and consumed the sacrifice that Elijah prepared. (1 Kings 17&18)

When you are up on a mountain it has a very special feeling. The occasion here in Isaiah was no different. The people here wanted to meet with God and learn from Him. They wanted the Lord to teach them and they were determined to walk in the paths of the Lord. "He will teach us of his ways, and we will walk in his paths." What a wonderful thought this is for us to climb up the mountain to get alone with God. The mountain is a place away from the hustle and bustle of life to focus on where we are at with God. Ask God to cleanse you from all your sin and ask Him to fill you with His Spirit. You will come back a new person with a new focus and greater desire to live for God.

The voice of God!

Genesis 22:1-14

"Abraham....went unto the place of which God had told him." Genesis 22:3

Abraham was known as the friend of God and there was a reason for this. He lived his life in such closeness to the Lord. Here was an occasion when God spoke directly to Abraham and he heard His voice. Sometimes the Lord is speaking to us and we don't hear His voice. We can be so rushed that we don't have time to listen to his instruction for the day. We want to listen to many voices, to advise, help and guide us, be it a friend, parent or pastor. But the best voice we need to listen to is the voice of God.

Abraham received a message that many of us would find it hard to accept. He was to go to a place where he would not go if left to himself. Have you ever been in a situation or a predicament when you have to decide about going somewhere? You don't want to go, the challenge before you is almost unbearable, yet deep down you know God is telling you to go. For Abraham this was the most difficult decision and the hardest place for him to go, yet it was the place of blessing because that is where he passed the test with God. Deep down if God is speaking and telling you to go, then go with the assurance that the Lord is with you and He will prepare the way for you.

IMPACT *Daily readings*

Our personal responsibility

Ezekiel 3:15-27
"But his blood will I require at thine hand." Ezekiel 3:18

An example of hypocrisy is whenever we pray for the salvation of our loved ones and then do nothing by way of telling them about Christ. This is just empty talk. We are responsible for our loved ones. Once the Lord puts them upon your heart, pray, and then follow your prayers with action. We must do all in our power to pull our loved ones from the fire of hell.

You may think you can never do this, well if you think like this, in your own strength probably not. But in the power of the Spirit of God we can do anything. To do anything in God's name we must be filled with the Spirit of God, which will make such a difference in your Christian life and walk. If you feel you cannot approach the person that is in your heart, then I would suggest you write them a letter and pour out your heart to them. When you do this then you are free from your responsibility.

Ezekiel was sent as a "watchman" to warn the people and this was by no means an easy task. You may not be successful in your task but then God is asking us to be faithful not successful in our walk with Him. Begin today by seeking to unite your family in Christ, it will amaze you what the Lord is willing and able to do through you!

God leads His people

Exodus 13:17-22

"And the LORD went before them by day in a pillar of a cloud, to lead them the way; and by night in a pillar of fire, to give them light; to go by day and night."

Exodus 13:21

As we look through the scriptures we read of how God continually led His people. On this occasion God used a moving cloud to guide the people during the day and a pillar of fire at night. The people moved only when the cloud or pillar of fire moved.

Sometimes we can become impatient whenever we are seeking guidance. Quite often it can be a case of doing what we want and then asking the Lord to bless it. God often tests and tries our patience to see if we will wait on Him. It can be tragic if we move on too quickly without knowing the will of God in our lives.

Waiting time is never wasted time. Always be ready to move the minute the cloud moves. God still leads His children today. His will and way are perfect for your life. Just like the saints of old prayed for guidance, we must do the same. God knows exactly when you have to move on. Just ask Him to let you know! For now though maybe it's time to be still and wait, but the time may come, maybe even tomorrow, to move on to the next phase or chapter of your life.

Are you prepared to leave your comfort zone to move into the complete unknown if God says it's time to move home, house, job, relationship... whatever it may be?

IMPACT *Daily readings*

Let's be honest!

Ecclesiastes 7:15-22

"For *there is* not a just man upon earth, that doeth
good, and sinneth not." Ecclesiastes 7:20

Sometimes it really bothers me that no matter how good we try to be we are often never good enough. No matter how much we want to keep our minds pure and clean, it is often a battle. No matter how determined we are to keep our bodies in good shape it is such a struggle. No matter how much we want to love and even like that person, it is such a challenge.

This verse is reminding me so clearly of our human nature, that no matter who we are, and no matter how good we try to be we will still sin in some form or another. This verse tells me that sinless perfection is impossible. Yes, we can strive to be holy and Godly, lament, weep and repent over our sin but so long as we are passing through this world we will still sin. The question is do we hate our sin, does it grieve us at the very core of our hearts? While we will never be sinless we can certainly strive to sin less.

Sometimes we can look to the best dressed man in church as our example of how to be Holy. This very person could be a wretch. Rather, look to Christ as your example, we will never be like Christ, yet we can strive to be like Jesus. All we should ever want to be, is to be like Him.

God protects His people

1 Samuel 7:13-17

"The hand of the LORD was against the Philistines all the days of Samuel." 1 Samuel 7:13

Sometimes we think the Lord will only use and bless those who have been saved from lots of sinful living. Sometimes we think the best testimonies to listen to are those who have had a very sinful background. While it is good to hear how the Lord saves such people, nevertheless, I think it is more interesting and extra special to hear how the Lord saves a child and ever since that time, they have sought to serve the Lord all the days of their lives.

Samuel was such a boy. Samuel lived a wonderful obedient life, seeking the will of God in all things. Ever since his childhood he lived a God fearing life with a deep and sincere reverence for the things of God. God was pleased with his life and therefore it is no surprise that the Lord honoured him.

God fought Samuel's enemies because Samuel pleased God with his life and living. Therefore if we seek to please, honour, respect and obey the Lord in all things will He not fight our battles too? Today many Christians have lost that fear and respect for God, that fear of offending a Holy God. Many today are careless in their walk with God. Many are living so close to the world they might as well be in it with little or no evidence of morals or Christian standards. While growing up, the enemies of temptation, greed, lust, selfishness overcome them and soon their lives are ruined as it is sin which dominates in their lives.

Can we from this day forth be challenged to live that God fearing, old fashioned Christian life again as Samuel once did?

IMPACT *Daily readings*

The prayer room

2 Kings 4:8-17

"Let us make a little chamber, I pray thee on the wall." 2 Kings 4:10

Elisha was man who journeyed around quite a lot. The Bible tells us there was a very important lady (a great woman) who asked Elisha to come in and dine with her and her husband. The woman recognised him as a prophet, a holy man of God. She suggested to her husband that they should make a room for the prophet, so any time he is passing their way he could stop by, rest, study, pray, do whatever he had to do. The room was to be furnished with a bed, table, stool and a candlestick. A perfect little room and all that Elisha would need.

There are different homes around the country where I would stop at and stay the night; they break up the journey well, especially while in the middle of doing missions in certain areas. This is very much appreciated, so I know how Elisha must have felt. On the other hand have you a special room in your house, a quiet room, a room where you can relax and pray, even called a prayer room. We have so much in our homes these days, so many things to occupy us and sadly there is no room for prayer and the reason often is because there are too many distractions. Can we be challenged afresh to make a little room in our house where we can pray to God every day? He will bless you for doing that.

IMPACT *Daily readings*

Feeling powerless? Ask God for help!

2 Chronicles 14:1-11

"Help us, O Lord our God." 2 Chronicles 14:11

King Asa begins his reign by pleasing the Lord, verse two tells us that he '...did [that which was] good and right in the eyes of the LORD his God.' He smashed idolatry by breaking up the images and altars of other gods. He took a stand for God where he was. He commanded the whole country to seek after the Lord God of Heaven. He protected the city so effectively that all attacks were evaded. He sought the Lord in everything he did and the Lord prospered him for it. Even in the small things of life to major decisions, it is always good to seek the Lord.

All was going well for Asa until one day he came under attack from an army of one million soldiers. The first thing Asa did was to cry unto the Lord for help. He acknowledged that he needed God even though he felt powerless and afraid. He admitted he needed help. He rested on the Lord and in the Lord's name he went forward into the battle which was, humanly speaking, an impossible task. Even though Asa's army was only one third of the size of the enemy, he defeated them because the Lord was with him and helped him. When the Lord fights our battles, nothing is ever too big for Him. When all seems to be against you, remember what Asa did, and take it to the Lord in prayer.

Be confident

Isaiah 30:15-21

"In returning and rest shall ye be saved;
in quietness and in confidence shall be your strength." Isaiah 30:15

There is a lot to be said about quiet people and at the same time a lot more can be said about loud people, as you can often hear them before you see them! The Bible has a lot of wonderful verses tucked away in some obscure chapter and when you first read them, you wonder what it is all about? Have you ever woke up in the morning and wondered how you are going to get through the day because there is so much to do and accomplish?

There is an old saying; 'if you ever want something done, ask a busy man to do it, because he knows how to prioritise his time and will get so much more done.' Sometimes we can become stressed because of a busy day or even a stressful life. I don't think that's the way the Lord planned it, it just seems to have become the way we are. When we get stressed out, we often become weak, which makes this verse so relevant because it tells us; in quietness and in confidence shall our strength be. God is our strength; the joy of the Lord is our strength. Keep Christ as your focus, keep talking to Him throughout your day and you will find much more ease and also realise at the end of it you have accomplished more than you thought you would.

Tomorrow may never come

Proverbs 27:1-11

"Boast not thyself of tomorrow;
for thou knowest not what a day may bring forth." Proverbs 27:1

Life is something we can all so easily take for granted. I suppose in many ways it is both natural and necessary to plan ahead in our lives. However it is important to remember our plans are made subject to the will of God. This is why we often see the letters D.V. after a planned event.

Life can be going so well today and yet at the same time tomorrow our world can completely change. This is why we are warned not to boast of tomorrow in our own strength, because reality is, tomorrow may never come for some of us. When we plan and speak of tomorrow, we should always make it subject to God's will, acknowledging the Lord in our plans.

At the same time there is a lesson here about the brevity of life. Imagine if today was your last day on earth, would you live it any differently? Would you speak to anyone about their soul? Is there someone you would make things right with? Don't leave something until tomorrow that you could do today. It's not always a good idea putting something off, especially witnessing to someone; you might well miss your opportunity as tomorrow may be too late. If the Lord is putting someone upon your heart, lift the phone or go to them, they could be waiting for you. Best of all the Lord will help you speak for Him, He will bring all things to your remembrance, it's called unusual help and the blessing that follows is unreal. Trust me!

IMPACT *Daily readings*

The secret of strength

Psalm 55

"As for me, I will call upon God; and the LORD shall save me. Evening, and morning, and at noon, will I pray, and cry aloud: and he shall hear my voice." Psalm 55:16-17

Have you ever wondered what the secret is for living a victorious Christian life? The secret is not some hidden formula that comes from man; rather, the secret is the blessing that comes from God when we spend time with Him alone in prayer.

Have you ever imagined what might happen if the people of God would "pray and cry aloud" in the "evening and morning, and at noon." What wonderful things might happen! As I think of myself, all of my failures can be traced back to my neglect of the place of prayer. Oh the evening, the morning and the noon might be transformed by His presence. How easy it is to rush right into the day and forget for a moment to take time to pray!

How we need to remember that no matter how blessed we may be in our Christian experience, if we neglect the throne of heavenly grace we do so at our peril. Let us then with God's help move forward by getting back to the blessed habit of lifting up our hearts in prayer to Him at all times but especially in the "evening, and the morning and at noon." Talking to Him freely and openly in the "evening, and the morning and at noon."

Can you be challenged today, that at the beginning of the day, the end of the day and at noon you will spend quiet time alone talking with God? Try it to see what great things will happen as the Lord hears your prayers!

The day of rest

Genesis 2:1-1-9

"God......rested from all His work..." Genesis 2:2

Sunday is a day when we worship God in church more than any other day of the week. It is known by many as the traditional Sabbath, Sunday being the day when the Lord Jesus rose from the dead, the day when the disciples met together to worship was the first day of the week. God rested on the Sabbath day, therefore the Lord's Day, the Sabbath day; Sunday is also known as the day of rest. It is a day of rest for many reasons, physically and spiritually.

When the Lord made us, we work, we rest and we sleep. The Sabbath was made for man and not man for the Sabbath. Today most people disregard Sunday as a special day made for us. Many Christians today say they can hardly find time to read and pray because they are so busy during the week. Then on Sunday they say it's their free time, family time and time for everything else except for God. So the danger society faces today is gradually phasing the Lord out of society, family and eventually our lives.

Then the Lord looks down from Heaven and sees His people living without Him, yet we are taught that our aim and purpose in life is to 'honour, glorify and enjoy the Lord for ever.' How can we enjoy the goodness of the Lord when we continue to live our lives without Him? Sunday is a special day set aside from all the rest when we can worship the Lord in the beauty of holiness. A day when we should try to switch off from everything that is not necessary or important, things can turn us away from focusing on the Lord. A Sunday well spent brings a week of contentment and remember 'Godliness with contentment is great gain.'

IMPACT *Daily readings*

Three times a day

Daniel 6:1-23

"Daniel kneeled upon his knees three times a day, and prayed,
and gave thanks before his God." Daniel 6:10

Daniel is a great inspiration for prayer. We must remember in Daniel's day he was forbidden to pray to God, which is why he was thrown into the lion's den. Even though it was forbidden to pray, Daniel still prayed. Today we are allowed to pray and still we don't pray. The disciples asked the Lord Jesus to teach them how to pray. Sometimes we need to ask the Lord the same question and never be ashamed to do so.

Daniel was very disciplined in his prayer life. This is the secret of the Christians life, his encounters with God. One of my failures in my walk with God is not praying enough. The most important thing any of us can do is spend time alone with God. Every day, week, month and year we all have victories and failures. Surely there comes a time in our lives when we need to make a solemn covenant before God to secure times of secret prayer. Just like Daniel, this will only come about and happen if we are disciplined in our efforts. Daniel went to the window and prayed three times. Even publically he was not ashamed of his Lord, even to the point of death. Muslims, Hindus and a host of other religions are not ashamed to pray to their gods in public, why then are we timid, ashamed, embarrassed when it comes to our God? Quite often, failure in the Christian life can be traced back to a lack of secret and daily prayer.

That's far enough

Deuteronomy 3:15-27

"Get thee up into the top of Pisgah, and lift up thine eyes westward,
and northward, and southward, and eastward, and behold it with thine eyes:
for thou shalt not go over this Jordan." Deuteronomy 3:27

For forty years Moses led the children of Israel through the wilderness to the Promised Land. He had now come to the border and pleaded with the Lord to let him travel into it. But it was not to be so. He had now seen it with his eyes and how beautiful it looked. But there was a time when Moses was angry and sinned against the Lord and for this reason he was forbidden to enter the promised land, rather he was to instruct one of his soldiers, Joshua, to continue leading the people on into the Promised Land. All that lay before them was the river Jordan, but that is as far as Moses got to.

Sometimes we can go with God to a certain place or a certain length in service. We plan to go on further and that's good, but sometimes God says "that's far enough" which might be hard to accept. Moses wanted answers, he wanted to go on, but the Lord had to tell him, "Speak no more to me of this matter." Sometimes we have to leave things with the Lord even when we don't understand why. Be careful not to push the boundaries when you know God is telling you it's far enough.

Meditating upon the law!

Psalm 119:97-104

"O how I love Thy law! It is my meditation all the day." Psalm 119:97

The old lesson of Christian living is still the best lesson. If you live close to the Word you will live close to the Lord and if you walk close to the Lord you will want more of His Word. The real challenge today is, do we have this double desire of both the Lord and His Word? Sometimes the excuse we often use for failing to read the word is because we don't have time. Is this really the reason or is it because we no longer have the heart? We live in a day when people are losing heart. The joy you once had is no longer there, the excitement and enthusiasm has all but gone. The zeal for souls, for God to work and save is no longer paramount for you.

Maybe there is someone or something taking the place of Christ and Christian living in your life right now. We can be in real danger of completely losing the desire for God's precious word. If we no longer love the law of God, then there is a real danger and concern for our spiritual walk, we can be, if not already in a backslidden state. This is a place where we don't really want to go. Just like a computer needs to do a scan and search the computer for any viruses, ask the spirit of God to do a scan in your life, right to the core of the heart and have the precious blood of Christ applied upon your life afresh.

The little foxes in your life

Song of Solomon 2:1-17

"Take us the foxes, the little foxes, that spoil the vines:
for our vines have tender grapes." Song of Solomon 2:15

A farmer's worst nightmare is when animals break into his fields and run wild through the crops destroying everything in their path. I remember being in Australia where the farmers dreaded kangaroos. They were so big, and with their long tails they made a huge path of destruction as they hopped their way through the massive paddocks of crops.

Here in this verse, we read about foxes, especially little foxes, destroying the vines. The lesson here is about sins in our lives, not big sins but little sins. These can often go unnoticed. Maybe we are aware of them but think no-one else is. This can be very very dangerous. It can be as simple as looking at something on the internet, simply browsing around and then you find something which you know is wrong to look at. You have a choice, either to click out of it, or click into it. It may be something small and everyone else does it you think. Do they? This type of problem has the potential to destroy relationships, marriages, careers and many other things. It may be a small habit but unless you click out of this small habit, whatever it is, you will have potentially a huge problem. What you need is to apply all your little sins and bigger sins afresh in the precious blood of Jesus. "The blood of Jesus Christ, His Son cleanseth us from all sin" (1 John 1:7)

This will help you conquer your sinful habits. Pray to the Lord and ask him to help you resist them!

IMPACT *Daily readings*

Who are we trying to please?

Proverbs 16:1-16

"When a man's ways please the Lord,
He maketh even his enemies to be at peace with him." Proverbs 16:7

From my own experience, I have realised that when you do something from your heart with your heart then it will be honourable to the Lord. If we have enemies, they will often watch us from a distance; the secret is not to focus on them but rather on the challenge at hand. The Lord can restrain your enemies to such a degree that they can be at peace with you. This is hard to believe, but not only is it a wonderful bible verse, it is a fact too; I have found this to be the case for me now for many years in my ministry.

It is very easy to try and please everyone at the same time, but reality is if you try to please everyone you will eventually offend someone. The only person we need to really aim to please is the Lord. If we only try to please people, then we can come short of pleasing the Lord.

Sometimes in order to please the Lord, it may cost you, but to stop short of pleasing the Lord it may cost you far more. Keep in mind the words of the Lord Jesus, "I do always those things that please Him." He was, of course, referring to His own Father. (Read John 8:29). The question is am I willing to go through with God, whatever He is challenging me to do? I know there is someone I have got to speak to, but I am afraid of what they might say or how they might react. Did you know God specialises in taking away your fears because He says 'fear not' because I am with you. Keep pleasing the Lord with your life, Let others see Christ in you that they will be so afraid, they will stand back in awe and say this person belongs to Jesus.

Let us go!

Numbers 13:21-33

"Let us go up at once and possess it; for we are well able to overcome it." Numbers 13:30

When the famous missionary David Livingstone was exploring Africa, where no white man had ever gone, a missionary society was deeply impressed. One of the leaders wrote to Livingstone: "Have you found a good road to where you are? If so, we want to send other men out to join you." Livingstone's reply was significant! "If you have men who will only come if there is a good road, I don't want them. I need men who will come if there is no road at all."

Are you prepared to, "make a road for God" where such has never been? Many today are looking at and considering the practicalities of missionary work. The finances need to be right otherwise it will never work out and I will be considered a fool. Even within fundamental circles this is the thought of so many. Can the God of Abraham, Isaac and Jacob not look after his children today as he did afore time? Sometimes we look at provision instead of the God of provision; we look for the road instead of being prepared to build a road.

Caleb stands out, for all time, as the one man, with Joshua, who was prepared to go forward; yet the people were about to stone him for being willing! Human nature has not changed. If you really endeavour to move forward for God or do something that may go against the grain of some, don't expect a clap on the back! To do something extraordinary for God will require Holy Ghost courage! If you are not prepared to abandon yourself completely to His claims on your life and be delivered from the fear of man, you may never do anything worthwhile for God. Together with Caleb and Joshua, I say "Let us go!"

IMPACT *Daily readings*

Have you asked the Lord?

Joshua 9:3-15

"And the men took of their victuals and asked not counsel of the Lord." Joshua 9:14

Joshua, as God's chosen leader had a brilliant career. There was no blot on his character as he meditated day and night on the Word of God. This was the secret of his success as he led the Children of Israel into the Promised Land.

The inhabitants of Gibeon heard of the advancing army of Joshua and realised they would soon be slaughtered. They then advised a cunning scheme. When they arrived to Joshua's camp, they did not look like warriors. Rather they arrived with tattered clothes and moulded bread, pretending they had come from afar off. They were so convincing by their words and appearance, that Joshua and his soldiers were completely fooled. Joshua's big mistake here is that he did not consult the Lord about it all. The Word tells us: "they asked not counsel of the Lord." This appears to be the only mistake made by Joshua during his leadership.

Later, when the men of Gibeon were found out to be deceivers, the Israelites could not kill them, as they had pronounced an oath to allow them into their company. Instead, the Gibeonites were forced to become labourers in the camp. There is a single warning in this story. Never make a decision, especially an important one, without praying much about it. When you pray and the Lord knows your heart, then the Lord is sure to open up the way before you.

Ask the Lord for discernment to see and know, the way in which He would have you to go.

IMPACT *Daily readings*

Rejoice in the Lord!

Isaiah 61:7-11

"I will greatly rejoice in the Lord: my soul shall be joyful in my God." Isaiah 61:10

A certain choirmaster was putting the members of his church choir over a hymn which spoke of heaven, and also warned of a lost eternity. He instructed them: "Now, when we sing about Heaven, let your faces light up with joy; but, when we come to the solemn part, your usual expressions will do!" This is quite funny as one would imagine the scene, yet in many ways it can be true. So many Christians are down in the dumps, everything seems to be gloom and doom with them.

Christ Jesus has set us free, free from the law, bondage and sin and yet many live as if they are still locked up with all three. There is nothing as discouraging to listen to as Christians continually yapping about some wee thing that nobody else really cares about. Try to be a person that turns the conversation around to something more positive, something about the Bible, even more about Jesus. When we look at ourselves there is little to be joyful about. When we look at the world it is even more discouraging, yet like Isaiah when we look to the Lord and all that He has done for us and means to us then it will change the conversation. Isaiah not only rejoiced but he greatly rejoiced in the Lord. With God he was completely happy. Are you completely happy with the Lord or do you need something more? Godliness with contentment is great gain the scriptures tell us.

IMPACT *Daily readings*

The Lord meanest good to you

Genesis 32:1-12

"Return unto thy country, and to thy kindred, and I will deal well with thee."

Genesis 32:9

Many years from his brother Esau. Now Jacob wants to return, returning back with his wives, children and great herds. He is a little worried as to how Esau would react, after all the reason he ran was because his brother was going to kill him. But in the end he couldn't have imagined or dreamed about it having a better outcome.

Then the Lord intervenes and tells him that all will be okay and that he would deal well with him. Many Christians worry so much about so little when the whole time all is going to be okay. This a real test for our Christian lives, are we trusting or worrying? The less we trust, the more we worry and the more we worry the less we are trusting in God. The promise that the Lord will deal well with us does not rule out trials, troubles, testings, tribulations and afflictions. But it does promise the He will be with us and that 'all things work together for good to those who love God.' The dealings of God are hard and difficult to explain at times, the question so often asked is why, why, why? One day face to face with Christ your King, you won't need to ask why; you will just smile and say now I know.

What does Sunday mean to you?

Exodus 20:1-17

"Remember the Sabbath day, to keep it holy." Exodus 20:8

Sunday should be, for the Christian, a special day. It is a day set aside for Christians to worship God. It is a day when we come together to publicly worship God. It should be a joy, not a chore. Some people are out so late on the Saturday night that they are too tired on Sunday to really worship God. Others see it as a time to have a snooze, is this not an embarrassment to the preacher and an offence to God?

Not only is Sunday a day for going to church, it is a day that is different. God has given us this day; the Sabbath is for man and not man for the Sabbath. This day is when we should rest our bodies, a day spent switched off from the world, and things other than necessity should not be done on this day. God forbids us to work unless out of necessity and care should we be working. God knows our bodies are not built to work every day of every week of every year. The fact that our lives are so busy throughout the week, Sunday is a great opportunity to spend more time with God, reading and praying about the past and coming week. God Himself rested on the Sabbath day; He alone should be our focus, motivation and reason for honouring the Sabbath day by keeping it holy.

Let's do something

Deuteronomy 31:1-13

"And that their children which have not known anything may hear,
and learn to fear the Lord your God." Deuteronomy 31:13

The challenge is ever before us to do something more for God every year. Some have yet to do something for God. Every year brings a whole new generation of children, every child is already one year older, every child has a heart that becomes that bit harder towards the things of God. That's why the challenge is very great to reach the rising generation for Christ.

In my life, while having different experiences of ministry, I find reaching the children to be the most rewarding and the most fruitful. Children are like little sponges; they can be so easily persuaded in so many ways, why not persuade them to follow Christ? Salvation is of the Lord, only Christ alone can save the children, but it is through the foolishness of preaching that they will know they are sinners. How then shall they hear without a preacher? Who then will go and tell them? Opportunities today are great to reach the children for Christ. If we miss them, we will lose them. This is our opportunity; let's make it count for God.

Not only the children, young people, adults and older people too, still do not know the way of Salvation. Just like in the day of Moses, there was a generation who did not know anything; we live in a generation when many people do not know anything about God. Someone has got to tell them. Will that someone be you? There are so many who do not know that Christ has died for them. Let's challenge our hearts and do something more for God.

IMPACT *Daily readings*

Men in mini-skirts!

2 Samuel 10:1-5

"Tarry at Jericho until your beards be grown, and then return." 2 Samuel 10:5

King David, out of consideration for Hanun, whose father had died, sent a number of men with a message of sympathy. Nahash, Hanun's father, had shown kindness to David. However, when they arrived, some of Hanun's officers became suspicious and completely misunderstood the mission of David's men.

When the sympathisers arrived, Hanun's men caught them and shamefully treated them, shaving off half their beards, and cutting off their garments in the middle, right up to their bottoms, hence the title 'men in mini-skirts'. This may have looked funny, but these were men of war and consider for a moment how ashamed and humiliated they were, especially when we know the reason for their visit.

When King David heard of it, he sent a message to the men to wait at Jericho until their beards grew back again. David immediately ordered Joab and Abishai, his well-chosen generals, with an army of men, to battle. The revenge was fierce and a terrible slaughter took place.

Has there been a time when you have been ashamed, and there was nothing you could do to stop it, when you have been totally humiliated? Sometimes in life this happens, it can be very cruel; life unfortunately can be cruel and unkind. We don't always have control over what happens to us; however we can pray for the Lord to cleanse us afresh and to purify us once again. The Lord Jesus tells us, "Tarry ye in the city of Jerusalem until ye be endued with power from on high" Luke 24:19.

There are times when we just have to get alone with God and talk to Him about these things; He alone has the answer to life's problems because He is the answer to all things.

Cleansing must be done!

2 Chronicles 29:1-11

"...sanctify now yourselves, ...and carry forth the filthiness out of the holy place."

2 Chronicles 29:5

Quite often a child would follow in his father's footsteps, with a desire to do what he does, but on this occasion it was different. After old King Ahaz died, his son Hezekiah reigned and he wanted to do things right before the Lord. Within the first year of his reign he reopened the doors of the house of the Lord and whatever state it was in, he repaired it. What a challenge this is before us. Many of us are given responsibility in our jobs and positions to take a stand for the Lord, by honouring his name. I remember contacting a school principal about doing an assembly, three times I made contact and she kept putting it off, not wanting to upset the system, yet testifying about how God had put her into her position. Within a few years she was forced to retire early on medical grounds. The school is now much more open for the gospel as I have since been allowed to do a week long Bible Club since her retirement.

Very often there needs to be a cleansing before there is blessing. Some well meaning believers can be a hindrance to the furtherance of the gospel without even realising it. Although in our passage before us it was very serious, there was filthiness in the camp and it needed to be cleansed. When there is sin being covered up, we have a responsibility to speak up. As believers God has chosen us to stand up for Him to do what's right, to be an influence for good, God and the gospel. The Lord has chosen us to stand up for Him to serve Him with all of our hearts. We ought to do that, start with our own hearts then we will see the filthiness of sin all around us.

IMPACT *Daily readings*

Watch out for yourself

1 Samuel 19:1-17

"...because his works have been to thee-ward very good." 1 Samuel 19:4

David and Jonathan were best friends. Even though King Saul was Jonathan's father, he hated David very much and was extremely jealous of him. He was now so determined to kill David; it became his number one priority. Jonathan met up with David and advised him to "Take Heed" as he was now in daily and constant danger. We can learn so much from David, he heeded the advice that was given to him.

There are many examples in scripture of individuals who were given advice but never took it, like Samson, Demas, Peter and Solomon. There were warned to take care of themselves to watch out, to take heed. They refused and in most cases tragedy came their way. Notice here as Jonathan was advising David, he told him to hide in a secret place not a social place. In the secret place we can find time with God, pour out our hearts and wait on the Lord. Many run to the social place to be with people, instead of the Lord. Very often the social place will keep us away from the secret place. In the social place you will often find Godless people. If we continue to spend time with Godless people, then God will become less important to us. This is the beginning of the slippery slope and believe me you don't want to start sliding down this. It is not a selfish thing to watch out for yourself, rather it is a sensible thing. If you have been cautioned recently, then take heed to yourself. If others are in danger, then prayerfully advise them to take heed, before they make shipwreck.

IMPACT *Daily readings*

What you see is not always what you get!

2 Kings 2:16-22

"The situation of this city is pleasant...but the water is naught,
and the ground barren." 2 Kings 2:19

From a distance the city looked very pleasant to the eyes; the scenery was very beautiful. But on a closer look; all around the city was barren. Is this not the mistake that so many young men and women make today? They see someone and are attracted by their outward appearance by the way they look. They are so absorbed by what they see they do not take time to look around them at the emptiness and barrenness it will bring into their lives. Such young men, happily married are often led away by the lust and desires of the flesh to what eventually becomes barren and unfruitful, wrecking many a wonderful marriage.

We can also think of the church here, many a fine looking building with all the furniture to go with it, yet on a closer look that's all it is, pleasant to look at, yet barren. Often there is little water, little evidence of souls being saved or Christians being stirred up and challenged to serve God. The church today is very pleasant, people immaculately dressed looking the part, but the ground is dry, little or no fruit is evident. Everything is pleasing to look at but is there any evidence of the Spirit of God? Everything is dry and barren. Worse still we can become like this, look the part, speak the language but that's all. There is no real evidence of the working of God's Spirit.

How did Elisha make the bitter waters sweet by pouring in the salt? Salt brought cleansing, purification and healing. Sometimes there needs to be a cleansing. This is often painful but necessary for healing to begin. Often then after the healing the blessing will come.

Will you allow the Lord to search you today for barrenness to see what hinders the blessing in you?

The mighty hunter!

Genesis 10:1-9

"Nimrod.....he was a mighty hunter before the Lord." Genesis 10:9

Imagine being described as a mighty hunter before the Lord. This is the title that Nimrod got, as one of the descendants of Noah. Being a mighty hunter, Nimrod would have made good preparation. He would prepare his bow and his spear, ready for action and expecting to be successful in his catch. Can you imagine him going out in the morning, seeing a deer and running after it to catch it, or a pigeon and throwing a stone to kill it? Nor, did he ask the Lord to bring the animal along and hold out its neck so he could kill it.

Yet today, in so many churches this is what the churches are expecting God to do, bring people along without them making any real effort to bring them in. The Lord Jesus commands us to go out to get them, we are to be like Nimrod, prepare well and go searching. We may find no one but at least we have got to make the effort. Believe me from my experience, when you go out and reach souls and God brings them in and the Holy Spirit works in their heart and they leave the meeting converted, it brings special joy, the soul winner's joy. Then you will want to go again and again reaching souls, precious souls for whom Christ died. Nimrod, was a mighty hunter before the Lord, always keep the Lord as your focal point. Nimrod may not always have walked in the way of the Lord. He became proud and self-centred. However the description of being a mighty hunter for souls before the Lord is worth considering.

Led by a child

Isaiah 11:1-10

"A little child shall lead them." Isaiah 11:6

Many parents have been brought to saving faith in Christ as a result of their children. This is one of the reasons I have devoted almost my entire ministry reaching children with the gospel. Not only is it a very rewarding and fruitful ministry, it is extremely essential. I often wonder why churches pour their entire efforts into adult missions, especially when only a few unsaved people would come to the mission. When there is a children's mission, it is so difficult to get helpers and volunteers. At the same time one might get upwards on one hundred unsaved children at that mission. I have heard a minister go on and on for weeks about a man getting saved and yet when two children were saved at the children's meeting he never even acknowledged it. Is this because he was not the human instrument that God was pleased to use to reach them?

When a child is saved, they can live their entire lives for God. Through children, parents can be reached where the church will never reach. Most Christians today were saved as children, why not then use every effort that comes our way to reach the children with the Gospel. Children will say things that adults are afraid to say. They will tell their friends they need to be saved, they will sing and quote scripture to their friends without being intimidated or embarrassed. Could you? I remember a little girl getting saved at a school Bible Club we had in Ballymena, as a result her mother came to Christ because of her little girl getting saved. Seek every opportunity to reach the children if you want to reach the parents.

IMPACT *Daily readings*

Satan can be in the crowd!

Job 2:1-7

"Again there was a day when the sons of God came to present themselves before the LORD, and Satan came also among them to present himself before the LORD."

Job 2:1

Whenever one reads the book of Job, especially the first two chapters, it is amazing how this man never flinched in his walk and relationship with God. He must be the man who has suffered the most human and personal loss in the world. He lost his animals, thousands of them, all ten of his children, even his wife told him to curse God and die. His body was covered in sores so that when his friends came to visit him they didn't even recognise him.

This was all the work of Satan. Verse two tells us that he goes to and fro throughout the earth looking for opportunities, easy targets. Today you may face your greatest test from Satan. He will do anything to taint or harm your relationship with Jesus Christ. He knows he cannot steal your soul but he will do all in his power to steal your body and harm it in whatever way he can. He will want you to question God about everything until you will be so close to giving up on God and will deny your faith. What will you do when it happens, even now, can you rise from the ashes like Job and say I know my redeemer liveth?

Protected by the angels

Psalm 68:12-17

"The chariots of God are twenty thousand, even thousands of angels:
the Lord is among them, as in Sinai, in the holy place." Psalm 68:17

Have you ever pondered the thought that there are thousands of angels? When we become a child of God, not only does the Lord promise not to leave us or forsake us but God also has angels looking after us. This is such a comforting thought that the Lord thinks about us in such a way. When we are in peaceful or dangerous situations in life the Lord has His guardian angels looking over us to protect us.

Won't it be a wonderful thing when we look back from Glory and see how we were delivered by the timely intervention of an angel? Maybe driving along in the car while tired and you suddenly wake up realising you have just fallen asleep, who do you think woke you up? Maybe you are walking down the street or around your house and an incident happens just before or after you get there, why has your timing been so perfect? Has not God allowed this to happen? I think of my own life on many occasions especially while driving. I remember waking up so shocked that I had fallen asleep. What shocked me most was the fact that I drove around a bend while asleep, I wept as I got out of the car thanking God for preserving my life, that's why I believe the Lord sends His angels to watch over us because they watch over me. "He shall give his angels charge over thee, to keep thee in all thy ways." Psalm 91:11

Time to rest

Ruth 3

"Shall I not seek rest for thee, that it may be well with thee?" Ruth 3:1

The book of Ruth should be read in one sitting, it really is one of the most beautiful love stories in the entire Bible. In many weddings today, vows are centred on the words of Ruth to her mother- in-law Naomi. As we read it we find that Ruth has been to see Boaz, who was to be her future husband. When she returned, Naomi, her mother-in-law, gave her good advice: "Sit still, my daughter, until thou know how the matter will fall." Ruth 3:18

Sometimes the most difficult thing to do is to sit still. The natural tendency is to do something. Are you like this, when something goes wrong you run around everywhere, talking to everyone trying to sort the whole thing out yourself. Why not learn from this today the importance of sitting still. By doing something you could do the wrong thing. It is good sometimes to be patient and wait on the Lord. Sitting still is a difficult thing to do especially if you are always on the go.

The Psalmist wrote in that very popular Psalm 46:10, "Be still and know that I am God." You may be at a stage in your life right now when your life seems to be shattered, falling around you. Your very faith rocked to its core. Can I remind you how much God cares for and loves you. Remember the words of the Lord Jesus during the storm at sea, when He simply spoke to the wind and the waves, "Be Still." Be still, and wait on the Lord my friend. It will be worth waiting, believe me.

IMPACT *Daily readings*

Wise or foolish

Proverbs 11:18-31
"He that winneth souls is wise." Proverbs 11:30

Since the day of my spiritual birthday, I have sought to win souls to Jesus Christ. It is my life's desire, calling and a worthwhile ambition. It may seem like foolishness to the world whenever they are challenged about salvation and about getting saved. Many Christians have never spoken once to someone about the importance of getting saved.

The Lord puts great emphasis upon this important work. In my own life many would see me as a fool. Yet deep within my heart, I would rather be a fool for God than have the earthly praise of man. I believe the only reason we are here on this earth is either to accept or reject Jesus Christ as Saviour and Lord. Once a person puts their trust in Christ, they are a new person and a new creature in Christ. Old ideas, desires and reasons for living should all pass away and everything should become new. But have they? Many Christians today are living so like the world it is virtually impossible to tell the difference between a clean living person and a born again believer. A born again believer should be on fire for God seeking to rescue souls from the pit, the fire of hell and eternal damnation.

From today onwards, aim to take every opportunity to win everyone you know and everyone you meet for Jesus Christ! Once you do and they start getting saved, then you will get a taste of soul winner's joy and it is the most delicious taste ever. Then the Lord says in His word that you are wise. Like me, you may be a fool to many people but in God's eyes, you are wise. Who would you really rather live for and listen to?

Please don't go with them

Numbers 22:1-12

"And God said unto Balaam, Thou shalt not go with them." Numbers 22:12

Every generation of Christians are faced with the decision to go to certain places and with certain people. These people may be our friends; they may be innocent in what they are trying to do. But the place you are going to and the company you keep may not be edifying for you.

Balaam was a prophet who was asked to curse the Israelites that were come upon them. He rightly refused. But then the peer pressure kicked in, the love of money and this world's riches and pleasures became too much for him. When God told him not to go, he went. His end result we find in Numbers 31:8, he died by the sword.

The temptation today to go places is probably greater than ever, everyone is given the invitation to go to some sort of social gathering. As you pray the Lord may lead you and tell you not to go, your conscience will tell you it is wrong. But the temptation becomes great; the pressure from your friends becomes enormous, just like it was for Balaam. The question is what are you going to do, especially when God's word tells you not to go with them? The word of God is always a good test in these matters.

IMPACT *Daily readings*

The test of tithing

Malachi 3:1-10

"Bring ye all the tithes into the storehouse....." Malachi 3:10

Most minister or pastors would encourage their people to give their tithe into the local church. The tithe is ten percent of your earnings. This sounds a good way of giving your tithe. However, before doing this I would make sure your money is being well spent and distributed. Many churches are very good at giving to those in need especially missionary organisations. Others however are not so good, they are happy to take your money, but it seems to be all put into the bank and eventually grows to a very large sum. Unless there is a direct need I would be very reluctant in helping to make a rich man rich, especially when there is so much need out there.

The real challenge is for us to give our money to the Lord and to his work. We must not lose out in this command from God, that every Christian should give ten percent of their earnings to the Lord. How we give it may vary, but remember it is a command. The local church ideally should be the place, providing it is distributing it fairly. If it is not, I would then send it to some good Gospel outreach, where they will not only appreciate it and it will be a great financial blessing to them. The real challenge for you however is, are you tithing ten percent of your income to the Lord?

I can't cope

Lamentations 2:1-19
"Their heart cried unto the Lord." Lamentations 2:18

Once there was a young couple who met and they seemed to fall in love with each other very quickly. They had so much in common and just enjoyed each other's company so much. He was a soldier and often travelled. One day they decided to make a challenge to see how deep their love for each other was. The test was for a whole weekend, they were not allowed to contact each other in any way from Friday lunchtime until Monday the same time.

The first couple of hours seemed okay for them as one was sure the other one would give in. But as time went on, one was as determined as the other, nothing came through the first night, or all day the next day. The pain for both of them was getting stronger, the day seemed long and the second night dragged and still none of them gave in. With two nights gone there was one final night to go, minute by minute went by, the pain of not being able to communicate was now unbearable, until suddenly the message came through, "I can't cope! Please can we stop this?" How relieved they were to be in touch again!

When I read that story I thought to myself, imagine if God set that challenge for us. That we were not allowed to communicate with Him in any way. How long could we last? Would it get easier as time went by or would it get more difficult? Would there be any pain? Would you miss Him so much that you would cry for Him to come back? Would the pain become so unbearable that it would bring us to breaking point, until you would cry unto the Lord, *"I can't cope!"*

The powerful presence of God Almighty

Judges 6:1-18

"The Lord is with thee, thou mighty man of valour" Judges 6:12

It seems as we read this account that when the angel spoke to Gideon, there was no sign that the Lord was with him. The children of Israel had been miserably defeated by the Midianites. Defeat seemed to be on every hand: and they were found hiding in holes, dens and caves in the mountains. Terror had overcome them! Yet the Word of the Lord came to Gideon, "The Lord is with thee.....go in this thy might." God used Gideon and the people were delivered.

This is so encouraging, so relevant and up to date. Maybe you are suffering defeat from whatever source; friends letting you down, finance no longer available or the future seeming uncertain. Everything you put your hand to seems to fail and nothing seems to be working in your favour. Like many, you seem to be at a dead end with nowhere to go. Everything seems hopeless and discouragement sets in. Well, just before you throw in the towel can I remind you that God is with you! Here the Word of the Lord reminds us, "The Lord is with thee...go in this thy might."

Go forth again in the power of God, cleansed in Jesus' precious blood, and the enemies of God will surely be scattered. The Spirit of the Lord came upon Gideon; He can also come upon you. Don't give up and don't despair. Be strong in the Lord! Pull yourself together and keep going on for God.

IMPACT *Daily readings*

Be not afraid of people

Isaiah 51:1-12

"I, *even* I, am he that comforteth you: who *art* thou,
that thou shouldest be afraid of a man *that* shall die." Isaiah 51:12

There was a time in my life when a lot of people were talking about me and generally gossiping. These people would never phone me to discuss what they were talking about and when I challenged them they of course denied any such talk. There was one such time however when the rumours were very great and it was beginning to affect my ministry in a small degree. To be a servant of God and a follower of Christ one needs to have very strong hide to take all the kickings so it's not the first time I asked the Lord to give me the hide like a crocodile or a buffalo.

However on one such occasion when I could hardly take any more a friend of mine whom I haven't spoken to in a long time suddenly texted me the above verse. The Lord used it to comfort me, and to convict and challenge me as to why am I afraid of men, when the Lord is on my side. These people are only men, and one day they will die and return to the dust like everyone else. This verse gave me so much encouragement to keep going on for God. If ever the Lord puts a verse of scripture on your mind for someone, send it to them immediately as it may be their life line. Also if you are afraid of people for the position you are in and the stand that you take stop being afraid of them and ask the Lord to take away that fear from you. He can and He will do it.

A different light

Genesis 1:1-12

"And the evening and the morning were the first day." Genesis 1:5

Here is something very interesting for us to consider. Our day begins with the morning and ends with the evening. We wake up in the morning and go to sleep in the evening and sleep through the night. Its natural progression is from light to darkness. Look carefully at the text "and the evening and the morning were the first day." The progression is from darkness to light.

What a wonderful picture this is for God's child. He is travelling not from light to darkness but from darkness to light, a light that shineth more and more unto the perfect day. The darkness of our sin is behind us and the glorious light of Christ is before us. We are in the light because He is the light. Even though we still live in a dark world, so stained and polluted with sin, remember we are nearer than ever before to the never ending day of God's everlasting light. God provides not only light in even, but praise His name, His Son, Jesus is the light to Heaven. The closer we are to Christ, the dimmer the light that is in the world. Where is your candle burning? One candle can't burn in two places and light two paths.

Spiritual wealth

Deuteronomy 33:1-10

"Yea, he loved the people; all his saints are in thy hand:and they sat down at thy feet; every one shall receive of thy words." Deuteronomy 33:3

Here we find Moses speaking to the children of Israel before His death. He was reminding them how he met the Lord on Mount Sinai. He was reminding them how much the Lord loved them, sometimes we can forget this simple message that, "God loves you" To be known and owned personally by God makes you the richest person on this earth. How wealthy is the child of God! Whenever we think of all the spiritual blessings we have in Christ Jesus, how wealthy we really are. We have so much to possess in Christ today. Even before the beginning of time God loved you and He will love you forever.

We are loved by Him and protected by Him, "all saints are in thy hand." We are surrounded by the fingers of God, hidden in the hollow of His hand, we that are saved are eternally secure and safe in the hands of almighty God. The people, like Mary sat at his feet and what a place to be, to learn of Him and to be like Him so that everyone can receive His words. We all have different needs, God has your portion, go to Him and get it, at His feet we humbly bow, what a wonderful, all caring Saviour who loves us.

The Lord will hear you when you cry!

2 Chronicles 20:1-10

If, *when* evil cometh upon us, ...in thy presence,
and cry unto thee in our affliction, then thou wilt hear and help." 2 Chronicles 20:9

King Jehoshaphat had great reason to fear. A great multitude of people were coming against him and his people to battle. He realised he didn't stand a chance against the Moabites and Ammonites; so he wisely "set himself to seek the Lord" and called his people to prayer. As they were praying and because they called upon the Lord in prayer, the Lord came to their aid and mightily delivered them from the enemy.

If you read this portion in Scripture, Jehoshaphat appointed singers to go before his army "to praise the beauty of holiness" and exalt the name of the Lord. As they were singing, the Lord sent ambushes against the enemy. What an encouragement this is to the child of God facing a terrible enemy. No matter what your enemy calls you or threatens to do to you, God can deliver you from them. The lesson is simple; be earnest and keep prevailing in prayer over your enemy and then sing the song of faith that God will deliver you from your enemies. If God did this in the past He can surely do it again for you! After all the Lord never changes. "I am the Lord, I change not."

Real friendship

1 Samuel 18:1-15

"The soul of Jonathan was knit with the soul of David,
and Jonathan loved him as his own soul." 1 Samuel 18:1

Here we have two of the greatest friends recorded in the Bible. It says the soul of Jonathan and David were knit together. This is something deeper than a normal friendship. This a friendship that has a kindred spirit, one that is more like a love for one another, feelings for one another. A love that one continually thinks upon the other one, longs to be with them, would do anything for them. David and Jonathan had this type of love, even stronger than a brotherly love for each other. When they hugged together, it was special!

They could talk about anything, spend so much time together, never get bored with the other one. They could laugh and cry for each other. Jonathan would naturally become the next King after his father Saul but because of his love for David, he stood aside and let David become king, so much was his love for David. They even made a commitment with each other that their friendship would remain until the day they died.

It is wonderful to find someone with such a love and kindred with each other. Such people are very hard to find. It cannot be made or forced; it must be there from the start. To have the Lord at the centre of such a friendship is very special. It is nice to feel wanted and even to be made special. If God has brought such a person into your life, thank the Lord for them; remember they could be an angel in disguise. But the bond of love that comes from it can often be really hard to explain, but then not everything in life needs to be explained, some things are best left the way they are.

The powerful seed

Ecclesiastes 11

"In the morning sow thy seed, and in the evening withhold not
thine hand" Ecclesiastes 11:6

As an evangelist I am greatly encouraged by the fact that it is nothing to do with me regarding the results of preaching the gospel. The power is with the Word and not the preacher. Sometimes we think that if a very popular preacher comes to take a gospel mission then droves of people may get saved. He may attract droves to hear him, but he certainly will not alone see them saved. God must do His work in a sinner's heart.

Likewise for those who labour behind the scenes for souls, whether teaching Sunday school, outreach of whatever description, remember that you cannot win souls in your own strength. Salvation is of the Lord, but we must keep sowing the seed. Many a person has been saved years later after hearing the gospel preached. The seed had been planted and one day many years later, the person got saved. In some of my missions it is no strange thing for a child to come and tell me five days into the mission that they called upon the Lord on the Monday night of the mission in the quietness of their own home. I had brought forth the Word as faithfully as I could and left it with the Lord and in the mean time the Holy Spirit was doing His work calling that little child to himself and in child like faith that child responded and trusted in Christ for Salvation. The seed is powerful and all we are asked to do is sow the seed, in season and out of season. Sometimes for our own humility the Lord with holds results until we are out of the picture so He alone can have all the glory!

Discouraged!

Psalm 43

"Why art thou cast down, O my soul?" Psalm 43:5

Do you ever stand on the bathroom scales and are almost afraid to look because you know what it is going to say? We all have the challenge to control our own weight, easy to put on and much more difficult to lose again. We all have the determination to lose weight, we have plans, ideas but unless we put our plans into action, our weight will probably stay the same and we will continue to feel bad about it. Sometimes I stand on the scales, don't look and imagine a weight and it makes me feel great!

Although on a more serious note there are times when everyone has a bad day, or goes through difficult times in their lives and rightly so, they are cast down. One time a man was having a really bad time in his life, he was feeling really sorry for himself and wondered was life really worth living. He went to tell a friend that he was going to end it all. The friend asked him seven questions. The man was to close his eyes and answer the questions to himself. Do you have a wife? Do you have children? Do you love your wife and children? Do you have a home? Do you have a job? Do you presently enjoy good health? Do you believe in God? With this the man began to cry, opened his eyes and told his friend he was a selfish fool, only thinking about himself, realising what he had in this world, so much, when many others had so little.

Why are you cast down? Sometimes it is good to sit down and begin to count everything we have in the Lord; He really has been so good to us. When we really do this, rather than being cast down may we be standing up praising the Lord!

The peaceful flow

Isaiah 32:15-20

"And my people shall dwell in a peaceable habitation...and in
quiet resting places." Isaiah 32:18

One of the things I love to do especially in the summer time is to sit on the bank of a river and watch the water flowing by. It is one of the most relaxing and enjoyable things to do. It's a good time to sit and think and to ponder over things, especially just to sit and spend time with the Lord. One thing I notice is the river is always so peaceful, it never stops, just keeps on flowing. Even though the wind may be blowing, the rain is falling, still the river keeps flowing.

Isn't this a wonderful picture of the Christian in the world? We should just keep going on for God, no matter what is going on in this world, just keep flowing for God. The river has a source and it will never rise higher than its source, likewise there are maybe people out there who look to you as their source, as their example in the Christian walk. If you stop flowing, then they too will slow down. This is why you must keep flowing, the water bumps its way around stones, through mud and dirt and even death. Are we not the same, we've got to keep going on. Maybe you lack peace in your heart, yes you might have Jesus, but you have no peace. This is not what the Lord desires for you, He wants you to have His peace upon you. Try not to get caught up and entangled in the affairs of this world; remember the peaceful flow of the river. Life will go on regardless of how you feel; you may as well take the peace that God gives.

Jealousy!

Song of Solomon 8:1-16

"Jealousy is cruel as the grave" Song of Solomon 8:6

Jealousy is a terrible sin that starts in childhood and is found in the oldest of people too. Even ministers and churches are often jealous of each other for whatever reason. Solomon treats it like death, so cruel is jealousy, just like an open grave. It is a deadly sin in the sight of God, satan has and will continue to use it, just like the tenth commandment, it is the sin of coveting, wanting something for the sake of having it, jealousy is someone else having something when you alone desire it. Many a good friendship has been broken and even marriages wrecked because of someone being jealous. If you suffer from this sin, you need to start praying hard. It often breeds resentment and bitterness.

In the book of Numbers, chapter 12, Miriam and Aaron became jealous of Moses, their brother. Either it was his wife from Ethiopia or how God was using Moses that caused the jealousy. However the reason, God was so angry He smote Miriam with leprosy to teach her a lesson. Whatever you are jealous of today, I would suggest you cry out with David of old: "Create in me a clean heart, O God, and renew a right spirit within me." Psalm 51:10. The cleansing may be drastic, but God will bring the deliverance. It needs to be acted upon quickly.

Mother!

Proverbs 31:1-31

"The words of King Lemuel, the prophecy that his mother taught him." Proverbs 31:1

There is nothing given to us to know who King Lemuel was or anything about him. His name however means 'dedicated to God' or 'belonging to God'. The lovely thought found here is that he has preserved, for all mankind, the wise counsel which his mother gave to him. This proverb is very inspiring to read.

Sometimes as we grow up we tend to despise the counsel of our mother. I remember especially during my teenage years, when going out on a Saturday night, I would have to give a fairly detailed plan of where I was going that night and who with. I often dreaded coming home, I knew mum would be up and if she wasn't up she would come into the room, while I pretended to be fast asleep, I often had to go over where I was and who I was with, the stories seldom ever matched. Looking back now my mum was just glad to see all her boys come home, one by one, all seven of them. My dad on the other hand, just snored his head off and knew boys are boys, they'll be all right, but mum would have been worried, anxious and concerned, naturally as only a mother would.

The chapter talks about a virtuous woman, it is any man's dream and desire to find one of these. Praise God, I have one; my mother on the other hand is another virtuous woman, for her price *is* far above rubies. Money can never buy a mother's love, care and attention she gives to her children. The chapter talks about doing good, rising up early and sitting up late, working willingly, bringing the food for the family. She was one that feared the Lord greatly and taught her boys to fear the Lord.

The best a mother could ever do is teach her children the fear of the Lord!

The boy who prayed

Genesis 21:1-21
"And God heard the voice of the lad" Genesis 21:17

Whenever Abraham and Sarah got frustrated waiting on God giving them the promised son, they got so impatient that they acted in a most unusual manner. Sarah came up with the idea for Abraham to have a child with their servant Hagar. As a result, Ishmael was born. This brought tension into the home especially after Isaac was born as Sarah became jealous of Hagar. All sorts of problems resulted and came into the household. When Ishmael began to tease Isaac, Sarah could take it no longer and demanded that both of them leave the house with no coming back.

Both Hagar and her little son walked and walked off into the dessert. Before long her water bottle became empty. It was hot and they had no food nor water to drink as the bottle they had soon became empty. The bible tells us that Hagar cast her son under bush and began to weep; she honestly thought they were going to die. Then we read in verse 17, that "God heard the voice of the lad" and opened Hagar's eyes so she could see a well of water, from which she and her son drank and lived. It is interesting to note that it was the voice of the boy that God heard. The name Ishmael incidentally means "God will hear." The lesson is simple, that God hears and answers the prayers of a child. He cares for them, answers their prayers and meets their needs. "Take heed that ye despise not one of these little ones." Matthew 18:10

IMPACT *Daily readings*

Turning aside

Exodus 3:1-12

"And when the Lord saw that he turned aside to see,
God called unto him....." Exodus 3:4

This incident in the life of Moses was to be the turning point in his life. He had no idea what lay before him, but he was the one God had chosen to lead His people through the wilderness. When the Lord saw that Moses turned aside to see, He called him aside to see. God then spoke and called to him out of the midst of the burning bush.

Sometimes in the business of our lives God needs to turn us aside to speak to us and get our attention. The danger is that we can be so busy in our lives that we miss out with God. You are not alone here, everyone seems to be busy these days doing their own thing. The devil is happy with this; he wants to see you healthy and prospering in life. When this happens we then don't need to take the time to spend with God. So the real challenge is when God has a plan for you and you are too busy, he may need to set you aside to get you to turn aside so that you may take the time to hear from the Lord. It may only be then, when we turn aside that the Lord will speak to us. We must hear the voice of God as He speaks to us. We hear His voice as He speaks to us as we read His Word.

IMPACT *Daily readings*

Benjamin's blessing

Deuteronomy 33:1-12

"And of Benjamin he said, the beloved of the LORD shall dwell in safety by
him; and the LORD shall cover him all the day long,
and he shall dwell between his shoulders." Deuteronomy 33:12

Benjamin is described here as the beloved of the Lord, just like John was in the New Testament. Sometimes we tend to only think about the important people like Joseph and forget how the Lord loves others. To be known as someone who not only loves God but that is loved by God is a blessed thing. One of the greatest privileges is to dwell with God, to have God as our companion and as a true friend, one who sticks with us and by us. When others come and go the Lord remains truly faithful.

Benjamin is described here as one that the Lord would protect and cover all the day long and that he shall dwell between His shoulders. This reminds me of the lost sheep in the New Testament. When the shepherd found it, he put it between his shoulders and rejoiced. How protected and cared for the sheep must have felt, to be so close to the shepherd. Is it your desire to be really blessed of God like Benjamin was? We can be because the Lord doesn't change, he says of Himself 'I am the Lord I change not.' It is us who need to change. Are you prepared to change?

God will meet the need!

Psalm 50:1-14
"For every beast of the forest is mine and the cattle upon a
thousand hills." Psalm 50:10

Since stepping out in faith in 2007, we often wondered what it would be like to see God help us and supply our every need. Well we have to say He has done just that, without having a wage or salary we have been on the road now in what is our fifth year and we have never been busier in the work of God. I remember a man called at our house and told us the Lord had put us upon his heart to pay a bill for us. I remember asking him, what sort of bill, electricity, phone, food? He said any bill you have? I then looked at Joanna and told her, I have a bill that would do and proceeded to give him our rates bill, at almost £1000. He took it, paid it and that was many years ago. Our Heavenly Father has riches beyond our expectation, and is abundantly able to meet our every need, whatever that may be.

The Lord does not provide for our greed but rather for our need. The Lord knows our heart and our need better than we know it ourselves. The Lord says, "I am the LORD I change not." If He could look after all the great men and woman of the Bible and all the Christians both great and small, can the same God not look after you? After all the Lord said, "I am the same yesterday, today and forever." Sometimes we do not trust in the Lord enough to meet the need, we tend to worry too much. I believe worrying is an offence to God because when we worry we are no longer trusting in the Lord to help us and supply what we need. Sometimes we should try to worry less and begin to trust more, it will make a huge difference in our walk with God.

Be courageous

Joshua 1:1-9

"Be strong and of a good courage; be not afraid, neither be thou dismayed:
for the LORD thy God *is* with thee whithersoever thou goest." Joshua 1:9

Joshua had just become the new leader after the death of Moses. This was a very daunting task, to lead the children of Israel, over two million of them at this stage. In the first nine verses of Joshua, we have the Lord instructing Joshua, these verses are full of encouragement. The Lord reminds Joshua that he is not alone, that He was with him and would not forsake him. The Lord not only tells Joshua to be courageous but to be very courageous. He knew it was going to be a tough battle ahead and was reminding Joshua to keep the focus, stay close to the Lord and He would give him the victory.

This is a wonderful picture of the Christian life today; we also are in a battle. In our own strength we will never win, but when the Lord is with us we will have the victory, therefore it is possible to live a victorious Christian life. Many today live in fear, yet the Lord says "be not afraid." We have here the promise of God's presence. Fear is a terrible thing, fear of the unknown. Many today worry about so much. If you worry that something is going to happen it probably will, otherwise you wouldn't worry about it. On the other hand if you seek God and pray earnestly about a matter, then there may be a different outcome. The secret is to be like Joshua, keep the focus and never take your eyes of the Lord. He is forever with His children.

A definite prayer

Genesis 24:7-21

"O LORD God of my master Abraham, I pray thee, send me good speed this day, and show kindness unto my master Abraham." Genesis 24:12

Abraham's servant was sent on a journey to find a wife for his son Isaac. When he made his way to the country he was going to, he had no idea where to start looking. How could he possibly find someone who was willing to leave her family to go and marry a strange man?

When the servant got to the outskirts of the city he began to pray. He was very specific and definite in his praying. As he sat by the well, he prayed to the Lord and told Him, that he would ask a girl for a drink of water from the well. This seemed like a normal request, but the real challenge and almost impossible request was that, if the girl offered to give all ten of his camels water also then this would be the girl. This would mean physically carrying up to 100 buckets of water. Today if a fella asked a girl for a drink of water, she would probably tell him to go and get one himself. This seemed like an impossible task he was asking.

Then a girl came along just as he finished praying. "Excuse me, would you please give me a drink of water?", the servant asked. The girl replied and willingly gave the servant water to drink and told him to rest and she would draw water for his camels as well. This story is totally amazing. This girl was Rebekah who later became Isaac's wife. Start praying with definite prayers and see God work in your life. God never changes!

Hammer it home

Isaiah 22:15-25

"And I will fasten him as a nail in a sure place." Isaiah 22:23

D.L. Moody believed in constantly repeating the text during his message. He said about this: "It is better to spend my time driving home one nail than trying to hammer in ten tacks!"

In order to drive a nail in, it needs to be hammered home. It should be like that when we preach the Word of God. It needs to be "hammered home"; to be repeated over and over again until it gets through to those who listen. It's like teaching a memory verse to children, repeat, repeat, repeat until they have it memorised word perfect. Don't be afraid of sounding repetitive, it is not vain talking we are talking about or a form of praying that would grieve those in your company because you keep repeating yourself as if God has a slow memory. We are talking about the Word of God, if you have a responsibility to share or preach the Living Word of God, hammer it home until it penetrates the heart. As you hammer, pray that God will do His work at the same time.

It's also good practice to memorise scripture to each other. Keep trying to memorise until you have got it word perfect. God will bless your soul as you seek to learn His Word.

Fresh oil required

Psalm 92

"I shall be anointed with fresh oil." Psalm 92:10

Another great secret I learned in the Christian life is to be filled with the Holy Spirit every day. Whenever a person gets saved, becomes a Christian the Holy Spirit comes and dwells within them, lives within their heart. When a person is genuinely saved the Holy Spirit remains within you. But there is a difference when we are actually talking about living the Christian life. We need to be filled afresh with the Spirit of God to live the Christian life, to be active for God to serve the Lord and to speak for Him. We cannot do this in our own strength. We need topped up every day.

Just like a car engine without oil, it still looks like an engine but without the oil it is useless. Likewise Christians who are saved will always be saved but without the infilling of God the Holy Ghost upon our lives we will be useless and ineffective for the Lord. This is something we need to do everyday to be effective in our Christian life. Ask the Lord today to anoint you with fresh oil.

"And be not drunk with wine, wherein is excess; but be filled with the Spirit." Ephesians 5:18

Fight discouragement

Isaiah 42:1-7

"He shall not fail nor be discouraged." Isaiah 42:4

Everywhere we go people seemed to be discouraged, more now than ever before. Is it because we expect more and more from man? We just get continually disappointed until we are so discouraged we fall into a depressive mode. My friend, man is man, and he will let you down and fail you. He is only human. Contrast this to God, He is God, He will not let you down nor will He fail you.

Discouragement comes from every side, especially from professing Christians. Every time you want to do something for God, they will pour cold water over your idea. Either because they are lazy and don't want to do it themselves, or they are jealous because they didn't have the idea and will not receive all the attention as they might like to have. So the best thing to do is to stop you doing it and it won't be done and they couldn't care less. I know all about this and believe me I speak from experience. I generally have the attitude to act first and then ask questions later. It may not be the correct way of doing things but it gets the job done and that's what is important at the end of the day. If we do not overcome discouragement then discouragement will overcome us. You don't want to go down that road; it can be a long road to recovery. A discouraged Christian is like a wounded soldier and can be very little use to God in the battle.

Bring down the giants

Joshua 15:1-8

"At the end of the valley of the giants" Joshua 15:8

We all have giants in our lives; these can be giant people that intimidate us, giant temptations that often cause us to yield, giant habits that are too big for us to stop or just giant problems that nobody knows about. Of ourselves we cannot fight these giants; they are too many and too strong. Therefore we either take these giants on or let them have the victory over us.

Sometimes we give up on our giants as if we cannot overcome them. They just seem too big and impossible to bring down and conquer. Remember David and how he defeated his giant. The Lord helped him and so the Lord can help you today. Bring the giants before the Lord today and confront them in the name of the lord. He will help you; let the Lord be your strength. If you don't overcome these giants today then they may overcome you, once they begin to press you, you will become weaker and weaker and soon will have no or little strength left to fight. There will always be giants in our lives, they may be little flies that land on us that begin to grow and grow until they become enormous giants. Sometimes there is only one cure for a fly...here endeth the fly.

Beware of the whisperer

Proverbs 16:24-33

"A whisperer separateth chief friends." Proverbs 16:28

Have you ever noticed a person whispering in the company of people? Why are they whispering I often wonder, is it because they have something to hide that they don't want everyone else to know about? I remember as a child my mum would often scold us for whispering, probably because she wanted to know what we were talking about.

We need to beware of the person who whispers when in the company of people. How true is our verse today- "a whisperer separateth chief friends," and it has been proven time after time. There are whisperers, gossipers, and slanderers who mingle with the people of God, often professing to be Christians, whose tongues are set on fire by the devil. An awful lot of damage can be done by whispering, that's how rumours start and these can often destroy the best of good people.

Are you guilty of whispering or even being in the company of a whisperer, the person who you nearly have to stick your ear to their mouth, because you can hardly hear them and they don't want anyone else to hear them, in case the person they are talking about is listening. When you listen to the slanderous reports of whispering and gossip they tend to be believed. Therefore you will find yourself keeping a distance from the person who the story was about even though there is no foundation to the story. This is how good friendships are broken up. Keep yourself pure in all things; this includes your mind from the gossiper who loves to be active for the devil in causing division by spreading rumours and tales that very often are hurtful and untrue. Don't be a partaker of another man's evil deeds.

IMPACT *Daily readings*

Universal language

Psalm 103

"Bless the LORD, O my soul: and all that is within me,
bless his holy name." Psalm 103:1

Today it is so easy to travel to many parts of the world compared to one hundred years ago. Back home I find when you meet a believer; one tends to find out what denomination they belong to. When we find out it is different to the one we belong to, suddenly there is a step back approach, we no longer are just as interested in the person we just met.

Compare this to meeting someone else in the far side of the world on your travels. Suddenly when you discover they too are a believer, it's not so important what denomination they belong to. There is an excitement within you to say I've just met a Christian, even though they don't speak English and you don't speak their language, you know because they are reading their Bible which you recognise. Suddenly you point to heaven and shout Jesus, they smile and Shout "Hallelujah" and you respond with joy by saying "Amen" then you smile at each other, shake hands and hug like true brothers and sisters in Christ. For all you know you have probably met a monk or priest, and they too thought you were the happiest English speaking person in the world.

Let's not take away from the Hallelujah and Amen language of heaven. Sometimes the man made boundaries at home hinder real true Christian fellowship because someone worships in a different church or uses a different Bible. Have you noticed many of those people are more Christ like and love to talk more about the Lord that those in your own church and denomination. Let's continue to bless the Lord and be thankful for every true believer who comes along our path.

Lot the greedy man!

Genesis 13:1-13

"And Lot lifted up his eyes, and beheld all the plain of Jordan." Genesis 13:10

Lot 'lifted up his eyes', and looked toward the well-watered plain of Jordan. His very decision was based upon the green pasture and the wealth he could make from it. Lot wanted money and he got plenty of it. But as we read on, we see where his choice eventually took him.

There was once when a crowd of men came looking for him and he was so depraved and far away from God, he was willing to sacrifice his two daughters to them. The sin was so wicked upon Sodom and Gomorrah that the Lord was going to destroy it. "The men of Sodom were wicked and sinners before the LORD exceedingly." Genesis 13:13. God sent two angels to Sodom from Heaven, to pronounce their doom! This sinful crowd of men, homosexual men did not want Lot's daughters, rather they wanted the men. Suddenly they were all blinded as the angels pulled Lot back into the house.

This is why it is so important to know God's teaching on such sin as homosexuality. We live in a day when all sorts of sinful life styles are becoming more 'acceptable'. Both the Old and New Testaments forbid such perverseness in God's eyes. God destroyed Sodom and Gomorrah; it wasn't because He didn't like the buildings, rather because He hated the sin of the people who lived there. There was no one else who followed the Lord, Lot never influenced one person for God, so his original decision to go there in the first place was for greed and certainly not for God.

Whenever we make decisions in life, is it for greed or most of all for God?

IMPACT *Daily readings*

It's the way you look at the situation

Ecclesiastes 11:1-6

"He that observeth the wind shall not sow;
and he that regardeth the clouds shall not reap." Ecclesiastes 11:4

Many years ago, two shoe salesmen were sent to Africa in order to expand their business. Within a few days, the first salesman called his home office: "Returning home. Nobody here wears shoes." The second salesman also sent word to the office: "Send more shoes. Market wide open. Nobody here has shoes."

It is the way we look at every situation that determines what we will do. If you say to yourself that person will never get saved, there is no point in talking to them about the Lord, it is very likely they won't get saved unless the Lord graciously intervenes. "Two men looked out from prison bars; one saw mud, the other saw stars." What are you seeking to do for God this year? We all have a responsibility to act upon our desires to do something for God. It is called our responsibility or human responsibility. The devil of course wants you to continually doubt your faith and anything you want to do in the name of the Lord. The lesson is simple; we must keep our eyes on the Lord and not on the gathering clouds. Always be motivated by faith and not intimidated by fear.

Time to pass on the reigns

Deuteronomy 3:21-29

"But charge Joshua, and encourage him, and strengthen him: for he shall
go over before this people and he shall cause them to inherit the
land which thou shalt see." Deuteronomy 3:28

Moses had led the children of Israel through the wilderness now for forty years. They had come to the river Jordan, the only thing that stopped them from entering the Promised Land was the Jordan River. But then God told Moses he was not to cross, rather he was to charge Joshua with the responsibility of leading the children of Israel across.

Moses was to encourage and strengthen Joshua for the task ahead. He was to pass on his responsibilities to Joshua. Sometimes this is a problem today, men won't let go of the reigns and pass them on to younger men. In some churches there are men, almost eighty years of age still leading children's work when the church is sitting full of young men with energy and freshness. Moses was to encourage and strengthen Joshua to the work. In the church today it seems to be the opposite, rather than encouragement there is discouragement and rather than strengthening, many tend to weaken others in the work. How we need to get back to the truths and examples of scripture and encourage and strengthen one another in the work. Would you be described as an encourager or a discourager?

Go forward!

Exodus 14:1-15

"And the LORD said unto Moses, Wherefore criest thou unto me?
Speak unto the children of Israel that they go forward." Exodus 14:15

Moses had led the children of Israel right until they faced the Red sea. They were in such desperation. Behind them was the slaughter of the sword, in front of them was drowning in the depths of the sea. Then the Lord commands "go forward" into the sea and of course to their amazement the sea opens up a pathway to the other side.

What are the lessons for us today, well first of all never go back when God commands, "go forward". To turn back is disobedient to God's commandment. If Israel had turned back they would have been destroyed, not the Egyptians. God's way seemed impossible but with God nothing is impossible. God promised to make a way and a way He did make. When the Lord tells us to go forward we must keep going on, He will make a way. We cannot see the way but He will make a way. God is only with us when we go His way. To disobey God is to depart from His way. You will know God's presence, help and guidance when you stay on the path He has planned out for you.

The sparrow's locking system

Psalm 84

"Yea, the sparrow hath found an house." Psalm 84:3

Have you ever considered a little sparrow, wonderfully and perfectly made? How the scriptures tell us that every time one of these little birds fall to the ground the Lord knows all about it. The great challenge goes to remind us that even though God cares for these little birds, how much more does He care for us.

Like me, have you ever wondered how a little bird can go to sleep at night while perched on a little twig at the end of a branch about one hundred feet in the air? Well, the marvel of it all is that God made a special little "locking system." There is a sort of a spring lock in the tiny bird's leg that cannot open. Whenever its leg is bent to sit down, the claws close in like a vice and this won't be released until the sparrow straightens its leg again. Totally amazing, isn't it, how our Heavenly Father designed these little creatures.

When you are afraid of falling, or even anxious about something, remember the little sparrow and especially the little locking system fitted within it to keep it from falling. Then this will help us to remember how we are locked in the arms of our loving Heavenly Father. If He cares for the birds of the air, how much more does the Lord care for those who love Him?

IMPACT *Daily readings*

The difference between man and God

Isaiah 44:21-23

"I have blotted out, as a thick cloud, thy transgressions." Isaiah 44:22

People often forgive but they seldom forget. What they forgive is often in the background ready to remind the other person of their fault. For many years in my Christian life I was terribly burdened with this. The weight and load of sin kept building and building until it seemed like an impossible burden to carry. Getting close to God was often difficult until I really and fully understood the power of the precious blood of Christ that was shed on Calvary's hill.

When we come to faith in Jesus Christ and get saved, He cleanseth us from all our sin. That is our original sin which we are born with and all our sin up until that moment is cleansed. However because we still have the nature of the old man before conversion, we are still prone to sinning and will still sin. Now the wonderful thing here is that when God forgives us He forgets all about the sin we committed. As far as the east is from the west He will remember it no more. This is the real difference between man and God. God forgives and forgets. Have your sins cleansed afresh today in the precious blood of Christ, there is still power in the blood..Amen.

Meet the captain

Joshua 5:13-15

"There stood a man over against him with his sword drawn in his hand.....
captain of the host of the LORD." Joshua 5:13-14

Joshua was a real warrior, always watching and protecting his people. One night he came across a man with his sword drawn, not recognising him as a friend or an enemy he called out to him. He soon realised that the man who had come into the camp was the Lord Jesus Christ. He as the captain was ready to fight with Joshua in the battle. Joshua immediately bowed before him and like Moses took off his shoes because the ground in which he now stood was holy ground.

Joshua thought he was alone, but no, the Lord was there with him ready to fight with him. Sometimes we can think we are alone in the battle, Christ is ever and always with us. Let the Lord go before you and hunt down your enemies and either silence them, disarm them or bring them to naught. Joshua was a great man of courage, but to know and have the physical presence of the captain of the Lord of hosts, how powerful that must have been, nothing would encourage you more in the battle than to know the presence of the Lord is with you.

IMPACT *Daily readings*

Acknowledge God in everything

Proverbs 3:1-17
"In all thy ways acknowledge Him and He shall direct thy paths." Proverbs 3:6

This is a great lesson for life and a favourite for many. Acknowledging the Lord in everything is surely pleasing to the Lord. Especially for seeking guidance in your life it is very important to bring everything before the Lord, whether it is your studies, relationship, home, church whatever it is bring it before the Lord. You cannot expect the Lord to help and bless you if you don't talk to Him about it.

We all need guidance and direction in life. There are many paths our lives could take, but God has a special path for every one of His children. The most common asked question is "how can I know I am in God's will right now?" The best answer is to try a different route and see where it ends up. If it all goes wrong then you had better go back to the original route. Of course with relationships etc. it is different. God gives His children perfect peace, if you don't have that peace about someone then it's probably not meant to be. Be open and honest with the person and most of all God. He tells us to acknowledge Him in whatever you are doing and He will help, guide and direct us. When God is in the situation, what is there to worry about? Godliness with contentment is great gain. Aim to be in that good, acceptable and perfect will of God for your life. It is a beautiful place to be.

Trouble free

Psalm 34

"This poor man cried, and the LORD heard him,
and saved him out of all his troubles." Psalm 34:6

The secret when you are in trouble is to take your troubles immediately to the Lord. When the Lord hears your cry, He will answer, help you and save you from your troubles. This is what the Psalmist here is telling us, we must fully trust in the Lord to help us. Going through life with continual troubles is a terrible thing; some of these cannot be avoided and therefore must be endured by some. We can ask the Lord for grace to help us through these difficult times.

Notice in this Psalm how often David mentions the Lord. In his difficult times he always remembered the Lord. This is a great lesson for us all to learn. He talks about blessing the Lord and he will continually praise His name. Telling those around him to exalt the name of the Lord together. How when he seeks the Lord, the Lord hears him, helps and delivers him. My friend what David's God can do for him, He too can do for you. The Lord encampeth round about those that fear Him. Do we fear the Lord as we should? To fear God is not to be afraid, but rather be afraid of letting the Lord down, to have the utmost reverence and respect to Almighty God. How He encourages us to taste and see that the Lord is good, blessed or happy is the man that trusteth in Him. When we cast all our cares upon Him as He asks us to then we should live a fairly trouble free life as far as this world is concerned.

Having God with you

Numbers 23:10-21
"The LORD his God *is* with him." Numbers 23:21

Have you ever read a verse of scripture really slowly, again and again? This is one such verse, as you do so you will find many wonderful truths imbedded in the verse. Even though Jacob was a scheming, twisted individual, cunning and crafty in character, God was able to take all this out of him when he met him in Penial and named him Israel.

Yet when God looks at Jacob He cannot see a speck of iniquity or a single trace of perversity. Why is this so? This is because He has blotted out all his transgressions and covered them in the righteousness of Christ. He remembered his sins no more, this is what God does. The Lord his God was now with him. Isn't this a wonderful thought to know that the Lord is ever with his children? In a day when many will leave and forsake you, Christ says, 'I will never leave you nor will I forsake you.' To have the presence and protection of God is very precious. To know our sins are forgiven and washed away in the precious blood of Christ is just wonderful. The challenge however goes out when we know and realise how much Christ loves us and walks with us. How much do we love Him in return and how close are we walking with Him?

The exact location!

Psalm 87

"The Lord shall count.... that this man was born there" Psalm 87:6

In Poland everyone has a name day and often it is celebrated more than a natural birthday. For the Christian the day they were born into the family and Kingdom of God should be more important than your natural birthday. Have you got a second birthday? Was there a definite time in your life when and where the Lord Jesus saved your precious soul?

I remember mine well! It was a Sunday afternoon in June, 25th June 1989 to be exact. I was 17 years old, ready to take on the world, had a head knowledge of Christ but no heart knowledge. My mum asked me if I would drive her to a gospel mission in a little hall, outside Lisburn. I loved driving and it wasn't a problem consenting to that. That night the evangelist Noel Grant was conducting his final night of a gospel mission. Being under serious conviction of sin for some time now, the Lord was calling me one final time. I responded to the call, repented and confessed my sin before the Lord and that night in that little hall was the exact location where I was saved! I have never forgotten it!

What about you? Do you have an exact location when and where you trusted Christ as your Saviour? Maybe someone was the means of helping you, never forget them. They have helped you, who now are you helping to bring to Christ? My Mum was the means, praise God for mothers who are lovers of souls. Not only mothers, but anyone who has a desire can be instrumental in bringing souls to Christ.

IMPACT *Daily readings*

Meeting afresh with the Lord

Isaiah 6:1-8

"Then said I, Woe is me! for I am undone; because I am a
man of unclean lips." Isaiah 6:5

Entering the temple to offer incense was the privilege and duty of the Levites. No one else was permitted to do this. King Uzziah transgressed, entered the temple to do this, as a result God struck him with leprosy. He continued to have this disease until the day of his death.

In the same year that King Uzziah died, Isaiah met afresh with the Lord. Sometimes the Lord will remove certain people and even replace them with others for His work to be accomplished. God often works in mysterious ways. We cannot and will never work out the mind of God and why He does certain things, when and how He does them.

Isaiah confessed that he was unworthy for this, saying he was a man of unclean lips. Often our lips are unclean because our heart is unclean. Following this Isaiah experienced a wonderful cleansing when one of the seraphim flew to him, having a live coal in his hand, and laid it upon his mouth. This was a radical, purifying work, brought about by the Holy Ghost. This is a very humbling experience. Brokenness before God is absolutely necessary if you are ever going to be used effectively to win souls. Isaiah met afresh with God that day and his life was changed forever.

Are you prepared for this test, to meet afresh, to pay the price, to go through with God?

IMPACT *Daily readings*

Led to death by a woman

Judges 16:1-31

"And it came to pass afterward, that he loved a woman in the valley of Sorek, whose name was Delilah." Judges 16:4

Probably one of the saddest chapters in all the Bible where we find a man of God, filled with the Spirit, who was a judge in the land and full of God given strength. Yet all in one chapter we see the fall and death of this great man. Samson had a weakness and it was his love of women, we read this from verse one. Even though he loved women, the chapter tells us he loved one woman in particular, Delilah. Many a great man has fallen snare to women. Even today many marriages are wrecked because of men loving and often lusting after the flesh. It is one thing to be tempted, but yielding to temptation is the beginning of the end. Even looking and lusting through the TV and internet will weaken any man or woman.

The Philistines wanted Samson dead, yet, no matter what they tried to do in order to bind him, he seemed to escape, he was stronger than a bull. He didn't have the physique of a strong man, otherwise the Philistines would know how he was so strong, but he just looked like any other man. The secret for Samson was that he was filled with the Spirit of God. The secret of his strength was in his Nazarite vow, in that no razor would ever come upon his head. The moment he revealed his secret, he lost his strength, lost his eyes and eventually lost his life. Even though he killed more people in his death than his life, he was lured into a trap by a woman who loved money. Through Samson's love for her, he revealed his strength and that cost him his life. The Christian needs to rely and fully trust in God everyday for strength. Beware of women and men who seek after you for deceitful means.

IMPACT *Daily readings*

Samuel grew

1 Samuel 3:1-19

"And Samuel grew, and the Lord was with him." 1 Samuel 3:19

Just a few verses before this it tells us that Samuel did not yet know the Lord (v7). This is the same with every child upon this earth that they do not know the Lord. Eli's two sons were grown men and they did not know the Lord. But the wonderful story of Samuel tells us that he came to know the Lord because as he grew, the Lord was with him. What great encouragement it is to know that the Lord is with us as we grow up and grow old.

This is why it is so important to know the Lord as our personal Saviour; something needs to happen to us, somewhere along life's way we need to get saved. I find the ministry amongst the children very rewarding, enjoyable and fruitful. Most children realise they are sinners and when they hear the good news of the gospel, they respond and get saved so as they grow they can know the Lord is with them. So much effort is made by churches today to reach the adults and so little emphasis upon reaching the children, the young adults of tomorrow. Let us learn from Samuel, a boy who heard God calling, gave his life to him and served Him all the days of his life. We need to reach the wee Samuels and Samanthas out there before they grow up, before it's too late.

Content where you are!

1 Chronicles 4:21-23

"There they dwelt with the king for his work." 1 Chronicles 4:23

The men here we read about were the potters in the king's courtyard. Their job was to keep the gardens well pruned. They dwelt among hedges and plants, probably unnoticed by many people, yet it was their job, their calling and they lived with the king for his work. It may have been a humble job, without much praise, yet they were happy in it, it was their place to be.

In the eyes of the king, their job was as important as those who worked with the king's horses or served in the royal courts. Many people today are not content with their jobs, in fact they hate their work. The Lord loves a contented people; the scriptures tell us that 'godliness with contentment is great gain.' Sometimes when we work we should have the attitude that we work for the Lord and not to man.

When we don't like our work, and we tend to moan and groan, then our testimony can be questionable because those around us who are not saved will be in no way attracted to the Christian life if they use you as an example as a Christian. Your job can be a lowly one, you work away and your work never gets noticed or recognised. But remember God has a plan for all of our lives, if He gave you the job in the first place, He has not forgotten about you. Life is not about being successful, it is about being faithful. It is your faithfulness that you will be rewarded for. So keep your head up, keep your focus on the Lord at all times and give your best to everything you put your hands to. The gardeners were seldom noticed, but the gardens looked stunning. It didn't just happen, someone worked away in the background.

Protected

Psalm 91

"For he shall give his angels charge over thee, to keep thee
in all thy ways." Psalm 91:11

When I was a child I was fascinated by this verse that the Lord has angels to guard over us. When I became a Christian although not till the age of 17, then this thought had an even greater impact upon me. The fact that God loved me so much that He sent His Son to die for me and then when I trusted in Him He has appointed angels to watch over me. There have been many times when I have found myself in awkward situations, sometimes even dangerous, not to mention dozing at the wheel of the car when I have been suddenly woken and wondered how I got up the motorway so quickly, a dangerous thing to do. It doesn't happen often mind you but from time to time. The point is I believe the angels took the wheel of my car and woke me up just in time as on one occasion I was driving so close behind a forty foot lorry.

Christian friend today, take great courage from what the Lord is teaching us and reminding us, He continually looks after His children. He cares more about you than anyone else would in this world. One thing Joanna loves about marriage is protection, the fact that I protect her from danger and make her feel safe and she knows I would protect her at any cost. It's our natural care of duty. How much more do our heavenly angels watch over and protect us. Next time you are praying thank the Lord for watching over you. To know His protection you must know the Lord!

IMPACT *Daily readings*

Determined to go

Ruth 1:1-18

"When she saw that she was stedfastly minded to go with her,
then she left speaking unto her." Ruth 1:18

Many wedding vows often use the words of Ruth to her mother-in-law Naomi. It is one of the most beautiful and touching scenes in all of scripture. Orpah is determined to stay with her people and her gods. Ruth on the other hand was willing to leave everything and go with Naomi. Even though Naomi pleads with her to stay with her own people, Ruth was still determined to make a new start in life. She said these beautiful words to Naomi, maybe with a tear in her eye and a lump in her throat, "Intreat me not to leave thee, or to return from following after thee: for whither thou goest, I will go; and where thou lodgest, I will lodge: thy people shall be my people, and thy God my God: Where thou diest, will I die, and there will I be buried: the LORD do so to me, and more also, if ought but death part thee and me."

Ruth was determined to go with Naomi and her mind was made up. It was such a wonderful love she had for her mother-in-law. It was a love until death itself. The lesson of course is not that we have to love our mother-in-laws to this degree, although some may but I have yet to meet them. These words are often used when young couples exchange wedding vows.

An even deeper love is on my mind though, and that is a love for Jesus. May we be determined and stedfastly minded to go with Him all the way in our Christian lives. May we be continually stedfast in our prayer lives, reading the Word of God and in our service to and for Him.

For Ruth it meant giving up everything for love. Am I willing to give up everything for my love for Jesus?

IMPACT *Daily readings*

My affliction

Psalm 31:1-8

"Thou hast considered my trouble: thou hast known my
soul in adversities." Psalm 31:7

Have you ever sat there all alone feeling sorry for yourself and thinking that nobody cares about you? Humanly speaking you could be right. Feeling sorry for yourself isn't going to help much nor does it make you the most interesting person to visit. However in the Christian life we have got to look at the bigger picture and focus on the One who does care. In fact the One who knows all about you, your situation, your condition, whatever way you are right now.

The Lord knows all about your trouble, He knows all about your adversities, more than anyone else does, in fact, better than you even know yourself. That's why we keep reiterating the point that it is good to talk to the Lord regularly in prayer. He knows and cares so much for you. Don't shut yourself of from Him. He wants to help you in your situation right now. We have got to acknowledge the Lord and how much we need Him in our lives. We need to surrender our entire beings to Him and let Him take total control of our lives. When He does, He does a much better job than we could ever do ourselves. Whatever your trouble, hand it over to the Lord, and cast all your care upon Him because He careth for you.

Are you feeling down?

Isaiah 38:9-16

"O Lord, I am oppressed, undertake for me." Isaiah 38:14

King Hezekiah, when he wrote these words, had spoken them when he was ill and in deep distress. God graciously answered his prayer, brought him through and added another fifteen years to his life.

There are times in our lives when we can feel 'oppressed'. When all the powers of hell seem to be attacking, sending confusion, pain, trouble, burdens and you just don't know where to turn for help. We can often think, am I the only person who has days or times like these? There are thousands of God's dear children who go through times like this, the same experience and maybe far worse. There is always someone far worse off than you are today.

Friends, doctors and medicine can be lots of help to people, but sometimes these are not always the cure, maybe it just takes time. This is your time to get alone with God and plead with Him to help you get out of it. Maybe not today but the day may come when you desperately need the Lord, don't be a stranger to Him, be in the habit of talking to the Lord every day. When you come to Him, He already knows your need, before you even ask Him. Then when you pray and the Lord helps you, don't forget to thank Him for setting you free, oppressed again you hope not to be!

Don't be afraid of them

Joshua 1:1-9

"There shall not any man be able to stand before thee all the days of thy life: as I was with Moses, *so* I will be with thee: I will not fail thee, nor forsake thee." Joshua 1:5

I personally take great courage from this text to know that the Lord is with us and when there are those who will stand up to oppose us, the Lord will be there to protect us. When you advance forward for the cause of Christ you can expect to be opposed, you can expect to make enemies and have people who will accuse you and ultimately try to bring you down. You must remain strong and calm. The winds of adversity will blow upon you, but you must remain steadfast, let them shout, let them mock, let them talk, but you must not flinch.

Just like God was with Moses so was He with Joshua and so He will be with us. Moses had enemies, those who made him mad and so did the great apostle Paul and so will you and so do I. Enemies from every quarter, those that are jealous, suspicious and envious but can I encourage you not to be afraid of them, God will protect and encourage you as you stand alone, and alone sometime we must stand. But to know God is with us is too precious to have it any other way.

The fall of Adam!

Genesis 3:1-16

"She took the fruit thereof, and did eat,
and gave also unto her husband with her; and he did eat." Genesis 3:6

Whenever someone is preaching or sharing the gospel, it is so important to refer to this portion of scripture. God specifically told Adam and Eve not to touch the fruit from this tree, it was forbidden. Along comes the devil in the disguise of a serpent and persuades Eve with his lies that she believed him. As a result of this one moment of disobedience, sin entered the world. "Wherefore, as by one man sin entered into the world, and death by sin; and so death passed upon all men, for that all have sinned." Romans 5:12

Everyone needs to understand where and how sin came into this world. As a result of the disobedience of Adam and Eve we are all born with original sin,which separates us from God, cannot enter Heaven and must be punished by death. "For God so loved the world that he gave his only begotten Son, that whosoever believeth in him should not perish, but have everlasting life." John 3:16

This is how amazing God is, that He is willing to forgive someone and completely forget all the sin and wrong things they have ever done. So many know so little about the Garden of Eden and what went wrong in that garden. How the fall of Adam has affected every single human being born into this world. Those who have never heard of the tree in the garden and especially the tree at Calvary are lost forever; those people are all around us everywhere. It takes courage to tell them, God will give you that courage, don't go in your own strength, rather go in the strength of the Lord!

The battle rages

2 Samuel 10:6-14
"Be of good courage, and let us play the men for our people,
and for the cities of our God." 2 Samuel 10:12

Like many times before, God's people were under attack. This time it was Joab and the men of Israel. In the heat of the battle, Joab shouts to the men to 'be of good courage.' They were to fight like men, remembering who they were protecting and more importantly who they were fighting for.

Sometimes we can be involved in the Lord's work and forget it is the Lord's work. When the battle rages and the going gets tough, when there is little fruit for our labours and not much happening, then we must remember it is the Lord's work. Especially when we are under attack from without and within, then we must remember that the battle is the Lord's. We must stand up like men and be counted. The work and people of God must be protected.

Often the work can be discouraging and disheartening. That's why it is so important to encourage one another in the Lord. Look out for others in the work. When they come across your path or the Lord puts them upon your heart, send them a message of encouragement. It could be just what they need at that very moment. So often we read in Scripture how they encouraged one another in the Lord. We all appreciate it, so why not give what you enjoy getting and encourage someone today?

The work is great!

1 Chronicles 29:1-10

"…..whom alone God hath chosen, is yet young and tender,
and the work is great." 1 Chronicles 29:1

Have you ever thought about your life and how quickly it is passing away? James states that our life is like '…a vapour, that appeareth for a little time, and then vanisheth away.' So it is with life; it really does pass by so quickly. Have you ever seriously talked to the Lord and asked Him if He has any special plans for your life? God chooses people and is pleased to use them for His special service. God will bring people into your life to give you opportunities to serve. Take every opportunity or God will give it to someone else and they will receive the opportunity to serve and be blessed. There is a job for everyone to do. Sometimes God uses and calls ordinary people for a special job which only they can do. If you are one of those people, keep an eye out and keep looking up for your opportunity. When an opportunity comes, grab it with both hands and don't miss out.

When David was speaking here, he was referring to Solomon, his son. Solomon was young and tender with his life before him, and he was in his prime to serve God. The work before him was great. The work of the Lord is great, not just great to be in. There is so much to do and time is short so the need is great for God's people to rise up and serve. People need the Lord; they need to be told of their need of Christ. God uses people to do His work, it is such an honour to serve Christ; there is no higher calling in this life. If He calls you, be sure to answer the call, because the work is great.

IMPACT *Daily readings*

Nervous about speaking?

Exodus 4:10-15
"I am slow of speech and of a slow tongue." Exodus 4:10

Some people hate the thought of speaking in public. The groom and best man on a wedding day are a good example of this as it really does make them so nervous and can even make them feel physically sick. This in many ways is normal! Most people are by nature not public speakers. Moses was making excuses before the Lord as he was not willing to lead the children of Israel out of Egypt, so the Lord used Aaron, his brother, as his spokesperson.

I remember when I was a child, the children in church were taking part in the service and I had to say a verse. When the time came, the leader had to pass me by and do it himself as I had disappeared! I was so afraid of going to the front that I hid behind my mum's skirt. I remember another time Mrs Douglas, my minister's wife, who looked after the children's meeting, asked me to tell the story. I prepared really well and wrote the whole story out, word for word, in about twelve A4 pages. As I got up to talk I was so nervous, then someone opened the door and the wind blew all the pages everywhere. I soon realised that using notes for a children's meeting is not the wisest thing to do. Once during Bible College, the students were taking a church service in Portadown; I was to do the reading. I was so nervous and shook so much I could hardly read the scriptures.

I soon learned the valuable lesson of relying totally on God for everything. He is my strength. He helps me and He can help you. This is my life's work now and I experience His help every single day of my life. When I am weak then He is my strength.

Early in the morning

Psalm 63

"O God, thou art my God: early will I seek thee." Psalm 63:1

There is a freshness about the early morning which cannot be recaptured at any other part of the day. Unfortunately it is becoming increasingly difficult for people to rise up early because with social networking and all the modern technology that most people have in their homes today. It makes it increasingly difficult to rise up early if we sit up late. It is a fact that our brain is much more active in the mornings as are our minds. Many will agree that much more can be done in less time in the mornings than any other part of the day.

When we study the lives of godly men and women, we invariably find that many of them rose up early in the morning to meet with God, some at four and five in the morning. Many of the Biblical characters also rose up early in the morning. Abraham arose very early to stand before the Lord. Jacob awoke at first light to worship the Lord. Moses was commanded to meet the Lord early in the morning at Mount Sinai. When Joshua was preparing to take Jericho, he was on the move very early in the morning. The Lord Jesus gives us a wonderful example to follow when He rose a great while before day in order to meet with His Heavenly Father.

Try to discipline yourself by rising early to meet afresh with God, if you do, a life of unknown blessing awaits you. If you want to hear from God, this is the best time to listen, when the entire world is quiet.

Do your neighbours know?

Deuteronomy 11:18-25

"And thou shalt write them upon the door posts of thine house,
and upon thy gates." Deuteronomy 11:20

If you were arrested and taken to court, would there be enough evidence to prove you guilty of being a Christian? If you happened to go missing and the police went around your neighbours to find out when they last saw you, what would they say about you? Do you think they would use the word "Christian" to describe you? Are the any markings around your home that might even suggest you are saved?

Are you embarrassed to shine for Jesus? Would putting up a verse of scripture in your home or office cause embarrassment or even offence to someone? Would that be enough for you to take it down in case someone gets offended? This is what is happening all around the world today, some individuals are offended by the sign of Christianity, so the pressure becomes too much so it is taken down. We are challenged here to take a stand for the Lord. When someone comes to our door, they should know even before they knock that we belong to Jesus. Sometimes we can be more concerned about the feelings of strangers than we are the feelings of Christ. When I go to a door and the first thing I see is a picture, Bible or something that tells me this is a Christian home, it fills my heart with joy. Other times when entering into a home, I look and look and then when I leave, sad to say I have seen no evidence that this home belongs to Jesus. In your home today, how hard would it be to find evidence of Christ living in your home?

Get out of the rut

Isaiah 32:1-9

"Rise up, ye women that are at ease; hear my voice,
ye careless daughters; give ear unto my speech." Isaiah 32:9

How many of us are just going through the norm of Christian living, living in a rut, with no real aim, focus or plans to do anything for God. You are the ideal Christian the devil loves. He knows that once you are saved he can no longer win your soul. So he likes to make sure you are preoccupied enough with your own life and leave the serving God up to someone else. Have you ever noticed every time there is a call and a challenge to go to the mission field it always seems to be girls who are willing to forsake all and follow the Lord?

The Lord is challenging women here that are at ease. Are you at ease with your Christian life, can you not be challenged to do something to reach the rising generation and the present generation with the gospel? Millions are going to hell because God's children will not take the flag and wave it to warn the people to repent and be converted. One day you will wake up all stiff and sore. The reason is because you are now old, with tears in your eyes as they fall to your pillow you will wish you had done something, gone somewhere while you were able and while you could.

Don't be careless with your life. There is blessing and pleasure in serving God. If you're stuck in a rut, give yourself a shake and get out of it. God needs you to serve Him. The Christian life is too beautiful and wonderful to miss out on all the blessings. Rise up my friend and catch the vision of God and His glorious Son who sets people free. Can you be challenged from today to endeavour to do something for the Lord?

IMPACT *Daily readings*

Clear direction

Psalm 78:38-52

"He...guided them in the wilderness." Psalm 78:52

The wilderness is a picture of the world. As the Lord guided the Children of Israel through the wilderness they had to keep their focus on the Lord. They were continually reminded that the wilderness was not their home; they had the land of promise to look forward to. Quite often they forgot that and they grumbled, mumbled and complained about their condition that they lived in.

There are many people around us today who are living in the wilderness; they have forgotten that we are just passing through this old world. We live as if we are here forever. Sometimes the Lord needs to throw in a few difficulties to remind us of the fact that this world is not our home we are just passing through. Sometimes when our Christian friends get all caught up in the cares of this world, we have the duty to remind them that we are not to make this world our home but rather to prepare better for our eternal home.

Likewise when we have unsaved friends and loved ones who are equally caught up in this world with their business and education, then use this as a great opportunity to tell them about the wilderness. It was only a journey that would last a certain length of time. Life is a journey and all of us are just passing through for a certain length of time. During this time we either accept Christ or reject Him. Maybe you are the only one to tell them, what stops you? Are you afraid or ashamed? The Lord Jesus tells us if we are ashamed of Him then He too is ashamed of us before His Father in Heaven. Go today and tell them about the land that is promised to all that call upon the Lord for Salvation.

IMPACT *Daily readings*

Never too old

Judges 1:1-20
"And they gave Hebron unto Caleb." Judges 1:20

Caleb was a man who followed the Lord fully; men like these are scarce today. Someone completely sold out for God. In order to be like Caleb there is a secret and that is the help of the infilling of the Holy Spirit of God. Caleb was so confident that he would possess the land from the day he left Egypt. He was an optimist, Christians today are full of pessimism and don't seem to rely on the confidence and power of God upon their lives.

All the other spies except Joshua declared a negative and dishonest report, but Caleb declared, "We are well able to possess the land." His faith was strong, he looked to God alone to help, he wasn't going to get defeated and depressed by the giants all around him. Sometimes we need to really learn the lesson of trusting and relying more fully on God to help us fight our battles. Surely the Lord hates gloom and doom Christians, the joy of the Lord is to be our strength, we are saved from sin, have the Lord with us and are guaranteed a home in heaven. Give me one good excuse for being down in the mouth all the time. You are never too old to do something for God, it may be the best thing you ever did and become the most blessed time in your life.

IMPACT *Daily readings*

Holding hands

Isaiah 42:1-16

"I the LORD have called thee in righteousness, and will hold thine hand, and will keep thee." Isaiah 42:6

Here in this text, we have a great and wonderful promise for the Christian. The Lord calls the Christian to salvation and promises to be with them, holding their hand all along life's way. When we fall or tend to wander off, He graciously pulls us back to Himself again. He also promises to keep us! What a great thought this is to stimulate and motivate you to go on living for the Lord.

We can be just like a little child who walks holding onto their father or mother's hand. The child is content holding on because they feel safe and secure as they walk. They know they are loved, protected and cared for. The parent on the other hand knows that while the child is holding on to them, they are really holding onto the child. Likewise this is what the Lord does with us. We don't keep Him but He keeps us!

When you are at your lowest, think about the above verse and read it slowly over and over again. "I have called thee;" so personal and so beautiful. "I will hold thine hand," He loves you so much, and He cares for you more than any other and more than you realise. "I will keep thee," just when you might think no one wants you, the Lord holds up His hand and says "I'll take you and I'll keep you and I'll hold onto you." The time has come when we need to place our lives once again into the loving, tender care of the Lord.

IMPACT *Daily readings*

Family problems

Genesis 21:1-21

"Wherefore she said unto Abraham, Cast out this bondwoman and her son: for the son of this bondwoman shall not be heir with my son, even with Isaac." Genesis 21:10

The story of the little boy Ishmael is certainly a very interesting one. The Lord had promised Abraham and Sarah that they would have a child, a son. But as time passed by, they were getting older and older and there was no sign of a child. So Abraham and Sarah became very impatient and thought they would come up with an idea to have a child. Sarah asked Abraham to have a child by her servant Hagar and Abraham did so and Ishmael was born.

Afterwards Sarah regretted what she had done and soon became bitter, jealous and envious over Hagar. Hagar was told to leave the household but soon came back again. When Hagar gave birth to Ishmael, Isaac was soon born to Abraham and Sarah. But when Ishmael began to tease Isaac, Sarah was so jealous that she put both Hagar and Ishmael out of the house. Can you see how many problems can occur over such a matter? I know some homes with a mother and six children, all of whom have a different father. This is not meant to be, nor is it a new problem in society. God's plan and will is marriage and a family within that marriage, then natural love should happen naturally without any preference over one child or the other. It is a good thing to be thankful for a stable marriage and certainly something to pray and to be thankful to God for.

Under pressure from the world

Psalm 37

"Fret not thyself because of evildoers,
neither be thou envious against the workers of iniquity." Psalm 37:1

Sometimes in the Christian life we can be put under a lot of pressure, especially when we look at other people. Everything with them seems to be going so well and maybe they are not even Christians. Even when we know a little bit about them, they are not good people. They lie, steal, curse, cheat and the list goes on. As we think about them, we can be intimidated easily because of who they are. Remember the Bible reminds us that greater is He that is in you than he that is in the world. The old devil will tempt you and tell you that life is much better for them than you. Jealousy is a terrible thing and we can so easily become jealous of those doing better than we are.

Unless we are strong we can easily give into this type of temptation. Maybe we will not become like them. We may not steal, lie or curse but becoming like them means we are slipping away from the Lord, our first love. This is one of the most dangerous positions to be in. When you start to grow cold in your heart as a Christian, then you can become very miserable. When you feel the pressure from the world coming your way, don't give in. Be strong and fight against it! Cry to God for help and He will give you the strength to resist and overcome the temptation.

Hidden riches

Proverbs 22

"By humility and the fear of the Lord are riches" Proverbs 22:4

God has wonderful promises, blessings and riches for his child. Most people sadly go through life without claiming them or finding them. One of the greatest problems today in the Christian church is pride. When God speaks through His Word to challenge, rebuke or chastise us, quite often the stinking sin of pride comes to the fore and we are no longer teachable.

The fear of the Lord is having utmost respect for God, not daring to challenge His authority. It is by taking His Word at face value, being totally obedient to Him, loving the Lord with all our body mind and soul. Humility is the opposite of pride; this alone is one of the greatest secrets to really discovering God and all His riches. The Bible speaks a lot about humility, I think because of the extreme dangers of pride and how pride has destroyed a lot of good relationships between families, churches and Christian friendships. The secret is if we get these both together, humility and the fear of the Lord, then we are going a long way with God. Discover some of the greatest riches He has us in store for us, something which our human wealth can never buy.

Going forward with God

1 Samuel 16:6-14

"And the Spirit of the LORD came upon David from that day forward." 1 Samuel 16:13

This was a special day in David's life. While he was away minding the sheep, all of his brothers were lined up before Samuel, wondering who would be the next king. Little did they realise that their little brother David was God's anointed. The brothers were all handsome, strong young men, but they were not God's choice. Sometimes we can measure ourselves up to others in the standard of the world's eyes, but this is not God's way of working. Take your eyes off the flesh of man and rather focus on the lovely Lord Jesus.

From that day forward, the Spirit of the Lord came upon David and he was a changed man. Why don't you give yourself afresh to the Lord, all that you have, are and ever hope to be? Something else happened that day, the Spirit of the Lord departed from Saul. We read it in the very next verse. God will always find someone for the job. We need to be so careful in our Christian walk as God could remove us and replace us at any given moment He pleases. This is a warning for us all, how in his disobedience to the Lord, God was finished with him. Now an evil spirit came upon Saul and troubled him and he was unhappy the rest of his life.

From this day forward we need a fresh anointing from God to seek with all our strength to go forward with and for Almighty God!

He took courage!

2 Chronicles 15:1-19

"He took courage." 2 Chronicles 15:8

King Asa was given good instruction from a man of God. This advice is found in verse two. The Lord is with us while we are with Him; if we seek after Him, He will be found. However, if we forsake Him, then He will forsake us. This is not referring to salvation but rather to the presence of God in our lives. Asa was being warned here because in chapter 16 verse 17, Asa relied on man instead of the Lord to help him. He actually died as a miserable back slider. This can so easily happen to any of us which is why it's so important to take counsel from friends and especially from the Lord.

However, in chapter 16 he did seek the Lord for help and the Lord helped him as he had done before. When Asa received counsel, he took courage and removed all the idols of the land. When he was in trouble he sought the Lord. This is good practice, not only when we are in trouble but in every situation we should seek the Lord. When someone comes our way to encourage us in the Lord we should take courage. Look out for others, to encourage them in the Lord so they too can take courage.

IMPACT *Daily readings*

Rescued in the desert

Deuteronomy 32:1-10

"He found him in a desert land, and in the waste howling wilderness; he led him about, he instructed him, he kept him as the apple of his eye." Deuteronomy 32:10

Have you ever imagined yourself stranded alone in the desert with no water, no shelter, the heat of the sun upon you and all you can see is sand and rocks everywhere you look? Certain death awaits you unless help comes. You will either starve to death or die of thirst that is unless the vultures spot you and start circling above you waiting till you drop.

This is like a sinner wandering about lonely on this earth. Yet God looketh down upon you as He did for Jacob to instruct and guide you. When the Lord looks upon us he sees us as one of His children, He wants to instruct us in the way He wants us to go, and not necessarily the way we want to go ourselves, He looks after us and keeps us as the very apple of His eye. God is interested in you, your health, family and most of all your walk with Him. Maybe you are walking afar off, lonely and feel like you're in the desert place, then let Him rescue you, call upon His name and He will hear and come for you. You must do this quickly before the vultures come and seek to destroy you; they come in many different forms.

Facing your enemy

1 Samuel 17:32-51

"David said to Saul, Let no man's heart fail because of him;
thy servant will go and fight with this Philistine." 1 Samuel 17:32

I think this is one of the most thrilling of all the battle stories in the Bible. To this day it still has children on the edge of their seats as they hear this wonderful story being told. Today is no different as God still has his man in the hour of need. You may not be the tallest, smartest, wealthiest, or most presentable but you may be the very person God will use. If you have no fear but God, then you are the man for the job. Who would have imagined such a young lad, a shepherd, taking on the giant Goliath? Humanly speaking this is impossible, but then with God nothing is impossible.

The battle is on today and we have many enemies. Are you willing to take on your enemies? Everyone seems so fearful and careful, not to offend. Who will boldly stand up and declare that Jesus Christ is Lord? Yes, it is easy to do it in church but now we have got to tell the world! It's a different story out in the world. David was away from the comfort of his sheep; the real battle was in the real world. Completely trusting in the Lord, he challenged, faced and defeated the giant.

God did not fail David, nor will He fail you. You may be in the minority but with God on your side, you are in the majority. We must be brave, very brave, to stand up and speak up for the Lord. The enemy is great and powerful, but we have the All Powerful, Almighty God with us! Go in His name and face your enemy.

What is it that makes you so fearful of speaking up for the Lord?

Walking God's way

Isaiah 30:15-21

"This is the way, walk ye in it, when ye turn to the right hand,
and when ye turn to the left." Isaiah 30:21

The beautiful thing about the Christian life is that a born again believer is led by the Holy Spirit. He guides us and directs us in our earthly pilgrimage down here. This is why it is so essential to listen to His voice when we are here on earth. The Holy Spirit abides and dwells within every believer. But to be really effective in our Christian walk and life we must be filled with God's Spirit every day of our lives. We must listen to His prompting and leading. We will often be challenged to go a certain way or to look in a certain direction. When we are tempted, we will feel the urge of God's Spirit saying, "This is the way, walk ye in it, when ye turn to the right hand, and when ye turn to the left." We will then know which way to go and in which way to turn.

The challenge of course is that once we hear His voice we need to heed it. Many believers drift in this matter and they become cold in their Christian walk. Soon the voice becomes faint, and they no longer hear the voice because they have decided to go their own stubborn way. God wants His best for you and for your life! Keep your ear open to His voice and what He tells you to do and where He tells you to go.

When is the last time you heard the still small voice speaking to you?

Little is much

Proverbs 15:1-21

"Better is little with the fear of the Lord,
than great treasure and trouble therewith." Proverbs 15:16

I used to be amazed at big houses, the big private ones. I used to try and imagine what it would be like to live in such a big house, with all the rooms upstairs and downstairs. As a child it sounded like the ideal place for hide and seek. Then as I look around me now I realise that all these big houses are only bricks and mortar like everyone else's, just a little bigger. I used to think that the bigger your house was, the happier you would be, but sadly this is not the case. I also realised the bigger the house the more it would cost to buy and furnish. In many ways it was the same with cars. I used to wonder how people can afford to drive all these big fancy cars. Then I realised just like the houses they had to pay them off month by month, just like most other people.

Many today have got a lot of wealth but at the expense of it, they also have a lot of trouble. A friend of mine, a business man, learnt this lesson in a hard way and rescheduled his whole business saying he would make less do. He is now putting the Lord first and by doing this to his amazement he would be as well off now as before without all the worry and stress. So like the verse says better is little with the fear and peace of God than having a lot of wealth which brings a lot with trouble. What would you rather have?

Divine direction

Psalm 37:18-25

"The steps of a good man are ordered by the Lord." Psalm 37:23

Sometimes we can read verses of scripture very quickly without stopping to ponder the true meaning or even the lovely personal encouragement they can be. Here is one such verse, 'the steps of a good man are ordered by the Lord.' Isn't it a tremendous thought even to imagine that our very lives, the very steps we take are ordered and directed by the Lord.

I believe like the will of God it starts immediately upon conversion, we start out as a follower of Jesus, desiring to love and serve Him with all of our hearts. We want to follow His way, His steps and His path. However the real challenge for the Christian is to stay on that pathway. Temptation is never far away; all sorts of reasons can cause us to leave the path that the Lord had led out before us. The question and real challenge before us right now is are we following close or afar off the Lord? The steps we take and are taking at this present time, can we honestly say they are ordered by the Lord? Sometimes we can easily say when all is going well, yes they are and when things don't go so well, they aren't but the real challenge is that we are able to keep walking in His way no matter about our circumstances.

IMPACT *Daily readings*

God will help me

Isaiah 50:1-9

"For the Lord GOD will help me; therefore shall I not be confounded:
I set my face like a flint." Isaiah 50:7

It is one thing to ask God for help and another thing knowing that God will help you. It is so easy to pray about a matter but having the faith to believe that the Lord not only hears but will actually answer you is a different matter. It is a wonderful thing to have confidence in the Lord as you go through your Christian life. In the Christian life we should always be confident in the Lord, He is wonderful. He wants to help you so much in everything you do, believe with all your heart that the Lord is interested in you. Isaiah was determined not to be beaten, not to be confounded as he went through life. Unlike many today, they are giving up on the fight, throwing in the towel and doing less and less for God. I'm the opposite; I want to run at the enemy, reach and do all that is within me to do what I can for God because I am confident and know that the Lord will help me.

Whenever you pray for something and it is within your means to do what you ask then go and do it. God is the God of impossibilities not the possibilities. Whatever you can do then go and do. If it is not meant to be then the Lord will close that door. Isaiah here set his face like a flint, he was fully determined to go through with God, and nothing was going to stop him. We should be like this in our Christian lives, fully determined to live out and out for God no matter the cost.

Watch out for the birds

Genesis 15:1-11

"And when the fowls came down.....Abram drove them away." Genesis 15:11

Abram was preparing a sacrifice unto the Lord at this time, but the fowls of the air were swooping down to devour it. Abram safeguarded his sacrifice by driving them off as they came. It meant that he had to stand watch over his sacrifice.

If you are making a special sacrifice, or offering unto the Lord as a Christian, or if you are deciding to do something for the Lord with your life in the form of time or service, especially if you are at the brink of fully surrendering your life unto the Lord, then I would suggest you watch out for the birds. The birds will come to you in many forms, shapes and sizes. Rest assured the devil doesn't want you sacrificing anything for the Lord and the best sacrifice we can ever make is our own lives for His service.

The greatest destroyer in the form of a bird believe it or not is the two legged bird, ever since the beginning of time this has been a great weapon used by the devil. Many a great man and woman have been destroyed by two legged birds. Marriages have been wrecked and broken, families broken up, churches ruined because of this problem. Learn from the birds of the air and watch and guard your life and testimony like a hawk. The birds come in all sorts of forms; even your work place may offer better pay and conditions to stop you stepping out. A nagging wife can also be a problem, so make sure you are honest with her from the beginning about what you want to do with your life. Be on your guard and watch out for the birds and they can fly in at any time, ruthless some of them to stop you going on and through for and with God.

IMPACT *Daily readings*

The Lord will help you!

Jeremiah 1:1-9

"But the LORD said unto me, Say not, I am a child: for thou shalt go to all that I shall send thee, and whatsoever I command thee thou shalt speak." Jeremiah 1:7

The word of the Lord came unto Jeremiah as a tremendous source of comfort to him at this time. Jeremiah was asked to go before the people and tell them a message from God. He was afraid of the people, what they might say and what they might do. Have you ever been in a situation like this? When the opportunity is given to you to speak up for the Lord, take it. You know the opportunity is given, it is a great opportunity, yet you are afraid to speak up for Jesus. Of course you are not embarrassed or ashamed of the Lord, but something still stops us from speaking up.

This is often what is missing and that is the realisation that the Lord is continually with His children. To speak something for Jesus we need power from God, we need His enabling, His help and words from the Lord to speak. The Lord God was reminding Jeremiah how well He knew him, in fact away before he was even formed or even born. God had a great plan for Jeremiah's life; He would help him and give him the words to speak. Jeremiah began to make excuses saying that he was like a child. The Lord told Jeremiah to go and speak unto the people and not to be afraid of their faces because the Lord was not only with him but would give him the words to say. Be like Jeremiah and ask the Lord to put words into your mouth and go and speak up for the Lord, don't be a silent Christian!

IMPACT *Daily readings*

The blessing

Numbers 6:22-27

"The Lord bless thee and keep thee." Numbers 6:24

This blessing is very often used when a child is being dedicated unto the Lord. It is a prayer unto the Lord for His guidance, protection and blessing upon you. It was given to those who took upon themselves the vow of a Nazarite. We can read more about the vows that Nazarites took in the book of Numbers, the vows were strict orders that God asked them to obey. This particular blessing came in a threefold.

"The LORD bless thee, and keep thee: The LORD make his face shine upon thee, and be gracious unto thee: The LORD lift up his countenance upon thee, and give thee peace." (Numbers 6:24-26)

If we are prepared to separate ourselves unto the Lord, then we can claim this blessing as well. There is often a high price to pay for total consecration, sanctification and living a Holy life. But remember God is always pleased with sacrifice and it is always good for us. It is a wonderful thing to have the blessing of God upon our lives. God keeps His children and watches over them in their going out and coming in. It is a wonderful thing to have the protection of Almighty God upon us.

Many today do not have peace! Even believers, struggle and worry about so many things in this world. They don't have or enjoy the peace of God like He would want them to. Maybe our faith is weak and we are no longer trusting God to guide us and help us. How do you think the Lord feels? Imagine you were walking a three year old child across the road and they refuse to cross because they don't trust you to keep them safe. How would you feel? Imagine how the Lord feels every time you start to worry and stop trusting Him.

Always thankful

Psalm 34:1-10
"I will bless the Lord at all times." Psalm 34:1

This is a tremendous challenge for any one of us to bless the Lord at all times. We live in a day when people seem to moan and groan all the time. Conversations can become negative and discouraging and the person talked about is anything but good.

The Psalmist on the other hand has the desire to praise and bless the Lord at all times. We should take on this challenge to see how far we can get. How many days can we go before we become negative and discouraging. The little chorus comes to mind to count our many blessings and name them one by one and it will surprise you what the Lord has done. Sometimes we can forget to count our blessings, many as they are. When we offer the Lord praise we glorify His name. (Psalm 50:23) If you have the habit of mumbling and grumbling, then ask the Lord to shake you out of it. It grieves the Lord seeing His children having an ungrateful, critical spirit. The next time you find yourself in a conversation that turns negative and your soul begins to be grieved, set yourself the challenge of turning the conversation around to one that pleases, blesses and glorifies the Lord.

Have you considered how much your negative attitude and such like conversations grieve the Lord?

Keeping short accounts

Lamentations 3:18-25

"The LORD *is* good unto them that wait for him, to the soul *that* seeketh him."

Lamentations 3:25

Sometimes we can be put off from praying and doing our devotions because we think we have to do them for hours at a time. If you feel like this then I would encourage you to keep short accounts with God. Little and often is a fruitful strategy and I would be in the habit of doing this. So many wonderful thoughts come floating into our minds and before our eyes we cannot help but immediately praise His name for it. On the other hand there is so much sin and ungodliness in the world all around us, our eyes, ears and mind continue to be polluted every day making it absolutely essential to have short encounters with the Lord as we seek to battle through these. But remember, the Lord is good to them that wait and to those who seek after God.

Many times in scripture we are encouraged to wait on the Lord. Patience is a very difficult thing for many people, myself included. Many today are discouraged and despondent in their daily lives. The weight and pressures of life and living seem to be on top of them. There are maybe problems with home, relationships, finance, friends, church and the list goes on and on. Maybe your heart is failing; you're at an all-time low. Keep short accounts with God; continue to plead with Him to help you in your situation. Be of good courage, He will give you strength, He will strengthen your heart. Wait, wait...keep waiting on the Lord, His timing, His plan, His will for you is perfect.

IMPACT *Daily readings*

The presence of God

Exodus 33:12-23

"My presence shall go with thee, and I will give thee rest." Exodus 33:14

Moses was given this wonderful assurance when he was asked to lead the Children of Israel. Moses was petrified of his own weakness; the Lord knew this and assured him of His presence. Without the Lord's help Moses would have been helpless, hopeless and most of all powerless. This is the secret of Christian leadership, being filled with the Spirit of God, because relying on our own strength we will not be strong enough.

There is a constant danger in this busy life, that many of us now live and lead, lives that we can neglect the presence of the Lord. This is essential if you want to know the Lord's blessing in your life. Moses would face many challenges and hardships to come, even his very own people would turn against him, more than once. This is why he would need the Lord. Life goes well until it stops going so well and turns out not so pleasant, these are times when we will need the presence of the Lord like never before. Just don't expect to live afar of from the Lord and then when something goes wrong, snap your fingers and the Lord comes running to your side. You might have to wait a while because the Lord does things His way in His timing; this is why we need to linger in His presence every day.

Don't miss the opportunity!

Ezekiel 33:1-20

"If thou dost not speak to warn the wicked from his way.....
his blood will I require at thine hand." Ezekiel 33:8

This surely is one of the most alarming warnings in the entire Bible. Basically from what I understand, every person we come into contact within a speaking and personal level we have to tell them about Christ the Saviour of the world, the importance of being saved and having our sins forgiven. If we fail to do this, then we are responsible for the soul of that person, and are guilty of blood guiltiness.

On the other hand we are told in the following verse, verse nine, "Nevertheless, if thou warn the wicked of his way to turn from it; if he does not turn from his way, he shall die in his iniquity; but thou hast delivered thy soul." This is the only way we can be free from this guilt of not telling them, it is by telling them. Remember you don't do this in your own strength; the Lord will go with you and help you. Pray about this, if there is someone you know, even dear to you, go to them and tell them. Be open, frank and honest. How they react and what they do is not your concern. If they refuse Christ, it is Christ they refuse not you. Whoever is on your heart, call them or go to them, before it is too late. Once they come into your heart, God puts them there, you are His messenger, what an honour and what a privilege to speak for Christ.

The love of a mother

Proverbs 23:19-28

"Hearken unto thy father that begat thee,
and despise not thy mother when she is old." Proverbs 23:22

The fifth commandment tells us to honour our parents. Following it comes a promise that the Lord will bless us with long life. Today many children take their parents for granted and often talk back to them and some parents are even forbidden by their children to go into their bedrooms. We are to listen to and obey our father; this is an instruction from the Lord. I remember as I was growing up there were many things I wanted to do and places that I wanted to go. I remember my father gently putting his hand on a lot of them, because he could see the mess I would end up in. It was hard and frustrating to accept when my Dad would overrule something I wanted to do, but he knew what was best, he didn't want to ruin my life, he wanted to save it.

The responsibility that everyone has is to love and look after their mother. Especially as you get older, so does your mother. We have got to look after them, provide for them, just as they have done for us. One day you will wake up and your mother will be gone. It is too late then to do something for them. Make a habit of calling your mother, buying her flowers; taking her out for a meal. I often say, I only take orders from two women in my life, one is my wife and the other is my mother. Never forget, neglect or despise your mother. You are here in this world because she brought you into it. There was a time when you needed her; maybe the time has come when she needs you.

Be honest with God

Psalm 142

"I poured out my complaint before him; I showed before him
my trouble." Psalm 142:2

When David was speaking here he was in constant fear while hiding in a cave. King Saul was pouring his entire efforts into capturing David. David naturally feared for his life. When his back was completely against the wall, we find him pouring out his heart to God. He was honest; there was no point in putting on a brave face pretending all was well.

How many of us often put on a brave face pretending all is well when deep down we know, that we are far from well. Just like David we find ourselves driven into a cave full of fear. The further you go into a cave, the darker it becomes. Sometimes we find ourselves hurting more and more, afraid, alone and embarrassed. David had the solution and the way out and he did the right thing in his hour of trouble. He poured out his heart unto the Lord.

Life is full of discouragements They will dishearten you to the very core if you focus on them and you will find yourself in the shadow of the cave. You don't want to go there! Rather focus on the light, the Light of this world, the lovely Lord Jesus Christ, the great Comforter who knows all things. Whatever is troubling you now, pour it out before the Lord. As the saying goes, "Better out than in!"

IMPACT *Daily readings*

Are you willing to be used by God?

1 Chronicles 28:1-9

"And thou, Solomon my son, know thou the God of thy father, and serve him with
a perfect heart and with a willing mind: for the LORD searcheth all hearts,
and understandeth all the imaginations of the thoughts: if thou seek him,
he will be found of thee; but if thou forsake him, he will cast thee off for ever."

1 Chronicles 28:9

The Lord had commanded King David to build a house in the name of the Lord, but because David was a man of war and had shed blood, the Lord needed someone of a pure heart. David was commending his son Solomon with this great task of building this house. David was instructing Solomon to serve the Lord with a perfect heart and with a willing mind. I have to be honest, my heart is far from perfect. Praise the Lord, the blood of Jesus Christ, God's Son cleanseth us from all sin. Solomon needed to be willing. God knows our hearts and it grieves the Lord when people are doing his work without a willing heart. They are wasting their time. When opportunity comes your way, are you willing to take it?

The Lord searcheth our hearts and understandeth all the imaginations of our thoughts. The Lord understands us and our thoughts, even when we struggle to understand them ourselves. Even when we don't understand ourselves, the Lord understands us. What great comfort the Lord brings to our hearts. Whenever we seek the Lord we will find Him, this is just amazing to know that the Lord wants us, even when we fail Him so much, He wants us, He is interested in us. Even when others reject us, God wants us.

What a thought at the end of this verse, if we forsake the Lord, He will cast you off forever. Don't leave the Lord out of your life. Keep Him in your plans, keep Him as your friend, tell Him everything, even your deepest thoughts, even the things you don't understand, God knows all about them. How great is our God! Advance and build!

IMPACT *Daily readings*

The morning watch

1 Samuel 11:11-15

"They came into the midst of the host in the morning watch." 1 Samuel 11:11

The Bible has much to say about rising early. I have found it possible to do more in the early hours of the morning than late mornings, afternoons or evenings. The mind is fresher, the body much more active and generally everything is much quieter.

Even in Scripture many wonderful things happened during the morning watch. We read about one of these times here in the passage we are focusing on. Saul and his army came upon the Ammonites in the morning watch and slew them, "until the heat of the day." Perhaps it would have been too late if they had waited until the heat of the day to commence the battle.

Also when the children of Israel were to cross the Red Sea, it was the early morning when the Lord troubled the host of the Egyptians. (Exodus 14:24) The lesson is simple; if we are to have success with God in our spiritual journey, then it must begin with the morning watch.

Perhaps you have so much to accomplish that you didn't take time to pray. You will soon realise that if you are to accomplish anything then you will have to take time to pray. Have you ever had one of those days when you seem to rush around with so much to do and at the end of the day realise you have done and accomplished very little? Try to start the day with the Lord and pray that you'll have a useful day. Live it like it's your last one here on earth. See if it makes a difference by looking for the morning watch.

From tomorrow start the day early with the Lord in the morning. Watch and see what happens!

Kept in perfect peace

Isaiah 26:1-13

"Thou wilt keep him in perfect peace, whose mind is stayed on thee." Isaiah 26:3

There is a lot to be said if you have got perfect peace in your heart. Many have got peace with God in their salvation but they do not have perfect peace in their heart, mind and lives. The latter part of the verse tells us that those who have perfect peace trust in the Lord. Worry is a terrible thing; this is why so many do not have perfect peace because they are concerned and worried about so much. Their mind is continually asking the question, What if? What if? What if? Concerned about their job, relationship, finance, health, children and the list goes on and on.

Can you honestly say you have perfect peace? The solution to having perfect peace is found in the verse, 'whose mind is stayed on the Lord.' When our thoughts and imagination are on the cares of the world and not the Lord, then we will naturally be concerned and worried. Try leaving all the things that bother you and fix your focus on the Lord until you will know and have that perfect peace, it truly is a beautiful thing to have perfect peace with God.

Under a waterfall there was spotted a little red robin on the branch of a tree. The waterfall was powerful in volume and sound, yet the little robin just sat there on the little twig, not one bit worried about the danger of falling in. May the Lord help us to trust in Him just like the little robin.

IMPACT *Daily readings*

My Redeemer liveth

Job 19:1-25

"For I know that my redeemer liveth." Job 19:25

There is probably no-one that suffered more humanly speaking than Job. It all seemed to happen to him in the space of a very short time. Blessed with a family of ten children, a huge farm and well respected in his neighbourhood. Then the day would come when all would go wrong, he would lose everything and yet at the end he was able to say these beautiful words, "I know that my redeemer liveth."

All in one day Job lost his sheep, cattle and camels, either they were stolen or burned with fire. Then news came to him to say that the building in which all his children were in had collapsed and all of them died. He himself was covered in sores, so bad were they that when his three friends came to visit him they didn't even recognise him. Job had lost everything, stopping short of his very life, then he stands to his feet, hand on his heart and looks to heaven and proclaims, "I know that my redeemer liveth." What strength and what courage that took for Job to say that. Not one word of complaint, anger or bitterness towards the Lord. What a challenge this is to all of us, the next time something goes wrong, remember Job and how he looked forward to the coming of the Lord Jesus. God knows all and one day it will all make sense, but until that time let us quietly wait until His glorious return.

A handful of dust

Genesis 3:7-24

"...dust thou art, and unto dust shalt thou return." Genesis 3:19

Have you ever thought about where you came from? Trace it right back to Adam and Eve and then just before Adam was dust. That's how God made the first man, from the dust of the ground. Then the amazing thing is, once we die, we return to the dust of the ground. The question then arises, where will we be the moment we die? In heaven with the Lord or lost in hell for ever. Yes, the body will return to the dust but we all have a soul that remains to be forever with the Lord or lost forever.

It won't matter how successful we were in business or how popular we were among people. Our success or popularity won't even come into question. What we did with our gifts, talents and abilities for the Lord, however, will. Sometimes and even most times we are all guilty of getting caught up with the affairs of this world. Years pass by and still we are in the race, the race of success, the race for fame and for fortune. What is it all about? Who is it all for? One day those words, those fatal and solemn words will be spoken, "Ashes to ashes: dust to dust." Then your time on this earth and world will all be over. How will you meet the Saviour? Will you say, "Lord I wish I had given you more?"

IMPACT *Daily readings*

How God guides His people

Isaiah 30:15-21

"This is the way, walk ye in it." Isaiah 30:21

I firmly believe that when a sinner gets converted to Jesus Christ, they are immediately in the will and plan of God. The time of conversion is beautiful as everything is so new and God is so real. The only desire for the new Christian is to love and serve God.

The problem however, for so many believers walking along the narrow way, there are many temptations to leave the narrow way and start wandering through the forest of life. Many stay close to the path, some keep the path in view and others wander so far from the path that they barely remember they were ever on the path.

The truly converted child of God will know they are genuinely saved when they wander from the path because the Holy Spirit that lives and abides within them will start gently prodding and whispering for them to get back on track. If we ignore the help and guidance of God's Spirit then we will start to get cold in heart, slide away from the call and will of God and in fact become very miserable.

Where are you now as you seek to follow God's path, plan, and will for your life? Are you wandering afar off, with the path barely in sight? Have you taken the time to listen to the inner voice of God, the unseen hand correcting and guiding you? Listen to the voice today, look for the guiding hand and obey the promptings of the Holy Spirit of God deep within your soul. Aim to get to the centre of the path where you can hear God whisper to you, "This is the way walk ye in it."

IMPACT *Daily readings*

Keep close to God

Genesis 12:1-10

"And there was a famine in the land: and Abram went down into Egypt to sojourn there; for the famine was grievous in the land." Genesis 12:10

Soon after Abraham arrived in Canaan a famine came upon the land and soon there was little food and the crops were failing. God had promised to supply Abraham's every need, but when the famine came Abraham gathered all his possessions together and went down to Egypt.

This was a great test for Abraham and he failed. Whenever the going gets tough this is when we must really call upon the Lord to help us. God had called Abraham into the land of promise; this was for his family and his inheritance. While all the heathen people moved down into Egypt Abraham just followed them, forgetting God's promises to him.

We are not to follow the ways of the world, maybe this was God's way of cleansing the land from idol worship by bringing a famine. What an opportunity Abraham had to prove God in times of difficulty, but he didn't take the opportunity to stand up for God.

Sometimes when trials and difficulties come our way we take the easy option and give in. God wants us to really come close to Him and not to follow the ways of the world. Even though we live in this world we are only here for a short time and while we are travelling through this world we must be focused on the one to come, Heaven. While we are journeying through this world the Lord has promised to lead, protect, guide and never to leave us. He is true to His promise, but like Abraham, we often make the mistake of walking away from God, right out of His will and doing what we think is best. Don't run from God, rather run to Him.

A clean heart

Psalm 51

"Wash me throughly from mine iniquity, and cleanse me from my sin." Psalm 51:2

The Psalmist was honest before the Lord. He knew what was bothering him; he knew that on the inside his heart was not right. My friend today we must be honest before the Lord. No matter how you look on the outside, it doesn't really matter because God looks at your heart. Maybe you are hurting, frustrated, angry, and jealous, the list could go on and on. In church on a Sunday morning it is so easy to dress up right and slip into the pew and look like a real Christian, who are you fooling? Why not be honest before the Lord and pour out your heart before Him.

Maybe you are living a double life. Living the Christian life on the outside and on the inside your heart is anything but pure. We live in a day and age in which sin is all around us and it no longer bothers us. Almost every main shop sells alcohol now and it hardly even bothers us. Almost all of us have computers at home. At the click of the mouse we can be viewing pornographic material of the most graphic manner, all within seconds. The devil has a field day here and many are tempted to look until they are addicted to looking. My friend if this is you, you have got to stop. It will destroy you. If your heart is no longer clean before the Lord, I would urge you right now to ask the Lord for a new clean heart. Ask Him to wash your sins away in His Precious Blood and start living afresh. It is easy to fall into the sinful traps of the world; it takes a real Christian to yield NOT to temptation.

IMPACT *Daily readings*

God's will or mine?

Joshua 24:1-27

"Choose you this day whom ye will serve...but as for me and my house,
we will serve the LORD." Joshua 24:15

Whenever we took our wedding vows we made the definite decision before the Lord to serve Him with all our bodies, mind, heart and soul. We had a choice to make, either we lived for ourselves and put the Lord second or we put the Lord first and asked the Lord to take our marriage and use it for His glory. Some see it as a sacrifice, we see it as an honour, when we realise what He has done for us. It is nothing too much for us to give back our lives to Him. He knows best what He wants from and for us.

Who are you serving today? I don't mean do you go to church on Sunday and live like a Christian. What to you is more important than the Lord? Is the television, internet, social networking more relevant to you than the Lord? Is reading books about the Bible more interesting to you than reading the Bible itself? Really the heart of the matter is, am I living in the centre of God's will contenting myself or am I in the centre of God's will living as He would have me live, doing what He would have me do and even dating or married to the person He would have me be with? There is a huge difference. Dating someone when you know it's just not right is wrong and will place your life out of God's will, doing your own thing, known as your will and not God's. If you expect God to work and bless your life, you had better weigh things up very carefully. The thought of being left alone on the shelf is not a good enough reason to rebel against God's Will.

IMPACT *Daily readings*

Watch yourself

1 Samuel 19:1-7
"Take heed to thyself until the morning,
and abide in a secret place, and hide thyself." 1 Samuel 19:2

Even though David was greatly respected by the people and loved by God, he still had someone who was so jealous of him that he sought to kill him. It was King Saul. The King's son, Jonathan, however was best friends with David and would often warn him of danger.

David had to be especially careful at night time as this was when the enemy often tried to kill him. How applicable this is for the Christian today as the night time is when Christians are often tempted to fall into sin. That is why the warning goes forth to "take heed to yourself until the morning." It is one thing to help one another along the way; however, we are all responsible for our own actions.

The television with all its channels today, the internet and everything that can be imagined, is only at the tip of your finger. At night time when you are alone and all is quiet, this is when the enemy of the soul comes in before your very eyes. No one can stop it but you; you are in control. Watch therefore and take heed to yourself! Many Christians today are falling, backsliding, giving up all because of the pleasures of the world. Don't be another one! Fight against the temptation that comes before you, make sure to resist the devil and he will flee from you. How we need to abide under the shadow of the Almighty, as recorded in Psalm 91, until the morning time when all will be well.

From today will you seek to watch yourself in order to stop from falling, like so many have before you?

The bigger picture

Genesis 50:1-26

"Ye thought evil against me, but God meant it unto good." Genesis 50:20

God's ways are not always our ways; He tells us this in His Word. That is why it is so important to understand that when something goes wrong, terribly wrong, God has a plan for it all. We cannot see it at the time but we must always think of the bigger picture.

In Genesis chapter 50, Joseph is reunited with his brothers again. He had the power to have every one of them killed, but he doesn't, rather he forgives them and says the verse for today "Ye thought evil against me, but God meant it unto good." His brothers tried to kill him, then sold him into slavery, but little did they realise the LORD was with Joseph. Joseph's life was not easy but eventually he was advanced to becoming Prime Minister over the whole land of Egypt. He in turn was able to invite his whole family to come and live with him and then we have the whole story of the Children of Israel, God's chosen people.

When something goes wrong in your life, whatever that may be, thank the Lord for the experience and ask Him to bless you through it. Nothing happens by accident, there is a reason for everything even if we have to wait till glory to find out the reason why. The question is: is your faith that strong that you can accept the way things are with you right now? God has a plan and a purpose for you!

IMPACT Daily readings

His determination

Psalm 18:1-12

"I will love thee, O LORD, my strength." Psalm 18:1

There was once a young postman who had a notion of a young woman. She worked in a shop and he was very determined to see this girl. Every opportunity he got to call into the shop he would take it. Every lunch break, every time he had a few minutes he would call in at the shop. He never bought anything, wasn't even interested in shopping, but daily found himself in her shop with the post.

When he arrived at the shop all he wanted to do was to see the girl, to hear her talk or laugh, this would just make his day. When she saw him and smiled he was so happy. Every day he left the post off at the shop he was so happy to have seen her. He was content that his journey was worthwhile. Then the next day came and he longed to make the journey to see her again and so it continued. His love for her continued to grow, it was often his motivation, determination and strength from day to day.

Have you ever had such determination to see someone you long to be with? What about the Lord? When you wake up in the morning do you desire to meet with the Lord every opportunity you get. After we meet with the Lord are we so happy and blessed that we just long to see Him again, just to feel His presence? When we don't meet with Him we will still go through life, but when we do meet with Him, life can be so much more enjoyable, worthwhile and satisfying. How much the Psalmist loved the Lord, the Lord was his strength.

How determined are you to meet with the Lord today?

IMPACT *Daily readings*

Speak to me Lord

1 Samuel 3:1-10

"Speak, LORD; for thy servant heareth." 1 Samuel 3:9

The story of Samuel is a favourite to many children. It pictures the life of a little boy who God spoke to and called into His service. While it is a beautiful story, there is more to it than God speaking to Samuel on that evening while he lay on his bed.

As we follow this thrilling story we learn that his life was the beginning of a life of remarkable obedience to the Lord. Many times we find ourselves disturbed in our sleep. We wake up and the Lord places someone or something upon our hearts. Looking back, we differ from Samuel as he answered God's call, many times we have failed the Lord by not acting. Every time God speaks, we may listen but often fail to go through with God.

God has a plan for every one of His children. Many today are outside the plan because when God sent the order through we failed to obey! Yes, we still live the Christian life, but it may be one with little blessing. Samuel's ears and heart were open that night. Quite often our ears are open but our heart is cold and not receptive to the command of God.

We need to live every day expecting to get fresh orders from the Lord. Samuel enjoyed a life of tremendous blessing and we can enjoy the same. Next time the Lord speaks, take it seriously and see what He has in store for you. It could change your life and the lives of others forever.

IMPACT *Daily readings*

Don't know what to do!

2 Chronicles 20:1-13

"We have no might against this great company that cometh against us;
neither know we what to do: but our eyes are upon thee." 2 Chronicles 20:12

The situation was quite frightening in Jehoshaphat's day. They were facing a terrible battle. They didn't know what to do and were sore afraid. The great comfort in this situation was that their eyes were upon the Lord. God is pleased when our focus is upon Him, even during our battles and difficult times.

The interesting point here is that although they did not know what to do, God gave them wonderful peace because they looked to the Lord for help, guidance and protection. This is a great and comforting lesson for us all to learn. Sometimes there are little and large problems that come into our lives. Most of these are to do with people and quite often we just don't know what to do or how to deal with it.

Especially if the problem is to do with a relationship that has formed or is forming then we need much guidance and wisdom from God when we just don't know what to do. Making decisions especially important, life changing decisions, can be difficult. That is why it is so important to talk to the Lord about it in prayer. Keep your eyes upon the Lord, focus and commune with Him every day. He will help you work it all out. Remember if you are His child, He is on your side and He wants the best for you. Your spiritual, mental and physical condition and well being is in the Lord's interest.

IMPACT *Daily readings*

Whiter than the snow

Psalm 51:1-7

"Purge me with hyssop, and I shall be clean: wash me,
and I shall be whiter than snow." Psalm 51:7

The Psalmist David when writing this Psalm was referring to the time when Nathan the prophet came to him, after he had gone to Bathsheba. Not only did he commit adultery against another man's wife and had a child with her, but he committed the terrible sin of murder having Bathsheba's husband delibertly killed in the battle.

David then went to his room and cried unto the Lord for mercy and forgiveness. He felt so bad he asked the Lord to take all his sin away and to blot out his transgressions. He asked the Lord to wash him thoroughly, completely from inside out and in his words to cleanse him from his sin. David acknowledged his sin before the Lord; he didn't hide it any more. His sin was ever before him, he had now such a guilty conscience. Not only did he sin against people, greater than this, much greater he sinned against the LORD. This is what happens when any of us sin; ultimately it is against the Lord.

David goes on to acknowledge how he was born as a sinner, and how his sin was separating him from God. His sin needed to be cleansed in the precious blood of the Lamb. He asked the Lord to wash his sins away, so he will be clean and become whiter than snow. There is only one thing whiter than snow, and it is a sinful heart washed and cleansed in the precious blood of the Lamb. Have you ever had this experience? It is the best thing that could ever happen to you, your sin and your guilt could be covered up forever in a moment!

One day at a time

Deuteronomy 33:24-29

"As thy days, so shall thy strength be." Deuteronomy 33:25

Sometimes when we look at life, we can begin to feel a lot of pressure. For example the financial pressure from your mortgage which seems to go on for years. Then when you think about bills, daily, weekly, monthly and bills that will come with children's education etc. There doesn't seem to be any way out of it and the reality is, there isn't.

However there is a solution that may help and that is to take one day at a time. It is good practice to take one day at a time. We don't know what a day may bring forth. Our health could be strong today and gone tomorrow as could our jobs, marriages, and the list goes on. This is why it is a good time to take stock of what we have, thank the Lord for it and take one day at a time instead of continually worrying about the future. The Lord will give us grace and strength day by day as we need it. It's always good and often necessary to plan ahead, but always remember in the will of God. Whenever I plan my meetings, missions and mission trips it is necessary to plan these many months in advance, this is essential but of course everything is in God's will. Sometimes people tell me to slow down or my strength will go down. This is maybe true, but I would rather wear out than rust out. In the Christian life we have got to keep going, God will give the needed strength everyday to keep fighting the battle.

IMPACT *Daily readings*

Continual striving

Genesis 26:15-22

"And they digged another well, and strove for that also:
and he called the name of it Sitnah." Genesis 26:21

Isaac went from place to place digging wells to feed his people and his flocks. Each place he came to he seemed to face contention. The first well, Esek, brought strife and contention and now the second well, Sitnah, brought more opposition.

Opposition intensifies when we succeed in getting the gospel water supply flowing. The devil will contend every inch of the ground and makes sure no advancement is made. The second well was evidently more contested than the first. It was so bad that Isaac had to forsake the new well and move to another site. Just like when the apostles were persecuted in one city they fled to another.

Isaac did not give up; he moved sites and kept on digging. He was forced to give up and retreat but he was crying 'no surrender' and kept digging. Today there are many battles within families and churches. There are those who will go against you and will try to force you out of your own home church. If it hinders your digging and your walk with God, don't rule out moving sites if it means keeping on digging for God, there is plenty of fresh water everywhere. The work cannot and must not be stopped, souls are perishing, they need to hear the water, the water of life.

No need to be afraid

Isaiah 12:1-6

"Behold, God is my salvation; I will trust, and not be afraid" Isaiah 12:2

This is a tremendous verse of encouragement for the child of God. For any Christian in the bondage of fear, for whatever reason, then this is a perfect verse for you. It is very personal; 'God is my salvation.' In other words, the Lord has saved me. Not everyone can say this; in fact most people in the world cannot say this because they do not know Jesus as Saviour and Lord. But the true believer who is truly saved can say: 'God is my salvation.'

Many Christians in the world today are full of worry and fear, even more so than people who are not saved. Maybe we have trusted in Christ to save us but not to look after us and keep us. Jesus is like a Shepherd and we are His sheep, He knows all of us by name, knows all our ups and downs, cares and fears. Why then do we worry so much about the unknown when God knows it all? Yes, we have put our trust in Him for salvation, but why do we not trust Him for looking after us?

Sometimes we worry because we are not trusting. Try it the other way because the more you trust Him with your life the less you will worry. Then you can really start to live and enjoy the Christian life, and what a blessed life it is!

IMPACT *Daily readings*

Pure determination

Joshua 14:1-15
"I wholly followed the LORD my God." Joshua 14:8

Caleb was one of those men who followed God at all costs. He often remembered the day when he and Joshua went to spy on the land of Canaan against fierce opposition. The other spies came back afraid of what they saw but Caleb and Joshua were ready to conquer. The secret for them was the Lord! He was with them and that is why Caleb wholly and completely followed the Lord his God.

Maybe you are going through a time of serious stress right now or perhaps you are facing a crisis that you never imagined would ever come to you in your life. The secret is staying close to an unfailing God! People and friends will let you down, but Jesus never will! Can you be like Caleb and in years to come look back and say that you wholly followed the Lord your God?

Perhaps you are going through or even facing a spiritual crisis in your life right now. In order to go through with God, it is going to bring misunderstanding and even a form of persecution from certain people, including friends. However, if you are serious about your Christian life and are fed up going through the motions, then the time has come for you to go through with God. Go forward in faith, having the confidence that the God of Caleb will go before you and prepare the way. It may not be an easy road and many bumps lie before you, but journey on you must with no turning back!

How determined are you to go through with God?

Expect an answer

Psalm 62

"My soul, wait thou only upon God; for my expectation is from him." Psalm 62:5

There are many today who will let us down and disappoint us. When this happens to you, you are not alone. We all have people in our lives that from time to time things don't work out and we have to go our separate ways. For most of the time it can be disappointment or let down for one side or the other.

The Psalmist states a wonderful thing that is worth us considering, he was telling us to wait upon the Lord, when others let us down as He will not. When others disappoint you, He will not, when others fail you, He will not. His expectation was from the Lord, God can meet our expectation, when others fall miserably short of it. On the other hand, many of us ask the Lord for things and we never expect an answer, then four hours later we forgot we even asked the Lord for such a thing. Why would the Lord be pleased to answer that prayer when you never even remembered what you asked Him for? The Lord sees our heart and knows how earnest we are when we pray and whether we pray believing and expecting God to work on our prayers. Whatever your situation, if you are serious, earnest, then wait on the Lord, He will renew your faith and strength, when you put your entire faith and trust in Him believing and expecting Him to answer.

IMPACT *Daily readings*

Ebenezer

1 Samuel 7:1-17

"He will save us out of the hand of the Philistines." 1 Samuel 7:8

The Philistines were a continual threat to Samuel and the people. Samuel told the people to prepare their hearts unto the LORD, and to serve Him only. By doing this he was confident that the Lord would deliver them out of the hand of the Philistines. When He did, Samuel lifted stones together and told the people to "raise our Ebenezer" and cry aloud, "Hitherto hath the Lord helped us." How important it is to acknowledge the Lord every time He helps us in everything we do.

While so much is going on around us, changing all the time, we must not lose our focus on the Lord. He is so good, He will not fail us. Look back upon your life and think about the many times He has delivered you and helped you. Never turn back on the Lord, never quit the Christian life. So many Christians feel like giving up and think about throwing in the towel and turning their back on the Lord. We must keep praising Him, thanking Him, worshipping Him, expecting nothing in return. Even if we continue to get beaten and slapped day and daily from friends and enemies then we must keep praying and praising God.

Sometimes when we are having a bad day it's good just to ponder over the goodness of the Lord and keep raising our Ebenezer unto Him. He has been so good and we have so much to be grateful and thankful for. Make a list of things you should be thankful for in your Christian life and soon you will raise your Ebenezer and begin thanking Him once again, He is a wonderful God.

IMPACT *Daily readings*

God chooses and uses the weak things

Proverbs 11:18-31

"He that winneth souls is wise." Proverbs 11:30

I personally take great comfort in this verse. I used to think it was only mighty preachers and famous evangelists who had the joy of winning souls for the Lord. This is not the case, looking back I was probably the lowest in my class at school. When I was at Bible college, I was never given the opportunity to preach as there were always those who were very able speakers. I soon learned the lesson that if I was ever going to be any use for God, I better let him take me and use me. After completing the training course with CEF in Switzerland, I soon realised the Lord was putting upon my heart the evangelisation of children.

Looking back now over the years, I have had the means and had the personal joy of winning hundreds of precious children to the Lord. Some of these were in classrooms, school assembly halls, camp sites, buses, churches and even in their homes with their mothers by their side. God often takes the nobodies of this world and uses them in a wonderful way. There are many humble believers, working away behind the scenes in the church, Sunday school or children's meetings. You are more influential than you realize teaching the Word of God to the children. Some sow, some water but ultimately God saves and giveth the increase. As Jonah acknowledged, Salvation is of the LORD. Keep at the work, maybe no one sees you doing your work; whether public or private, keep at it. You're maybe not wise in this world but in heaven, in the Lord's eyes you are wise because you are seeking to win souls. Praise His name for you!

IMPACT Daily readings

The Lord calls, holds and keeps

Genesis 28:1-15

" I am with thee, and will keep thee in all places." Genesis 28:15

Here is a verse that is so encouraging for every child of God. This is not a theological argument; it is a verse of scripture. It is a great promise from God that He has called you, will hold your hand as you journey through life and will keep you until the end before bringing you home to glory. Some take this as a "I'm saved, I can do what I like attitude." Be careful my friend because the Bible also tells us 'faith without works is dead' and that 'many are called but few are chosen,' therefore make your calling and election sure. Many Christians are sound and fundamental but as cold as steel. Whatever you may be, ask the Lord to fill you afresh with Calvary love and to give you a compassion for the lost and perishing souls all around you.

Sometimes we can go through the routine of Christianity and tick all the boxes, that is religion. Search the scriptures and find Christ, dig deep into the wells of Calvary love and find all the beauty that Christ has for you. So many wonderful marvellous verses to motivate, encourage and ignite your love for Him. Find these verses write them down and memorise them. Someday you may need them when things are getting tough. Then when the going gets tough, through Christ the tough gets going.

IMPACT *Daily readings*

What every home needs!

Genesis 35:1-5

"Let us arise, and go up to Bethel; and I will make there an altar unto God."

Genesis 35:3

Many today blame the world and the church for their children going astray. Yet when questioned there were very few times when parents with their children would read and pray. When Jacob built the altar unto the Lord there in Bethel it took a lot of work, lifting stones to make that altar. If we are going to have a real meaningful, worthwhile altar for the Lord then it is going to take a lot of effort and work. Just like the stones and the earth were moved, something may have to be moved. What are you willing to sacrifice, move or even change to make room for your altar?

There are many challenges upon the Christian today. This is life and this is the real world we are living in. We must fight against all the temptation that comes our way. We will fall but we have got to get up again and keep walking the walk, following the path that the Lord had laid out before us. The best thing to have is that precious time with the Lord every day. Be open, be honest with the Lord. The altar was the place where all sin was confessed and forgiven; this is an essential ingredient if we want to go on in our path with God.

IMPACT *Daily readings*

Love for the wrong reason

Judges 16:1-18

"The lords of the Philistines came up unto her, and said unto her, Entice him, and see wherein his great strength lieth, and by what means we may prevail against him, that we may bind him to afflict him: and we will give thee every one of us eleven hundred pieces of silver." Judges 16:5

This chapter tells us how much Samson loved Delilah. But as we read this very sad story of the destruction of a young man we find her love for him was for the wrong reason. She betrayed Samson for money, she became close to him, had courtship with him until he finally poured out his heart to her. This eventually cost Samson his life. Delia was only with Samson for money which was obtained by deceit. The moment he was betrayed, when the secret of his strength was revealed in his unshaven hair, he was captured by the enemy, made blind and eventually died with the enemy. Delilah got her money; we don't read any more of her, her mourning, her regret, nothing like this.

There is nothing as beautiful in the world as true love, in riches and in poverty, in sickness and in health. On the other hand there is nothing as sickening as when someone takes advantage in pretence over the other for monetary gain. How careful we must be in our relationships that we enter into them with the right motives and intentions. Samson once was a champion with God, his relationship with Delilah was the beginning of his downfall until she eventually destroyed him. Your partner in life will either make you or break you; this is why it is so important to pray for God's leading and guiding for His choice of a life partner for you.

The clean heart

Psalm 51

"Create in me a clean heart, O God; and renew a right spirit within me." Psalm 51:10

An old saying goes "an apple a day keeps the doctor away". A better one would be "a Psalm a day keeps the devil away." Every Psalm is so full of devotional thoughts and encouragement that once you read them, you just long more and more for God in your life. Have you ever had a genuine desire for a clean, pure heart? This is what the psalmist was asking for here.

For the blood of Jesus Christ to be applied there must be a repenting and forsaking of all known sin. There should be a true hatred and remorse for your sin. Only then will God apply the power of the blood of Jesus upon you. Only God can create, and therefore only He can create a clean and pure heart. We cannot do this ourselves. Naturally from the moment we are born, our hearts are sinful, impure and unclean. Most people make the mistake here of trying to clean up their old lives like they are cleaning out a garage or storeroom. By doing this in our own strength, we then choose what to throw out and what to leave to another time. The natural man needs his sin dealt with supernaturally. How powerful it is then that the power of the precious blood of Christ needs to be applied, not only to our past sinful life, but our present impurity and sinful condition! "The blood of Jesus Christ his Son cleanseth us from all sin." (1 John 1:7)

Temptations and failings will often come as we walk through this old sinful world but like the psalmist we must have that desire to have a clean heart before the Lord. God will then enable us to walk in the Spirit and therefore not fulfil the lusts of the flesh. Through Christ we can have the victory every day.

Do you have a genuine desire for a pure, clean heart?

IMPACT *Daily readings*

I love my master

Exodus 21:1-6

"I love my master...I will not go out free." Exodus 21:5

Under Old Testament law, it was the custom for a slave to go free after serving his master for six years. However, if the servant did not wish to leave, he would say, "I love my master...I will not go out free." The master would then inform the judges of the day, after which he would make a hole in the ear of the slave at the door post. It was a sign that the servant would be his for the rest of his life.

The slave would become so devoted to his master that he wants to stay with him the rest of his life, he now loved his master. This is the way it is with the Christian, if you were given the choice of leaving Christ and going back to the world, what would you choose to do? Would you say like the slave 'I love my master, He is my Saviour, I have no desire to turn back because I have decided to follow Jesus, no turning back, no turning back.' He had freed us from the sins of this world, let us then serve Him with all of our hearts, holding nothing back, loving our Saviour and our Master more and more every day.

The devil's weapon

Deuteronomy 1:9-21
"Fear not, neither be discouraged." Deuteronomy 1:21

Discouragement is without doubt the greatest weapon the devil can use against the Christian. These are days in which more and more people are getting hammered with this weapon. He is having a field day and getting plenty of overtime these days. When we hear of someone being discouraged, don't gossip about them, rather make it your business to call round and visit them. Just tell them you were thinking about them and call round for a chat. That visit, no matter how short it may be will do more to bring your friend back on to the road to recovery than you realise.

The devil has a lot of tools he uses as his weapons and even uses Christians to fire them without them even realising it. These tools include; malice, hatred, envy, jealousy, sensuality, gossiping, tale bearing and deceit. More than any of these is the greatest weapon called discouragement. Continual discouragement will eventually lead to depression unless it is overcome. If you are a victim to discouragement then my friend you must pray and ask God to help you defeat it. Claim the Power of the Precious Blood of Christ over your body, mind and soul afresh. Then in the name of Jesus be encouraged and go forth once again in the battle. Please don't quit, I ask you in Jesus name, "please don't quit."

Fight against depression!

Psalm 42
"Why art thou cast down, O my soul?" Psalm 42:5

We live in a day when more and more people seem to be depressed, especially among Christian people. We only have one short life to live for God here on earth and some people spend it down in the dumps of despair. I wonder what impact Christ has really made on them.

The famous Martin Luther often suffered from fits of depression, not surprising with one having made such an impact for God during the reformation. One day, his wife entered the room, wearing a black veil and a black gown. As Luther looked at her in surprise, he asked the reason for such an appearance. She replied that she was mourning the death of God, for by the way he was behaving, it was as if God was dead. It wasn't too long before Luther was his jovial self again.

Are you living as if God is no longer alive? The Psalmist tells us later on to, "Hope thou in God, for I shall yet praise Him..." Whatever is pulling you down, whether physical or mental, lift your eyes up to God a fresh and cry for mercy to be renewed in the body, mind and soul. Fits of depression may come in vain; but they all must be conquered in Jesus name!

IMPACT *Daily readings*

The empty seat

1 Samuel 20:11-23

"Thou shalt be missed for thy seat will be empty." 1 Samuel 20:18

This was a tremendous test for David as he had been invited to a meal by King Saul. David knew his life was in danger and realised it was a trap to lure him to the King. David and Jonathan had become the best of friends. There was a serious strain on their friendship as it was the King, Jonathan's father who wanted to kill David. Jonathan was the only one David could trust, Jonathan knew also that David was God's anointed and was willing to stand aside and give David the throne. When David refused to come to the meal at the King's table for his own safety, Jonathan said, "Thou shalt be missed for thy seat will be empty."

A friend of mine once left a dead apostate church because it no longer preached the Gospel. When people noticed his seat empty they soon understood why and it spoke volumes. Are you in a dead church where you no longer get anything from the preaching? The best way to make a stand is by leaving an empty seat. Another challenge here is that one day our seat will be empty at home and at church. Will people even notice? What sort of impact are we making for God here on earth? When our seat becomes empty it's too late to do anything else in God's name. Go quickly and do what you have to do, leave your comfortable seat if you have to. If you're just a pew warmer, it may keep your minister happy but what about the Lord, is it not important what He would have you do?

IMPACT *Daily readings*

A natural concern

Genesis 24:1-6
"But thou shalt go unto my country, and to my kindred,
and take a wife unto my son Isaac." Genesis 24:4

Abraham was getting on in years. His son Isaac was still not married, he was forty years old at this stage, so Abraham was naturally concerned for Isaac and the future generation of his family. He then instructed his servant to go and find a wife for his son Isaac.

The question of natural concern is an important thought. Are we concerned about the life of the people we love and care for? Do we honestly seek God's best for them? Sometimes jealousy can creep in and deep down in our hearts we don't really wish the best for someone we know. Maybe they are in a relationship that makes us jealous because we don't have it. There's an old saying, 'if you make your bed you lie in it.'

Rather we should be concerned for others with a genuine and godly concern for good in their lives. This surely is the scriptural and Christ-like way we should be. Try seeking and seeing the good in others and life will treat you better. Confess any known or intentional sin right now and start living the Christian life afresh. Pray for young ones today, that they will find the right partners and enjoy beautiful marriages. If there is ever anything that is rocked at the heart and core of society, it is marriage, the centre of the family unit, an institution owned, blessed and created by God.

You don't have to be weak!

Isaiah 40:28-31

"But they that wait upon the LORD shall renew their strength;
they shall mount up with wings as eagles; they shall run,
and not be weary; and they shall walk, and not faint." Isaiah 40:31

There are times in our lives when we become weak; physically, emotionally and even spiritually. Sometimes we can almost feel like giving up. So much discouragement seems to come our way and continually dishearten us to the point when we feel like throwing in the towel. We are at the point of crying defeat and surrender! When I was growing up the cry was "no surrender!" So it is with the Christian life as we must not give up on God! We must battle on to the end.

The word "renew" in our verse today signals change. The secret is waiting on the Lord. When we feel like giving up, then it is often the case that we are weak spiritually. We need to simply wait on the Lord and then our strength will be renewed, and changed us for the good. We must get back to reading His Word and pouring out our hearts to Him as this will renew our strength. Maybe you have failed God in some way you think is unforgivable. God will forgive you and will remember it no more. He wants you to come back to Him; He is calling you, waiting for you to come. He has so much in store for you, His child. Maybe you are weak now, but tomorrow is a new day! Wait on the Lord and He will make you strong once again. Once again you can soar like the great eagle far above all your problems, difficulties and tears. Are you prepared to wait upon the Lord? He will help you.

Maybe we are trying to live the Christian life in our own strength? Try waiting on God...He will give you real strength that comes from above, to have within!

IMPACT *Daily readings*

Always be ready!

Joshua 8:1-4
"Be ye all ready." Joshua 8:4

Here in the life of Joshua he was commanding the people to be ready. We can learn so much from these very challenging words. Using these words "be ready", the one thing we must be ready for is the return of the Lord Jesus Christ. Nobody knows the time, date or the hour when Christ will return to earth to take His people home. How important it is for each one of us to live a holy life separated unto the Lord and be ready to meet Him when He comes or be ready to go when He calls.

If we knew that Christ was to return to earth tonight is there anything in our lives we would change? Is there anyone I need to speak to?, to ask forgiveness from,? witness to? Are we not to live our lives today as if it's our last or as if Christ should come tonight or tomorrow?

God is holy and asks His people to be holy also. Strong and subtle temptations are all around us. In ourselves we are weak. We cannot fight these in our own strength. God desires us to have that closer walk with Him. The closer we are to God, the more conscious we will be of our sin. We will have that desire to be purified in His precious blood.

This is wonderfully possible through the power of the precious blood of Jesus (1 John 1:9) and the power of the Holy Ghost. Why not come afresh today and plead the blood that Jesus shed for you and for me? Why not know cleansing and from today desire to live that life that brings you closer and closer to God.

Remember those who helped you

Proverbs 10:1-16

"The memory of the just is blessed" Proverbs 10:7

As we look back upon our lives we remember individuals who helped us along the way, especially in our Christian life. I can think of faithful Sunday school teachers who would come every Sunday to instruct children from the Bible. I remember in particular one man called Peter Crory, probably the most influential man in my early Christian life. Peter was the general secretary of the YMCA in Lisburn. The YMCA was situated in the centre of Lisburn town. I would call at lunchtime, a great place for cheap food, while I was at the local college. Peter was married to Pauline and they were both on fire for God! The love of the Lord Jesus shone from them.

I remember the day Peter came along and introduced himself. I was deeply impressed with him taking an interest in my life. I was just a recent convert at this stage. Peter asked me if I would like to help out at the youth club on a Monday and Wednesday night. I was glad to help out and grateful to have been given an opportunity to do so. He sent me on so many training courses, sent me on my first international mission trip to Holland, and gave me an opportunity to spend a whole summer working at a camp in America. Most of all, he gave me the opportunity to pray out loud publicly for the first time, as we prayed each night before the youth club started. Is there someone in your life that you have good memories of? What about those who were instrumental in bringing you to the Saviour?

In years to come, will there be someone who will thank God for your life and for the influence of good you had been to them? Never be afraid to draw alongside someone and encourage them in the Lord! It could change their lives forever.

IMPACT *Daily readings*

Praise, prayer and preaching

Psalm 65

"Praise waiteth for thee, O God, in Sion." Psalm 65:1

The Scriptures have so much to say about praise. In fact any time you are feeling down in the dumps then try praising God. If you are able to do so with your whole heart and lips then you will soon start to feel much better. This is like a good gospel meeting, praise prepares people for the Word of God and when Christians continue to pray that the Word will have free course then it will cause them to continue to praise God as the blessing will follow.

Every time when we pray and God answers our prayers then it is a good time to praise His name. God loves praise. Sometimes we go through life and don't praise God enough. Sometimes with Joanna we just talk about all the Lord has done for us and we can't help but praise Him every time we acknowledge His goodness towards us. Even when you pray and there is no answer, praise the Lord anyhow, and when you pray and the Lord answers you in a way which you don't expect and you don't seem too happy about the outcome praise His name anyhow. This will please the Lord more than you realise and He will continue to work everything out for your good. Keep praising the Lord!

Enoch walked with God

Genesis 5:18-24

"And Enoch walked with God: and he was not; for God took him." Genesis 5:24

Today we think it is hard to be a Christian with all the challenges and temptations in the world. We seem to be so busy, can hardly find time to read and pray and going to church seems like such a chore.

Well in the days of Enoch, the world was full of sin and wickedness, yet here we find a man who chose to walk and talk with God. Sometimes we can blame our circumstances and make excuses for not walking with the Lord the way we should. Times for Christians have been much harder than what they are today. It is too easy to be a Christian today, there often lacks real commitment and devotion to the Lord because it is too easy. There is often a price to pay for that closeness with God and few there are who are willing to make the sacrifice and pay the price.

Enoch had the desire that he would please the Lord and this is recorded in Hebrews 11:5. We must realise that the more we desire to please the Lord, the more we may displease others. Closeness with God can often bring distance from others, even those close to us. Life is full of challenges; we all face them from different sources. Enoch disappeared when he least expected it. Don't get 'caught on' trying to be a Christian, rather live as one ready at any moment to be 'caught up' with Him.

To live an effective Christian life, one needs to be filled with Holy Ghost power, which alone comes from God. Ask Him for it today, to see the difference it really makes.

IMPACT *Daily readings*

The secret of blessing

Deuteronomy 28:1-15

"And thou shalt not go aside from any of the words which I command thee this day, to the right hand, or to the left, to go after other gods to serve them. But it shall come to pass, if thou wilt not hearken unto the voice of the LORD thy God, to observe to do all his commandments and his statutes which I command thee this day; that all these curses shall come upon thee, and overtake thee."

Deuteronomy 28:14-15

This is a solemn warning to obey the word of the Lord. The secret of the blessing often depends upon our attitude to the word of God as to how we treat and respect the word of God. In order to respect and obey the word of God we need to hear it and read it. That is why it is so important to go to a church where great emphasis is put upon the word of God and the preaching of God's truth. Reading the word of God is also very important; if we fail to do this we starve our own soul of manna from Heaven. It is also important to take heed to the word of God once we hear it. The Lord puts emphasis upon delighting in the law of God, not just for the sake of it but reading and listening to the word of God should be a delight. How we need to start reading, hearing, honouring and delighting in the precious word of God.

God's wonderful providence

Genesis 24:15-28
"I being in the way, the LORD led me." Genesis 24:27

This is a wonderful story of God's providence at its very best. Abraham clearly instructed his servant to find a wife for his son Isaac. He was to go to a certain place and find a suitable girl who would be willing to leave all and marry Isaac, someone whom she had never seen. This would mean that Abraham would be praying for a good wife for Isaac. Isaac would be praying for the right girl. The servant would be praying that he would find the right wife for Isaac and no doubt Rebekah would be praying that someday, her life would change forever.

Well it did, because one day when she went to the well, as she did normally, God clearly led the servant of Abraham there and to this girl Rebekah. It is a wonderful thing to know God's providence upon your life. This is when God brings His perfect plan in your life. You know it because you could never have arranged it yourself. I do not believe in such things as coincidence or luck. This then makes God's providence even more real and special. I know it because I have experienced it for myself when I met Joanna, back 10th September 1993, as I was in a little cafe in the main square in Krakow, Poland. Suddenly a girl all dressed in white with a red bandana on her head, stood on the huge window ledge. To me, it was as if an angel flew down from heaven, I fell in love with this girl, didn't even know her name, let alone a Christian saved five months earlier.

Are you at the stage in your life when you can honestly say, I want the Lord to lead me in His perfect way! Do you realise you could meet someone today, anyone, even a servant, sent by God who could change your life forever? Or you could be that person sent by God to change someone else's life forever!

IMPACT *Daily readings*

Whatever you do, do it with all your heart!

2 Chronicles 31:15-21

"And in every work that he began in the service of the house of God,
and in the law, and in the commandments, to seek his God,
he did it with all his heart, and prospered." 2 Chronicles 31:21

Hezekiah was now commanded to build the house of the Lord. It was his generation to influence them for God. He broke down all the idols and images and brought the people back to God again. He did that which was good, right and truthful before the LORD his God. What speaks to and challenges me in this verse though is that whatever he did for the Lord, he did it with all his heart.

Whatever opportunities come your way to serve the Lord, do it with all your heart. There is nothing as bad as doing something with half-heartedness, it's just as bad as having no heart at all and is an offence to the Lord. Whatsoever thy hand findeth to do, do with all thy might the scriptures tell us. When you serve the Lord with all your heart, you will love serving Him and will just want to keep on serving Him.

There was a blessing that came with this; because Hezekiah served the Lord with all his heart, the Lord prospered him. God hasn't changed, I know from my own experience, that when we serve the Lord with all our soul, might, strength and most of all our heart, the Lord will bless us and prosper us. To serve the Lord with all your heart, you receive a joy which no man can give you. This is the deepest privilege and honour we can receive on this earth, to walk in the will of God serving Him with all of our hearts.

Whatever you do for the Lord, make sure it is with all your heart. Don't give the Lord the crumbs of your life. Give Him everything; He gave His everything for you!

Perpetual prayer

Exodus 30:1-10

"And Aaron shall burn thereon sweet incense every morning...
a perpetual incense before the LORD." Exodus 30:7-8

As Moses journeyed through the wilderness, God commanded him to build a tabernacle. It was made with such marvellous and beautiful detail. Within the tabernacle was the altar of incense. There perpetually, morning and evening, it was kept burning by Aaron the High Priest.

This continual burning of incense speaks to us of our prayer life. God desires that the continual incense of prayer and praise should reach His throne in Heaven. Can we be challenged afresh to go back to the place of prayer? Maybe the candle has been burning low this past while. Now is the time to re-ignite the flame of prayer! Don't leave it until tomorrow. Don't let the flame get any lower, or else it may blow out completely. Just as the altar of incense burned perpetually, may our prayer life take new life and burn brightly once again.

God is most pleased when His children talk to Him in prayer. He wants to know how you feel and what is on your heart. How do you expect God to help and bless you if you keep Him at a distance? Of course the Lord knows all about you! He knows what it is that is heavy upon your heart and the big decisions you have to make. All you have to do is talk to Him. The more you pray the more you will want to pray. The more you talk to God the more you will have to talk to Him about. Then your prayer life will be like the altar of incense it will just keep going on and on!

Watch your tongue

Psalm 50

"Whoso offereth praise glorifieth me:
and to him that ordereth his conversation aright will I shew the salvation of God."
Psalm 50:23

If you want to glorify God in heaven then sing praises unto Him continually with your lips. When you do this God will give you a wonderful peace in your heart, a tremendous feeling of being close to and in touch with Him.

On the other hand if we use our lips and tongue to murmur, grumble and complain then we glorify the devil. God hates a complaining and bitter spirit but the devil loves it. It is so easy to grumble and complain all the time! How important it is for us to order our conversation aright. Sometimes our lips need to be disciplined and our tongue may even need to be bitten because we are about to say something out of turn.

Maybe today you are in bad form, you have a grumbling spirit within you and you no longer enjoy the Lord the way you once did. Well then try to think about the Lord for a moment. Think about everything He has done for you. We can praise Him continually, for His wonderful salvation, His constant keeping power, His blessed Holy Spirit, the Comforter and His innumerable blessings on your life. We can thank Him for His good and continued hand of blessing down through the years,: His guarding and protecting hand over you right to this very moment and His blessing that often comes in disguise when we cannot understand the reason or way.

The list is endless and goes on and on. The joy of the Lord is the secret. Enjoy the Lord and then the joy of the Lord will be your strength.

Two sons!

1 Samuel 2:12-25
"The sons of Eli....knew not the Lord." 1 Samuel 2:12

There were three prominent high priests in scripture, each of whom had two sons, none of which followed the examples of their fathers. These three men were Eli, Aaron and Samuel.

The sons of Eli; Hophni and Phineas were disobedient, ungodly and immoral. The scripture describes them as the sons of Belial. Some of the sins they committed were stealing the money from the people as they entered the temple and to lie with the women as they came to the temple to worship. They were warned about their sin and Eli did not discipline them for doing wrong. As a result both of them were killed by the Philistines when the Ark of God was taken. When Eli heard the news he fell from his chair and broke his neck.

The sons of Aaron; Nadab and Abihu, offered 'strange fire' with incense, before the Lord. They were deliberately defiling the Tabernacle. They immediately died when God struck them both.

The sons of Samuel; Joel and Abiah, "walked not in his ways, but turned aside after lucre, and took bribes, and perverted judgement" (1 Samuel 8:2-3) Samuel had trained many young men for the ministry yet his own two sons were godless! Samuel lived a godly life, from the time that Hannah, his mother, brought him to the temple. As leader and High Priest of Israel, his life was unspotted. He really lived as a great example.

Not all children follow in their father's footsteps. How instrumental fathers are in the lives of their children to train them up in the way they should go. Parents have just a small window of time to influence their children as they seem to grow up so quickly.

IMPACT *Daily readings*

An angry man

2 Chronicles 26:16-23

"Then Uzziah was wroth, ...and while he was wroth .....
the leprosy even rose up in his forehead." 2 Chronicles 26:19

In my teenage years as I was growing up, very often I would have a bad temper, or become angry, often with frustration within myself. After my salvation at the age of 17, God wonderfully helped me deal with this. We read here in our text today that Uzziah the young King had an anger problem.

This chapter gives us wonderful insight into his life. He was liked by all the people, because they made him King. He built and rebuilt cities. He lived a life like his father that pleased the Lord. He sought the Lord in prayer and the Lord made him to prosper. He was also victorious in battles defeating many enemies; he had a mighty huge army. His name was known throughout the world as a powerful leader. He dug wells in the deserts and had lots of cattle and grape vines.

One rule, that no one including the King was allowed to break was the offering of incense in the temple. It was to be offered by the priests only. Uzziah was now at the stage in his life, that he thought he could do what he liked, he refused the warning from 85 priests not to touch it, but he got angry with them, very angry and the Lord smote him with leprosy until he died. Uzziah started off his life well with a wonderful upbringing and tremendous opportunities to serve the Lord. His life was even pleasing to the Lord but he threw it all away in a fit of rage. What a challenge this is to us all!

IMPACT *Daily readings*

Pure determination

Daniel 1:8-21

"But Daniel purposed in his heart that he would not defile himself." Daniel 1:8

What a challenge this is for any young person, or any person for that matter. Daniel and his friends were in the king's palace with a feast laid before them. It would have been much easier to do the same as everyone else and eat the king's meat.

Without realising it, every Christian is put in the same situation as Daniel was that day. However there is a major difference as Daniel was determined in his heart not to defile himself by eating the king's meat. Everyone is tempted to be defiled every day when the plate of meat is set before us. In our mind and heart we know it's wrong. But the longer the meat sits the more interesting it becomes. Just a little bit, just for the taste and before we know it we are like everyone else, full of the king's meat and often full of regret.

The meat I'm referring to is the temptation of the world and all the sinful pleasures that go along with it, everything from jokes, to movies and the internet. In our hearts we are determined not to go there but instead we find ourselves yielding to temptation.

Daniel and his friends were told to eat the meat and drink the wine in order to be like the others. Of course Daniel never gave in to such temptation and faired much better than all the others. The secret for Daniel was the Lord. In the den of lions and in so many other situations the Lord was with Daniel and protected him.

How easy it is to be defiled in these sinful and worldly days in which we live. Many Christians today live so close to the world it's so hard to tell the difference. From today may we be like Daniel and know God's power to keep us pure and clean. May we be determined not to defile ourselves but to seek purity of mind, body and spirit with God's help.

Don't stop short!

Genesis 11:27-32

"Terah died in Haran." Genesis 11:32

Haran is the place where Terah stopped on the way to the Promised Land. Had he not stopped, he could have made it to the land that flowed with milk and honey. Canaan was the place called the Promised Land. Abraham later made it there with his family. Haran can be a place where we can die, not just physically but spirituality. Many people, good Christians end up on the scrap heap, no longer useful or used by God. They are recycled and used by the devil for some other purpose.

Haran is the place where Terah stopped, gave up and died. Had he kept going he would have made the Promised Land. Sometimes we get to Haran and we feel like giving up, others can tempt us to come to Haran or go to Haran. That is why it is so important to be strong in the Christian life. The children of Israel turned back at Kadesh-barnea, on the borders of the land of blessing. As a result, they spent forty years wandering in the wilderness. Many today are just wandering about, blessing awaits them and because of unbelief, they neither see nor get the blessing of God upon their lives or ministry. Be careful that you don't arrive in Haran, the place that will slow you down and eventually bring you down completely Whoever, wherever or whatever it is, if it hinders your walk with God, run as fast as you can away from it.

Technology will never catch up with God

Isaiah 65:1-24

"And it shall come to pass, that before they call, I will answer;
and while they are yet speaking, I will hear." 7

Technology seems to be progressing at such a speed that it's difficult to keep up with the latest gadgets out on the market. A photograph can be taken and sent to the other end of the world and viewed within seconds. With your mobile you can talk with someone at the other end of the world and understand each other as if they were standing right next to you.

Yet to contrast modern technology with all its advancements we come to God. Someone who knows our thoughts, our mind and even our heart. Someone who knows what we want and what we need before we even think of it. Then think about us here. Suddenly we think of something we need to pray to God about. It maybe is personal, it maybe is public but none the less it's real. Then as you begin to talk to the Lord about it, He smiles and says "the answer is on the way even before you ask or call." With modern day advancements in technology I would say they are more like modern day distractions to real communication between man and God. Don't let your technology hinder your walk with God.

The way you say it!

Proverbs 15:1-13

"A soft answer turneth away wrath: but grievous words stir up anger." Proverbs 15:1

Communication is a wonderful thing when used. Whenever we think of the way technology has advanced today: Messages, emails, photographs, videos etc. can be sent across the world literally as they are taken. We live in an instant world; people want and even expect things instantly.

The verse today is simply talking about simple communication. Answering a question whenever we are asked can say a lot about the way we are. Sometimes we are asked a question and we can snap just like that, especially when the person asking the question is angry and frustrated. How you react to the person asking the question will either calm them down or make them even angrier. The secret to a wise person is not to start arguing but rather to answer softly and carefully. It will turn away wrath and anger. An insult is like mud. It will brush off much better when it dries. Let the mud dry. Wait until you both cool down. It may avoid a terrible argument, whenever we could very quickly stir up anger by speaking grievous words.

If you answer sharply with grievous words, this will have a natural reaction to make the other person angry. In my own experience, I remember I couldn't find something and was getting really annoyed and frustrated and in a rage I shouted at Joanna 'where is my passport?' In a quiet and soft voice, she then told me where I left it. Then it dawned on me and I went to where I left it and there it was. Always remember how we react whenever someone speaks to us. The way you speak to someone can speak volumes and be one of the greatest witnessing tools ever.

IMPACT *Daily readings*

Serve with gladness

Psalm 100
"Serve the LORD with gladness" Psalm 100:2

What a beautiful and challenging text we have before us today! Surely it is a terrible thing to get to the stage in life when we are serving the Lord with sadness instead of gladness. Many today have lost their joy, their zeal and their vision. God wants us to serve Him with gladness in our hearts. To serve God is the greatest joy we can have in this world. Many do not have this gladness in their hearts because their heart is in the world and the things of the world. We are supposed to be different and no longer of this world. That is why we should be glad to begin with.

Jesus is the King of Kings and Lord of Lords! When we come before Him, He wants us to have praise in our hearts and lips. Sometimes we can get so caught up with serving that we can be guilty of serving man, our minister or pastor, trying to please him instead of God. Everything we do in life we are to do it as unto the Lord and not unto man. Man can often disappoint us! But God never disappoints us. This is why it is so important whether in ministry, Christian service or Christian living to focus on the Lord and to serve Him with gladness. Maybe your heart is cold and sad today for some reason. Ask the Lord to give you back your joy as the joy of the Lord can be your strength. Once your strength is renewed then you can once again serve the Lord with gladness.

Stop rushing

1 Samuel 9:25-27

"Stand thou still a while, that I may show thee the word of God." 1 Samuel 9:27

Are you one of those people who runs around continuously, always on the go, hardly finding time to sit down and enjoy your meals? If so, then here is something for you, a timely message to urge you to slow down, just for a moment, so that you can take time to hear from God again.

Saul was the one with whom Samuel was speaking. Others were rushing on but Saul waited to hear the word of the Lord. The Lord has a message for you, but cannot seem to get your attention; you're always on the go, always in a rush. Life seems to be passing by before your very eyes and you can't get a moment. God says, "stand still a while." He has something to say, something for you to do.

In these days of technology people have never been so busy and yet have so little time for each other and even less time for God. Will you today, stand still, just for a while? Take time to be alone with God away from your friends, work and even family just until God has spoken. We can so easily miss out on His presence, His peace and His perfect plan for our lives. Many a person regrets making a hasty decision because they never took the time to stand still, just for a while, to hear from the Lord and what He has to say in His Word.

Do I find myself so busy rushing around, that I don't have time to stand still to hear from the Lord? Today all could turn out differently if you stand still and look in the WORD for the answer.

IMPACT *Daily readings*

A praying brother

Deuteronomy 9:15-21

"And the LORD was very angry with Aaron to have destroyed him:
and I prayed for Aaron also the same time." Deuteronomy 9:20

The Lord was very angry with Aaron and would have destroyed him but for the prayers of his brother Moses was he saved from death. Likewise Moses had a sister Miriam and when she was covered with leprosy, Moses prayed for her healing and she was healed. What blessing Moses was to his brother and sister when his prayers both saved and healed them.

What an encouragement this is for those of us who have brothers and sisters to keep praying for them. Like Aaron, one day they will have the judgement of God upon them, but try prayer. Just like Moses prayed for his brother and sister, God heard him and answered his prayers. You could be the only one praying for them and maybe that is what God is waiting for before he makes his move upon your brother or sister.

Christ is like a praying brother to us, He continually prays and makes intercession for us. Why then should we not intensify our prayers and start praying for others especially those close to us like our brothers or sisters. What a difference it would make in a family when one is saved, it could be the beginning of a family, community, town and country won for Christ. It needs to start with one, why not you?

IMPACT *Daily readings*

God will guide you

Psalm 143

"Cause me to know the way wherein I should walk." Psalm 143:8

The Psalmist had reached a crisis in his life! Right when he was in total desperation he cried: "Cause me to know the way wherein I should walk." There are times in our lives when we just don't know what to do. Maybe you have come to a time like this now. Maybe you are faced with a major decision about a relationship or college course, you have no idea what to do and are afraid of making the wrong decision. This is when you have to totally trust God to help you make the right choice.

Notice the remainder of verse 8 when the Psalmist says, "For I lift up my soul unto thee." Here was his secret. It was God and his communication with Him. He brought the Lord into the situation in his life. He needed help, needed guidance and he was wise when he sought the Lord for help. There can be no clear guidance until first of all we seek the face and will of God in the situation. We do this by pouring out our heart to God in prayer. This is not always an easy task; it takes time, honesty and humility. God desires what is best for you, but you must come as a child to a father and pour out your heart to Him. He is touched with the feelings of our infirmities. Tell Him everything and then watch Him at work in your life, working everything out for your good because He loves you.

God hates pride!

Proverbs 16:18-33

"Pride goeth before destruction, and an haughty spirit before a fall." Proverbs 16:18

God is a God of love but there are many things God hates and one of them is someone who is full of pride. Pride goeth before destruction is what this verse tells us and what a great warning and certain truth that is. I have known young couples where the man would boast how his girl would do anything for him, as if it were a dog he was dating. Within a short time he was on his own with nothing and his reputation as she had finished the relationship. I recall another, this time a minister who would boast how he had his congregation wrapped round his wee finger. No matter what he preached they all seemed to nod with agreement. This gradually came to an end as one by one those faithful servants left the church until the minister himself was forced to resign.

Pride is a terrible thing and sometimes we can get caught up in our pride and forget our humble beginning. There is nothing as distasteful as a proud, overbearing manner in a professing Christian. It usually preceeds a fall. So if you are the proud type and are loving it, watch out or you could come down with a bang. There is a lot to be said about having a servant's heart, willing to serve the Lord with body, mind and soul. Never think you are beyond reproach, any man that thinketh he standeth, take heed or you will fall.

Undo the heavy burdens!

Isaiah 58:1-14

"Undo the heavy burdens, and to let the oppressed go free." Isaiah 58:6

Many Christians today live with very heavy burdens upon them; maybe it's the constant care of a loved one, responsibility of a business, finance, raising a family etc. Have you ever realised that the Lord specialises in carrying our burdens for us? 'Cast your care upon Him for He careth for you.' We often carry burdens which get heavier and heavier each day. However, we don't have to carry them ourselves; the Lord will carry them for us if we just ask Him.

Verse 11 says that the Lord will guide you continually; not just yesterday and today, but tomorrow and every day after that as well. The Lord wants to guide us and carry our burdens; certainly to make them lighter than they are at the moment. To have the continual guidance of the Lord upon us is a wonderful thing. Don't go through life without the Lord; take Him with you, every step of the way. Make every day count for God; prove Him every step of the way because what He says, He will do. If He says He will make your burdens lighter then He will do that in His perfect will and plan for your life.

Pray for the peace of Jerusalem

Psalm 122

"Pray for the peace of Jerusalem, they shall prosper that love thee." Psalm 122:6

Back in 2012, I with some friends went to Israel; this was a very special joy for me to go to the Holy Land. There we met believers who worked with CEF in Nazareth. What amazed me was the size of the country, although not very big at all compared to all those countries around it, many of whom are enemies. Israel is constantly being attacked and hated by many countries throughout the world. This is a land were God's ancient people are from and He will protect them. This a lovely picture of how we are God's people and he will protect us even though we too have many enemies.

Jerusalem is a very beautiful city; it was very touching to stay at Nazareth, the place of Christ's birth and to make that journey to Jerusalem to the place of His death. The Jewish people of Jerusalem are still strangers to God because they are yet to believe in Jesus Christ for salvation. Many religions of the world and all different faiths want Jerusalem to be the centre of their activity. Pray for the peace of this city, that the inhabitants may find peace with God through the Lord Jesus Christ.

Making friends

Proverbs 18:10-24

"A man that hath friends must shew himself friendly." Proverbs 18:24

This is so true and is a basic rule of life, if you want to make friends you have got to be a friendly person. Have you ever met someone and you come away from them saying, "They are so unfriendly" well if you notice closely they probably don't have that many friends. This is not a general rule of life. But if you want to make friends with someone, there has got to be something that connects you, something you both have in common.

If you are always negative, pessimistic, and continually complaining about something then you will soon find most people aren't looking for new friends at that time. People generally like people who are friendly, happy, joyful and optimistic. Certainly if you are a Christian people should be attracted by your Christ likeness. It would be a terrible thing if your personality put people off becoming a Christian because of the way you are. The greatest compliment I have ever received was when I received a letter from a little boy at a school Bible Club who said, "I have just become a Christian because you have inspired me to become one." If there was one reason my life was worth living it was to bring that child to Christ, then it has been worth living. Try being friendly a little more and see what happens, but not with over excitement as that will put people off and they may think you are desperate or even a bit strange. On the other hand there are so many people out there who would love a friend and you could be that person.

IMPACT *Daily readings*

God leads the way

Isaiah 45:1-4

"I will go before thee, and make the crooked places straight." Isaiah 45:2

Have you ever had a situation in your life when things seem to go so wrong that you just don't know what to do? The pressures just keep building up and up and you never seem to get on top of them. In my life and ministry, this is one of the thousands of verses that the Lord uses to comfort and encourage me along the way.

Not only does the Lord say He will make the crooked places straight, He also says that He will go before us and make the way smooth. Sometimes we can be nervous about an interview or a meeting we have to take and after it is over we wonder why it went so smoothly? Have you ever thought that maybe the Lord went before you and made this crooked place straight?

So many times in my life I have come across what seems to be impossible situations, yet on reflection, the Lord put words in my mouth and ideas in my head preparing the way and continually making the crooked places straight. For a Christian to worry, it simply means they are not trusting in the Lord to help them along life's way. From today may we learn to trust more and worry less.

How many times can I remember the Lord really helping me in what seemed an impossible situation?

A great human test

Genesis 22:1-18

"And he said, Take now thy *son*, thine only son Isaac, whom thou lovest, and get thee into the land of Moriah; and offer him there for a burnt offering upon one of the mountains which I will tell thee of." Genesis 22:2

Abraham was put to the test like no human has ever been before. There is no one or nothing more precious to a man than his son. When Abraham was put to the test here in Genesis 22 we see this as something that would break the hardest of men at the thought of slaying his only son Isaac. Abraham was a wonderful man of God and the problem here, from what I can see, is that Abraham was now spending more time with his wee boy than he was with God.

This is a basic principle in the Christian life that the Lord must come first before everything and anyone else in our lives. Abraham went the whole way through with God in carrying out what God had asked him to do. The Lord asked Abraham to prepare his son Isaac for a sacrifice. That is exactly what Abraham did, he was willing to go through with God and he passed the test. Has the Lord ever tested your willingness to serve or do something for Him? With Abraham there was no excuse. Why is it with the Lord's people today there are so many excuses? What are we really willing to sacrifice and give up for the Lord, even something so close to us that we couldn't imagine living without?

Time to put things right

Psalm 66

"If I regard iniquity in my heart, the Lord will not hear me" Psalm 66:18

This is a powerful verse of scripture. This is talking about hiding deliberate sin in your heart and life and trying to keep going on as a Christian. The Lord is telling you that if you deliberately have unconfessed sin in your life and try to pray to me, "I will not hear your prayers." The Lord is not a fool as to be mocked. He knows your heart, He knows what you have been up to, looking at, talking about. It is time to come clean before the Lord, weep if you have to but it must come out. You cannot keep living a lie, honesty is a great thing and God hates lies, cover up and false Christians. Your lovely suit or nice dress means nothing to God if you are deliberately sinning and worse still have unconfessed, unrepented sin in your life, especially if you are conscious and aware of it. Does this not bother you? If you are truly saved then it should.

If you want the blessing of God upon your life and God's best for you, you have got to be honest and come clean before Him. He will not keep haunting you and reminding you of it, He will forgive you and put it all away as far as the east is from the west, He will remember it no more. But, you my friend must not hide sin in your heart. Many are not being blessed today because of sin, secret sin in the heart that enters through the eye gate, the ear gate and makes your heart unclean. It must be confessed and washed in the Precious Blood of Christ, come afresh and start afresh tonight, it's between you and God otherwise the Lord will not hear you. Surely my friend it is time to put things right.

Help from God in the battle

1 Samuel 7:1-12

"Ebenezer...Hitherto hath the LORD helped us." 1 Samuel 7:12

How many times can you look back when you were in certain situations and say, the Lord really helped me there? How often do we ask the Lord to help us in different situations? Is there ever a day that goes by when we do not pray or say "Lord help me?"

In this portion we have a wonderful occasion when the children of Israel were genuinely sorry for all their sin and wrong doing. They have asked the prophet Samuel to pray for them as they continue to repent before the Lord. Samuel gathers all the people together and begins to pray for them.

In the meantime the powerful Philistine army hears about all of Israel gathered together so they prepare for attack. When the Israelites heard what was happening they were afraid and pleaded for Samuel to keep praying. The Lord immediately intervened in the situation and sent a thunderstorm upon the Philistines.

Sometimes when we are in the battle the best weapon we have is prayer, while we pray, the Lord already has an answer and a solution. We have enemies all around us, many waiting for the perfect opportunity to attack us physically, mentally, emotionally or in whatever way they can to make sure it hurts. This is why is it so important to realise, the secret of winning the battle is praying throughout the battle. Then when all is calm and the Lord gives us the victory we can say "Ebenezer", meaning, the LORD has helped us.

Who or what would I consider to be my enemies? How can I pray that the Lord will give me the victory over them?

IMPACT *Daily readings*

Neglecting the Word of God

Psalm 119:1-18

"I will delight myself in thy statutes: I will not forget thy word." Psalm 119:16

How the devil loves it when we neglect reading the Word of God. Isn't it amazing that we have advanced so much with technology, with cars, phones and computers over the last few years? People should have so much more time to get things done, yet sadly in reality this is not the case. The Psalmist here promised the Lord that he would not forget the Word of God; he would continue to meditate upon it. This a basic fundamental lesson in the Christian life, just like food to the body, a bed for rest, the Bible is just as important for the soul.

The Psalmist actually delighted in the Word of God, it did him so much good, he learned so much about the Lord. Of course we can't remember everything we read, that's why we need to keep on reading. Like food, we have got to keep on eating to stay alive, if we stop eating we will starve to death. It is similar with the Word of God, in order to grow we have got to know, unless we meditate upon it we'll never understand and have knowledge of the deeper things of God.

Sometimes I become so busy in the work and I easily find myself living the Christian life in the flesh, this is so dangerous as very soon we become flat, and dated, lacking in power. This is when I realise I have been neglecting God's Word, maybe a day, a week, even a month relying on others to feed me, like church on Sunday. I've been honest with you my friend, now it's your turn to be honest with God; don't make it easy for the devil. Every time the Lord Jesus was tempted by Satan, He replied, "It is written." The devil eventually left him as the Word was too powerful. We need to use the same weapon, the Word of God is quick and powerful and sharper than a two edged sword.

Others depend on you

Proverbs 4:15-27
"Keep thy heart with all diligence." Proverbs 4:23

There is a saying that the river doesn't rise higher than its source. Without realising it, there are many people in your life who look at you as an example. What you say and do and how you react to a particular situation may have major consequences in other people's lives. With this in mind, it is so important that we watch our life and testimony like a hawk. How important it is for us to keep in close fellowship with the Lord! If we fail at something, then others may fail too! If we stumble and fall, others who look to us may stumble and fall also.

I remember in November 2011, I went with a team to China to smuggle Bibles from another neighbouring country. It was a really exciting adventure. Would we get stopped at the border or could we pass by without being stopped and searched? We crossed backwards and forwards many times sometimes getting stopped and other times getting through. After being stopped several times it was very discouraging. Stephen, who was the leader of the team, never lost heart once. He was always optimistic! "There's always another time, remember the last time when you did get across" he would say. Even though they would take almost everything, there were always a few Bibles smuggled through. "Focus and be thankful for everyone who makes it," he would say. Others looked to him for leadership and encouragement. If he went down the team would go down. He stayed strong and the whole team was united in their purpose throughout the trip. Others will be watching you today, so be careful and remember the bigger picture all the time.

We are either stepping stones or stumbling blocks.

IMPACT *Daily readings*

The greatest distance imaginable

Psalm 103

*"As far as the east is from the west,
so far hath he removed our transgressions from us." Psalm 103:12*

Here in this 103rd Psalm we have a note of praise throughout. What a blessed, spiritual tonic for the soul it is. Surely this is the most wonderful thought ever, to know that our sins are gone forever as far as the east is from the west and that we are surrounded with so many benefits and given so many promises from the Lord in His word. We have so much to thank and praise God for.

Through the precious blood of Christ, our sins have been forgiven. Christ dealt with our sins when we called upon His name for salvation. Our sins are all washed away in the precious blood of Christ, never to be remembered any more. How merciful God is, surely we cannot help but bow in complete adoration at His name. His name is wonderful! We tend to constantly remember our past lives, our sins and all the baggage that goes with it. But let's think about the power of God's forgiveness. As far as the east is from the west, this is surely the greatest imaginable distance. Are you willing to forgive someone this much?

Today, lift up your heart and praise Him that you have been forgiven; that the record of your sin has been forever blotted out. Isn't that just altogether wonderful! Maybe as you read this you have no assurance of having your sins taken away. Come to Jesus now and trust in Him alone to save you! He can and He will!

What else is there in your life you can thank God for?

Sit still

Isaiah 30:1-7
"Their strength is to sit still." Isaiah 30:7

There is strength found in being still. If you ever want to be strong in God, you will have to learn this valuable lesson. We live in a day when everyone seems to be running around with hardly time to say hello. Life is a constant hustle and bustle. Someone once said if you don't take time to "come apart," sooner or later you will "come apart"!

Some people keep telling me to slow down and don't do so many missions and Bible Clubs. I find the secret is to balance my time with rest, physically, emotionally and spiritually. For me it's as easy to do sixty missions in one year as six missions. Of course it takes a lot of planning and effort, but what doesn't. Souls are perishing, we need to reach them, God knows my limits and I ask Him to guide me and to limit me when I need to be limited. Right now I feel as if I am on the German motorway with no limits, going flat out for God.

Right now we are in Mexico, having a rest for two weeks, I am so rested I have written over one hundred pages of this devotional, as well as this playing volleyball, swimming, eating and resting on the beach and spending loads of time with Joanna. It is important to run well for God, but know your limits. You are only as good as your last mission or message. When you become tired it shows, when the battery light comes on, go and get re-charged. That's when you need to be still and come aside and rest a while like the disciple of old.

He loved her

Genesis 24:61-67

"Isaac brought her into his mother Sarah's tent, and took Rebekah,
and she became his wife; and he loved her:
and Isaac was comforted after his mother's death." Genesis 24:67

Isaac had never met Rebekah before. His father had sent his servant to find a wife for Isaac. When Rebekah agreed to go with the servant, we can easily see God's hand at work in her life. After she was introduced to Isaac, they got married. The Bible tells us "he loved her".

These are beautiful words. There is nothing more beautiful in this world than real genuine love. It affects our emotions, mind, and feelings. In fact it goes right to the very core of the soul and affects everything about us. Love is a God given gift and it is a natural desire for someone to fall in love not just with anyone , but rather with one special person God has chosen for you.

When you find that person and begin a relationship, your love grows deeper and deeper every day. That leads to marriage and then two become one flesh, then it truly is a most wonderful and exciting life! The real challenge and fear is knowing whether we have the right person or not. Many people worry and worry, and doubt and doubt. If you can live your life without that person, then you are not meant to be together. If your love doesn't grow stronger and deeper for each other every day, then there is something wrong. Isaac loved Rebekah; he would have done anything for her. Love cannot be bought; it is either there or not. If in doubt leave it. If God is in it, you can only win!

They will either pull you further away from God or closer to Him. Which one is it?

IMPACT *Daily readings*

The Lord will preserve you

Psalm 121

"The LORD shall preserve thee from all evil: He shall preserve thy soul." Psalm 121:7

This is another one of the great, wonderful and mighty promises we find in the Bible. When a person becomes a Christian, it is totally amazing what the Lord has in store for them, how He will look after them and most importantly, the promises contained in His Word for all of us who seek to follow Him.

We live in an evil world and there is no doubt about it! Right away when we think of all the sin, evil and bad things that go on the world, we have this encouraging verse, "The LORD shall preserve thee from all evil." For the people who have been saved recently from the world and all the snares and evil grips that once held you there, you have been set free! God will protect you because He has delivered you from the world.

Your soul has been rescued my friend and no one else can protect you the way the Lord can and certainly no one else can preserve your soul the way the Lord can. Your soul has been rescued because you have been saved! This is an amazing thought, that out of the millions of people in the world, God has saved you! You have called upon Him, now you are His child. He will look after you, but stay close to Him! Don't offend Him in any way and He will give you the desire of your heart.

IMPACT *Daily readings*

The brave young man!

1 Samuel 14:1-15

"We will stand still in our place...." 1 Samuel 14:9

King Saul was with his men, being taunted and laughed at by their enemies, the Philistines. The Spirit of God suddenly moved Jonathan, the king's son. He would never have got the approval of Saul to do what he did, so he acted alone with his faithful armour bearer. When Jonathan told his armour bearer what he was going to do, he replied to Jonathan, "do all that is in thine heart...I am with thee." How encouraging it is to have those with you in the battle, those who will go to the end, those who will fight till the death for the cause of Christ. There are two ways to be in the battle; either, stand and watch it or get into the middle of it. One is to talk about it and the other is to go and fight.

Jonathan seemed to climb up an awkward cliff at the amusement of the Philistines, then he charged them, killing at least twenty of them, his armour bearer following close behind him, finishing them off. The effect was great, there was a trembling and fear in the host and even the earth quaked.

Whatever challenges face you today, face it head on. Don't expect others to fight your battles for you. Sometimes we need to act. Others may not like it, nor may they agree with it, but, if the Lord moves you to act, to speak up, to do what needs to be done, then do it.

Seek the Lord about what you should do; then go forward! Listen to those incredible words from the Saviour. "Do all that is in thine heart.... behold I am with thee." The Lord never failed Jonathan and he will not fail you. As you go forward , stand still in your conviction that this is the way God would have you go.

Waiting on the Lord

Psalm 27

"Wait on the LORD: be of good courage, and he shall strengthen thine heart:
wait, I say, on the LORD." Psalm 27:14

There is a lot to be said about patience and waiting on the Lord. God teaches us so much about waiting on Him. He knows what is best for us. When we run on along in our own strength we can easily get tired and weary. When this happens then we can get frustrated and downcast. When this happens then we can get worried, deflated, discouraged and depressed. When this happens it can be a disaster so we want to avoid this at all costs.

The Lord wants to make you strong and to encourage you. This is why we must wait on Him. Take time to be with the Lord. It is vital in your Christian walk. Maybe your heart is weak, your countenance is very low and you are at one of those low moments in your life and it is not pleasant at all and there seems no way out. Well the lesson is the same. Wait on the Lord. Take your eyes of all others and fix your gaze upon Christ. Twice the word, "wait" is mentioned in this verse. The Lord is emphasising the point and the importance of waiting upon Him. Read the verse over and over again, in fact the whole Psalm. This is a personal favourite of Joanna's, it encourages her so much in her walk with God, it can do the same for you. Wait my friend, whatever you are going to do, wait until God gives you the nod.

Gathering the Manna

Exodus 16:11-21

"And they gathered it every morning." Exodus 16:21

Every morning for a period of time the Lord provided manna for the Children of Israel to eat. When they woke up in the morning the manna was already there for them. They were to eat it and it would give them the physical strength to live.

The manna is like the Word of God to us. It comes with freshness each morning that is why the Lord puts so much emphasis on the morning. This is the best time to seek the Lord. Breakfast is the most important meal of the day and yet so many people do not eat breakfast. Ask a Christian why they do not read their Bibles and pray in the morning and they will say that they do not have time. Yet they have time to use the toilet, shower, get dressed, check the phone and respond to text messages, drive to where they are going, spend the whole day there, come home, eat, use the toilet, shower, get dressed again, go out for the evening, come home, check their phone for the tenth time that day and then, crawl up the stairs, use the toilet again, get dressed for bed and zzzzzzzzz.

Have you ever had a day like I just described? Is every day the same? If so we've got a problem, we don't have time for God. Watch out my friend God is going to need to teach you a lesson, lay you aside so that you will take time. I suggest tomorrow morning you rise a little earlier and fill your soul with manna and start the day with the Lord. Otherwise you will grow cold, backslide and become a useless Christian.

Don't give up

Psalm 142

"I cried unto the LORD with my voice;
with my voice unto the LORD did I make my supplication." Psalm 142:1

There were many times in David's life when in total desperation he cried unto the Lord. In over half of the verses in this Psalm, David mentions the Lord. This is such a challenge for us to remember the Lord every day, especially in time of despair. When David wrote this psalm, he had been in great trouble. God had delivered him out of the hands of his enemies.

There are times in our lives when everything seems to be going against us, nothing seems to be working out and it just seems to get worse and worse. Are you having one of those days? Is this a time in your life right now when you are in great despair? Well then, look to the Lord and don't give up! David was one of the most harassed and oppressed men who ever lived, being pursued by King Saul and his soldiers for years, with enemies on every side.

Sometimes we can become so self-focused that we think we're having a bad day. Try to think of others as there are often others much worse off. The lesson remains the same however that the more we focus on the Lord, the less we will focus on ourselves. God knows your heart, He knows how desperate your situation is and He will step in at the right time and bring you through. His timing is not our timing, nor His ways our ways, but both His timing and ways are perfect.

IMPACT *Daily readings*

The challenge

Isaiah 6:1-8

"Whom shall I send and who will go for us?" Isaiah 6:8

This is one of the greatest challenges in the entire Bible, a call to forsake all and follow Christ. How easy it is to sing about such a challenge, how easy it is to pray about such a challenge, but now the time has come when we need to put feet to our prayers and go out for God somewhere to do something for Him. It may not be easy and you may not be popular. I learnt the hard way, I thought the whole church would stand up and applaud me for stepping out of the boat to serve God, in many ways other Christians became my worst enemy. Unless God's work is done their way they don't like it, but I believe God's work done in God's way will never lack God's supply, I have proved it for many years now. When God puts something on your heart, then do it, don't wait on the approval of man because you may never get it.

The challenge is great today, in many ways it's easier to be a missionary today than it was many years ago, in the sense of travelling. It used to take six weeks to travel to Australia, now you can be there in less than twenty four hours. Missionaries years ago relied more on the Lord I believe; today we have too much technology to rely on for help. Technology is good in many ways but can be a major distraction in many other ways. The question is, are you willing to go, go wherever God will have you to go? The best ability you can have right now is availability. Are you available? Are you willing? Will you go?

He spoke and it happened!

Genesis 1:1-31

"The gathering together of the waters called he Seas:
and God saw that *it* was good." Genesis 1:10

In January 2013, we went to Gambia, the west coast of Africa for a holiday. This has one of the nicest stretches of beaches in the world, pure golden sands, blue sea, cloudless blue sky and guaranteed sunshine. Every morning and night as we would walk, skip, jump and play along the beach we would be amazed at the creation of Almighty God. His handiwork is just amazing. Even as we would swim every day, the power and the crashing of those waves, they would toss you about like a tadpole in a pond, so powerful they were. Yet we read of the Lord Jesus, when he rebukes the wind and the waves during the storm on the Sea of Galilee. "Peace be still" He said and all was calm. The very God who spoke these seas into existence, even the seas obey His voice, it is marvellous, wonderful to see the majesty of His creation.

Sometimes in life we can always be in a hurry and rush around from day to day. We can miss out on the beautiful things in life, the very sand on the seashore, the shells, perfectly created, millions of them, yet all different. There are beautiful people around us every day, neighbours we don't even know, people in church we don't even get to know because we are rushing off to get our lunch. Try to see God in someone today.

Today make a special effort to see something of God's handiwork, His wonders to perform. God is truly all-powerful, all-knowing and all-wise God. I am so glad I am His child and He is my Heavenly Father. What a great God we serve. Don't go through life without Him, if you do, you alone will be the loser!

Purity at its best

Psalm 24
"He that hath clean hands, and a pure heart..." Psalm 24:4

The most important part of the human body is the heart. Once it stops working your life on this earth will be over. Unlike any other part of the human body, we can keep living if we lose or break something. However the verse is referring to the centre of our feelings and emotions rather than the physical organ of the body. This inner life is of the highest importance to every one of us and especially to the Lord.

How we live and how we look may have cost a lot of money, we must realise that they are of no value for eternity. There are many believers today who are dressed to perfection, yet, underneath it all, there lies an evil temper or a heart that is full of jealousy, anger and hatred. Sometimes we tend to forget the power that lies in the precious blood of Christ that cleanseth us from the very depths of our sinful nature, purifying and cleansing that which is unclean. David prayed "Create in me a clean heart, O God; and renew a right spirit within me." Psalm 51:10 We must guard our hearts at all cost. Once our heart is polluted by the world, flesh or the devil then we can be sure we will no longer enjoy the victory in Christ we once enjoyed. More than anything in this life look after your heart, in every aspect of it, once it is gone life is over and it's too late to start making changes then.

No restraint with God

1 Samuel 14:1-7

"It may be that the LORD will work for us:
for there is no restraint to the LORD to save by many or by few." 1 Samuel 14:6

While Saul and his six hundred soldiers waited and slept on the mountain, Jonathan decided to move on ahead to confront the Philistines. From the outside this seemed like a foolish thing to do, but as we read this portion of Scripture, God honoured his step of faith and defeated the Philistines that day.

Sometimes others will want us to wait and wait and wait to do something for the Lord. The time will come when we are so used to waiting that we will no longer see the need to move forward. The Lord is not limited; there are no restrictions with the Lord. It is not our business to save people, this is God's business alone. Our business though is telling others they need to be saved. Whether it is an individual or a group of people, whether it is a mission or a special service, there is no restraint on the Lord to save.

Sometimes we have got to make this journey alone and leave the others behind. Only Jonathan's armour bearer went with him that day. He encouraged Jonathan to do all that was in his heart and assured him that he was with him. So my friend, the Lord will be with you as you seek to go in Jesus' name! Many an able soldier with armour and sword stayed hiding in the mountain that day, but Jonathan went on ahead. Many an able preacher is hiding today, afraid to go, afraid to step out in faith just as faithful Jonathan did, but my friend you must go!

Always remember that salvation is the Lord's work. He alone can and will save!

God watches and cares for you

Psalm 33:18-22

"Behold, the eye of the LORD is upon them that fear him" Psalm 33:18

Many times in the scriptures we are reminded that the Lord looks after His children. We are told this so often and the fact that He never takes His eyes off us. I remember being at the beach one day with lots of people, thousands in fact, there was the lifeguard watching over the people and my friend was there with his son. While the lifeguard was generally looking out for everyone he had no real love for anyone. There was only one person my friend was watching out for without taking his eyes off and that was his son.

This is what the Lord does, He both loves and cares for us His children. Sometimes we can come to a stage in our lives when no one seems to care. Life can become lonely, problems seem to keep coming and no one seems to care. Can I tell you, yes there is someone who does. The Lord cares and He cares more for you than you will ever know. Better than this He keeps on loving and He keeps on caring for you. The eyes of the Lord go to and fro throughout the whole earth and at the same time, He never takes His eyes off you. In Psalm 37v15 we read: "The eyes of the Lord are upon the righteous, and His ears are open unto their cry." Don't cut yourself off from the Lord who loves you, not only does He see you and care for you but He always has a listening ear for you and your cry. Who else in this world cares for you like that?

Give me ten percent of your time

Genesis 28:16-22

"And of all that thou shalt give me I will surely give the
tenth unto thee." Genesis 28:22

This can be a touchy subject for many people. It is a clear command that ten percent of our income should be given to the Lord. Ministers would argue that it should be given to the local church and let them distribute it accordingly. Others would argue that the local church is very often narrow minded in its outreach so prefer to distribute it according to where there is need. However you look at it I think it is important as Christians to practise giving our ten percent to the Lord.

I would like to challenge you in a different way with this verse, it is not concerning money but rather time. Sometimes we can think that going to church on Sunday is enough to please the Lord. This is often as far as many Christians go in their Christian life. Can you imagine how the Lord feels after all He has done for us? Yet in return this is all many of us do for Him.

Have you ever considered giving to the Lord ten percent of your time, your day, week, month, year, life? What about your holidays? It's so easy to go to the sun and relax! What about a mission trip? This is making your holiday time a time when you can give back to the Lord and do something for others? Think for a moment like Jacob, of everything the Lord has done for and given to you. All he is asking for is ten percent of your time, talents, money and whatever else you can do for Him.

IMPACT *Daily readings*

Let the Shepherd lead

Psalm 80:1-19

"Give ear, O Shepherd of Israel, thou that leadest Joseph like a flock." Psalm 80:1

Sometimes we can miss the simplicity and the personal message God gives to us in His Word in relation to a verse like this. Here we are thinking about Joseph and through all his trials he never lost sight of the Shepherd. The Lord was with Joseph. The Lord today is with His children; He calls them, feeds them and protects them. It is a most comforting thought to know there is someone looking down on and after the sheep of His fold. When we wander, He brings us back and when danger comes He is there to protect.

To fully understand and appreciate what the Psalmist is saying here can easily be missed. He in effect is telling us how the Lord is his shepherd and he has need of nothing. How we ought to listen to the shepherd's voice. Contrast this to the Christian today, who has so much and at the same time is not really content. There is always something to mumble, grumble and complain about. Even though we know it's wrong, we still compare our lives and what we have to others. This is a great lesson in life to take our eyes off others and fix our eyes upon Jesus. When we have the Lord Jesus, then He is our everything. Sometimes the Lord will test us to see how much we love Him, trust Him and rely on Him. To fully test us, sometimes we need to lose everything we ever had to appreciate the only thing we ever need.

IMPACT *Daily readings*

Bathsheba!

2 Samuel 11:1-5

"And David sent and enquired after the woman." 2 Samuel 11:3

David lived a great life, described as a man after God's own heart. However we sometimes tend to point the finger at this point in his life when both the terrible sins of adultery and murder were committed, one leading to the other of course. When God sent Nathan to David, to bring the message 'thou art the man', the Lord was showing his love and mercy to David in forgiveness. Of course much sorrow and weeping was to follow as the child they had together died.

I have often thought why David is the only one to blame here, Bathsheba is hardly ever condemned. She was within distance of King David, why then did she expose herself to his notice, therefore tempting him? When the messengers went for her, why did she go so willingly without her husband's approval? When David offered to lie with her, she again did so willingly. Then after her husband's death, she easily consented to become the wife of David, no sign of remorse from her end.

Of course this terrible sin of David can never be condoned or excused but from a different focus point Bathsheba was the person and the means of causing this to happen on what would have otherwise been an almost guilt free life for David. She can never be excused for this. There are many Bathshebas around today, men are not always to blame, it always takes two, and many a good man has fallen as a result of a tempting woman. Everyone has their temptations, how we need to be so careful not to cross the line which we could live to regret forever!

Take your opportunity

Proverbs 25:10-25

"As cold waters to a thirsty soul, so *is* good news from a far country." Proverbs 25:25

Have you ever had the conviction upon your heart that you should speak to someone about their soul and their need to get saved? When such conviction comes to you, I believe it is from God. I suggest you respond and act immediately otherwise that poor soul may be lost and you will give account to the Lord some day for not responding to your responsibility. The Lord will help you and give you the words to say to them.

I remember when pastoring a church in Australia, I was greatly burdened for my eldest brother, who was unsaved and cared not much for his soul as he lived for the things of this world. He didn't receive the conversation very well and was quite annoyed at why I phoned him, to press upon his need of salvation. I came off the phone not feeling very well as he refused to get saved and pretty much cut the conversation short. However before the Lord, I did what I had to do by warning him of his soul and how he needed to get saved. Six weeks later that same brother was at a gospel meeting and waited behind and got saved, how delighted I was to hear such news.

Is there someone on your heart right now, a brother, sister, father, mother, aunt, uncle, and grandparents, still not saved? You are maybe the only Christian they know. You are maybe the only person there is to tell them. Are you going to act now? As you stand around their grave someday realising they are not saved, maybe so, because you never warned them about trusting in Christ and having their sins forgiven. They may hate you for it, but on the other hand they may be rescued for eternity because you told them.

IMPACT *Daily readings*

Will revival come?

Psalm 85

"Wilt thou not revive us again: that thy people may rejoice in thee?" Psalm 85:6

People often speak very glibly about revival. They have a conversation about it, pray about it then look out the window and nothing happens, then they wonder why? I ask the question, are the churches ready for revival? If a multitude of unconverted people came into church, a lot of church going Christians would soon feel very uncomfortable. Maybe that's why, we have become far too comfortable and have really lost the focus of God at work, sinners being saved and Christians set on fire for God. That's revival. When you go to church, do you go eagerly to hear a message from the Lord? Do you expect to be challenged and changed forever when you hear the Word of God preached? Maybe that's one reason why revival is not here.

One of Spurgeon's students once asked Mr Spurgeon why no one was getting saved during his preaching. Mr Spurgeon asked him, "Do you really expect someone to get saved after listening to you preach?" "Well, no, not really" he replied, that's your problem Spurgeon told him. You have got to preach with expectancy. I pray that every time I preach that souls will get saved. Every mission I conduct, I am disappointed when souls don't respond to the challenge of the Gospel. It is the greatest joy, especially when a child comes up to me at the end of a meeting and says, "excuse me Colin, will you show me how to become a Christian, because I want to get saved." The soul winner's joy is beautiful beyond measure, a taste of personal revival. May God send us all revival and may our hearts, homes and churches be ready to receive it.

IMPACT *Daily readings*

God keeps you safe

1 Samuel 22:17-23

"Abide thou with me, fear not...with me thou *shal*t be in safeguard." 1 Samuel 22:23

David was at this time on the run for his life from king Saul who sought to kill him. Even while David was looking out for himself, hardly knowing who to trust, there came another young man called Abiathar who was also on the run from Saul. David assured the young man that he would look after him and protect him. Isn't it wonderful when all seems to be going wrong for us, that we can take the time to look out for and help others?

Today is no different than in David's day; these are Godless days with temptation all around us. These are both challenging and difficult days for the Christian to remain pure and strong in the Lord. Subtle temptations come from every corner, especially from the internet. From the most innocent use to the vilest use the internet can be the sole means of destroying the strongest of strong Christians. Be on your guard; be careful on those lonely nights when you find yourself at the screen. The push of a key or click of a button may start you on a path that will be the means of your destruction.

It is when we are out of touch, and stray from a close walk with God in prayer and from His Word that we become an easy prey for the devil. So, be watchful today! Subtle enemies of your soul plan your downfall. Just like David offered protection to Abiathar, so God will watch over you, but you must stay close and don't wander off from Him or the enemy will get you.

IMPACT *Daily readings*

He didn't even know

Exodus 34:29-35

"And it came to pass, when Moses came down from mount Sinai with the two
tablets of testimony in Moses' hand, when he came down from the mount,
that Moses wist not that the skin of his face shone while he talked with him." Exodus 34:29

In January of 2011, together with my wife Joanna, we had the great joy of climbing to the top of Mount Sinai in Egypt. We could not help but think that this was the very place where Moses met with God. It took many hours to climb to the top and we travelled all night to get there for the early morning sunrise and what a splendid sight awaited us.

Moses had been alone with God, forty days and forty nights. Is it any wonder that his countenance shone and glistened with the glory of God? Moses himself was not conscious of his shining face, but when he came down from the mountain, the people could see his shining face. This is something we can all experience, the presence of Almighty God in our lives. Sometimes we can be so busy, so active even in the Lord's work that we can miss out on His wonderful presence.

Moses' face shone because he was in the presence of God. This did not come from him mingling with the world. Today we can also enjoy this same presence; it is a personal thing between you and God, being alone in His presence. Once there, you will never want to leave the warmth and joy of it. If you do, you will become cold and miserable like so many are today, far away from the presence of God. Like Moses, your face may have the radiance of Christ. You may not be aware but others will know that you have been alone with God.

When is the last time you felt the nearness, stillness and closeness of God?

A personal word

Psalm 119:105-112

"Thy word is a lamp unto my feet and a light unto my path." Psalm 119:105

It is very important to realise that the Word of God is a very personal book from God to us. It is very personal because this is how the Lord speaks to us today. If you want a message from the Lord, you will not find it on your phone or in the Newspapers; you will find it in the written Word. This is God's "text" message to us. If you want to know God's guidance, plan, will for your life, then I would encourage you to get into the habit of reading His Word.

I must admit the great challenge when it comes to reading the Bible is being consistent. In many ways, like running a race, but it's easy to quit running once you stop. The more you run the harder it becomes, but that's the challenge if you want to finish the race well then you must run well. To run the Christian race and not read the Bible is like running a real race in the dark, you will stumble and fall, get frustrated and just feel like quitting. Therefore the secret is that it is a lamp to your feet, to guide you, a light to lead you to the Light of the World, the One the book is all about, the One who gave Himself for you. Open the book today and read all about Him.

The enemy will hinder the work

Genesis 26:13-18

"For all the wells which his father's servants had digged in the days of Abraham his father, the Philistines had stopped them, and filled them with earth." Genesis 26:15

Whenever we think of a well of water, it is natural water, tasty water and straight from the source. Abraham had dug many wells of water as he travelled around. Water was a natural resource and yet to get it was hard work as sometimes it took a lot of hard digging.

Now the Philistines had come across them and filled them in with earth, therefore stopping the source and flow of water. However Isaac was determined to open the wells again. This was not going to stop him. Sometimes in the Christian life and the work of God there will be those who seek to hinder and stop the work. They tend to ask lots of questions, putting up barriers and obstacles all the time. The devil can even use Christians to hinder the work of God and sadly they cannot even see it.

Isaac never got deflated or discouraged; rather he rolled up his sleeves and got stuck in to the work to get the wells working again. Our fathers have kept the gospel flag flying from generation to generation. This is our generation, what are we doing to maintain and advance the work of God. Every generation has its enemies and its workers. I would rather be a worker for God, what camp would you be in? Let's seek to advance the work of God!

Failure not final

Psalm 145
"The Lord upholdeth all that fall." Psalm 145:14

It is a fact that somewhere along life's way you will fall. Maybe the fall will be small, gentle or you will come down with an almighty crash. I'm not talking about the physical fall, although it can be similar as any one of us can slip at any time or place. Likewise it is so important to watch your walk and where you walk. If you walk in snow or ice then the risk of slipping or falling is increased greatly.

In the Christian life, if we put ourselves in a situation of temptation then the risk of falling and giving into temptation will be increased greatly. For example if someone decides to go to a public house or a night club for the evening, then the temptation to drink will be increased greatly. Likewise the temptation to lust after the things of the flesh will be increased greatly as well as being bombarded with the music of this world. The internet is another source where one can easily fall. It is so important to be careful when one is searching and surfing the internet. In the click of a button, the heat of the moment, the weakness of the flesh can easily fail you and you will fall.

These are some examples of how one can fall. This can lead to guilt and the feeling of failure by letting someone close to you down, especially the Lord. If this has happened, go to the Lord immediately and tell Him all about it. Be open and honest with God. He will restore you and by His promise of a forgiving Saviour you will learn the lesson that failure is not final.

A terrible day

1 Samuel 4:15-22

"She named the child Ichabod, saying,
The glory is departed from Israel: because the ark of God was taken" 1 Samuel 4:21

One of the aims in the Christian life should be to give God the glory in everything we say and do. It is a sad thing when the Lord's presence is withdrawn from a situation because of sin. It is much worse though to know for sure that the glory of the Lord has departed.

Here in this lesson we read of a very sad state of affairs. Eli the priest had been warned many times about the behaviour of his two sons, Hophni and Phinehas. They were young priests in the temple of the Lord, yet they committed some terrible crimes and were not punished for them. Eli would not scold them, even after being warned many times to do so. What a lesson for fathers!

Israel had gone into battle with the Philistines only to be terribly defeated. Not only was Israel defeated, but the ark of God was taken and on this day both of Eli's sons were killed in battle. Later on the same day when Eli received the news about the battle and how both his sons had been killed, he fell off his chair at 98 years old, broke his neck and died. On the same day the wife of Phinehas, one of Eli's sons, gave birth to a baby boy. When she heard the news of this most terrible and sad day, she named the child Ichabod, meaning "the glory has departed."

This all happened because of the gross sin of these two men. Surely there is a severe warning here that God cannot and will not tolerate sin. Sin must be dealt with and someone must pay the price at a severe cost. How we need to be on our guard every day lest the glory of God depart from us!

Stay close to God

Psalm 139
"Thou hast set me behind and before..." Psalm 139:5

Whenever Moses was standing in front of the Red Sea with around two million people behind him he was faced with a dilemma. He could neither go forward nor back until the Lord told him to go forward. Here the Psalmist is speaking about a similar situation. The pressures were coming behind him and even greater pressures in front of him. Have you ever felt such pressure? Are you facing such pressure at the moment? Some people thrive when under pressure; others find it more difficult and hardly know how to cope with it.

Very often there are obstacles in front of us and the enemy behind us. We cannot fight these in our own strength; this is why we must stay close to the Lord. It is so important to be strong in our Christian walk. The devil will want to bring you down and keep you down. He will make sure you have a lot of trouble going on at the same time. Then he will want you to start blaming God for the way things are going for you.

The challenge here is to make sure the Lord is before us, within us and behind us. This is the greatest place to be in the Christian life, to be completely surrounded and protected by the Lord Jesus Christ. Every morning you wake up, ask the Lord to watch over you and protect you everywhere you go and in everything you do. Wherever you are, move forward in faith, don't worry or fear, hand your life completely over to God.

IMPACT *Daily readings*

Acknowledging God

Proverbs 3:1-10

"Trust in the LORD with all thine heart; and lean not unto thine own understanding. In all thy ways acknowledge him, and he shall direct thy paths." Proverbs 3:5-6

These two verses are probably the most quoted when giving advice to young people. When a gift is given, then often you will read these verses written inside to help guide the young person in life. I often wondered what these words really meant and why they were so often used. As one progresses in the Christian life then it is easier to understand the importance of these words.

Whenever we trust we have no need to worry but whenever we start to worry then we will find we are trusting very little in the Lord to keep us in the situation. When we start to worry we find that we are relying more on our own strength than that of the Lord's. We tend to bring God into some aspects of our lives but not all of them. Is this your experience quite often? We may always rush on and worry, but life seems to go on. Then think about the verse and read it slowly, over and over again until you fully understand what the Lord wants you to do.

The Lord wants all of our heart, not some of it or a part of it, He wants all! In all our ways the Lord wants to be acknowledged! In our going out and our coming in, plans, relationships and everything the Lord wants to know about these things. If you want the Lord's best in your life, then keep the Lord in your life.

The secret place

Psalm 91

"He that dwelleth in the secret place of the most High
shall abide under the shadow of the Almighty." Psalm 91:1

The subject of prayer cannot be spoken of enough for the believer. This is the secret place with God. No one has any advantage over another in this matter, as God is no respecter of persons; He favours no believer over another. Therefore we all must be personally motivated once again to get back to God.

He that "dwelleth", or continues to dwell, in the secret place will be given tremendous power and authority that other Christians know nothing of. So many are going through the motions and are missing out on so much, namely the secret place of prayer in the presence of God. Maybe now your relationship with God is at an all time low. Maybe you feel you have failed the Lord in so many ways and you seem to keep making mistake after mistake. Now, more than ever, is the time to return to the secret place with God and open and pour out your heart before the Lord. Remember God knows all about you and what you are thinking before you even ask. Surely then, there is no better and safer place for you right now than under the shadow of Almighty God.

When is the last time you felt the real presence under the shadow of the Almighty?

IMPACT *Daily readings*

The attack of the enemy

1 Samuel 31:1-6

"And the battle went sore against Saul, and the archers hit him;
and he was sore wounded of the archers." 1 Samuel 31:3

The great and mighty king Saul had finally been hit by the enemy archers. He was a man and then a King anointed by God to lead the people. He had departed from the Lord and was living in his own strength and wisdom. The Philistines severely wounded him on Mount Gilboa that day, which led him to fall upon his own sword and die. There the mighty king lay slain on the battle field.

The enemies of the Lord and His people are everywhere. We need to be constantly on our guard. The devil's archers want to wound and destroy you too. This is why we need to plead the protection of God every day and night to be upon us. The darts of the devil fly everywhere; someday they will stab us right in the back or even close to the heart. It is so important that we know how to use the shield of faith every day of our Christian lives.

Are the archers closing in upon you today? Are you under constant attack and being constantly harassed by the enemy from whatever source? Then you must plead the power of the Blood of Jesus over your soul, and resist in His name. "Submit yourselves therefore to God. Resist the devil, and he will flee from you." (James 4:7) At the name of Jesus, the precious and powerful name of Jesus every knee must bow. Fight the enemy and claim the victory! Whatever you do, stay both close to and in the will of God.

It's not really ours

1 Chronicles 29:10-19

"For all things come of thee, and of thine own have we given thee." 1 Chronicles 29:14

Have you ever thought for a moment that everything we own isn't really ours anyway? It all ultimately belongs to the Lord and He could take it all away from us in a moment if He chose to do so. Sometimes we can get so caught up with our bricks and mortar down here that we can lose out with God. Many people who once walked well with God have got so caught up with their business affairs that they are no longer a threat to the devil.

That's why the Christians deep in the heart of Africa are the happiest believers in the world. They have very little in this world but their little mud huts and a few tin saucepans to claim as their own. They have no pension to look forward to when they retire so every day they just bless the Lord for another day alive. I have seen these people with mine own eyes; I have been in their mud hut homes. All they want to do is praise the name of Jesus because He truly is everything to them. It is so humbling to see these people and then to go to their church on Sunday, after they walk for a couple of miles, they stand for over an hour praising and praying to God. What have we really given to the Lord whenever we see what He has really given us? We often think giving to God is ten percent of our money; this may be so but what about giving the Lord ten percent of our time every week. Imagine what could be done for Christ then!

What a thoughtful friend

1 Samuel 20:1-10
"Then said Jonathan unto David, whatsoever thy soul desireth,
I will even do it for thee." 1 Samuel 20:4

It is a wonderful thing in this world to have a friend who would do anything for you. It is better to have a few good friends like this than lots of general friends who would do very little for you. David and Jonathan had such a friendship. They loved each other zealously in the Lord. Ever since the day David killed Goliath this fervent friendship seemed to develop. It was strange in many ways because Jonathan was a prince, being the son of King Saul, yet he had so much love and respect for David that he desired David to be the next King. In fact Jonathan would have done anything for David as he promised him, "Whatsoever thy soul desireth, I will even do it for thee."

Is this not a picture of Christ and what He will do for His children? Does the Lord not have a similar fervent and tender love for His children? According to His will He will give you the desire of your heart and whatever your soul requires; encouragement, help, strength, forgiveness and power! He will grant such according to His mighty power as you ask in His will for such things.

David had an enemy who sought for his life; it was King Saul, Jonathan's father. You might think your problems are difficult and complicated. There have been and will be others who are much, much worse. David was on the run until the day King Saul died. Sometimes we have to face the fact and come to the reality that our problems are not going to go away in the morning and may be with us until the day we die.

It's good to have a friend to talk to, help and share things with but it's never a good thing to continually complain of your sorrow with them, else it may weary your friendship.

MPACT *Daily readings*

Follow the needle

Psalm 73:22-28
"Thou shalt guide me with thy counsel." Psalm 73:24

Have you ever watched someone sewing or knitting something? The thread always follows the needle every time. Where the needle goes the thread will follow, into the most unusual shapes, patterns and colours. When a pair of trousers or a shirt needs mended, it's hard to believe what a needle and thread will do. Yet when the sewer gets the thread and needle moving it's not long before the hole is covered up and one can hardly notice where it was. This is a lovely picture of what the Lord Jesus does to lives. Sometimes we need to be broken before we are mended. Do you ever ask yourself where would you be today, if the Lord never intervened in your life?

When we get saved we become like the thread, following the needle. The needle of course is a picture of the Lord Jesus and we want to follow Him everywhere we go. Everything we say, do and every place we go should always have the Lord in sight. Keep close to the Lord, talk to Him every day as you go through the day. The thread will never get through by itself, that is why it needs the needle to make the way more smooth. Likewise the Lord is pleased to use His children to do His work. When the job is done we don't physically see the needle, we see the thread, God's human instruments, yet without the needle it would be impossible. The Lord is pleased to guide and lead His people; He is the All Wise, All Knowing God.

Try tracing the Lord in your life!

IMPACT *Daily readings*

Don't lose the vision

Proverbs 29:1-18

"Where there is no vision, the people perish." Proverbs 29:18

During the summer of 1999, when Joanna and I attended the CEF training centre in Kilchzimmer, Switzerland, I was especially struck by one of the lecturers, Henry Berry, who led the work of CEF in Ireland for many years. With great passion he would love to shout, "Catch the vision, and when you catch the vision, don't lose the vision!" This had a tremendous impact upon me. When I saw the passion in his heart, it made such an impression. It was during that summer that we found our course in life, to reach children and young people for Christ.

Can I share this with you now and ask you what is your vision and passion in life? Not just your hobbies and interests but what is your vision? What about the souls of people, children, young people, married people, families and older people? People all around us are dying every day! What are your plans to reach them for Jesus Christ? People all around us are perishing every day because we have no vision to reach them for the Lord. Try to spend some time today wondering what happens to those around who die without knowing the Lord. The Bible teaches us they are lost forever in that awful place called hell, with no hope at all of escape. Continue to think of all those you know from school or college, friends, neighbours, relations. No doubt there are a lot of people we all know who don't know the Saviour of this world. Get a vision of eternity and the real value of their soul. When you get the vision, don't lose the vision!

IMPACT *Daily readings*

Give yourself unto prayer

Psalm 109:1-15
"But I give myself unto prayer." Psalm 109:4

The enemies of David were speaking lies against him to bring him down. He could have easily fallen into the trap of fighting with them, but rather we see him giving himself to prayer. In his distress David cried unto the Lord in prayer. What a simple yet altogether powerful lesson we can learn today from David.

In your workplace or however you spend your time, maybe even in church circles, there will be those who rise against you and in order to catch you out or bring you down they will lie about you. Lies are often easily told and even easier believed. We must pray that those who lie against us will be silenced and stopped.

When someone rises up against us spreading rumours and lies, it can be an awful, depressing and discouraging experience. God speaks many times in Scripture about liars and even says they will not inherit the kingdom of heaven. It is always good to use wisdom when confronting an enemy about telling lies against you. Make sure you have your facts right and always take a witness with you to keep yourself right. It is best to sort things out early on before it festers out of control. You may find yourself becoming increasingly angry and frustrated with the situation and that's why you must pray and plead to God for help to silence those who rise against you.

IMPACT *Daily readings*

Is God angry with you?

Isaiah 12:1-6

"Though thou wast angry with me, thine anger is turned away,
and thou comfortedst me." Isaiah 12:1

Sometimes when we are not living right before the Lord we can make Him angry. When we turn to Him for repentance and forgiveness then the Lord's anger is turned away from us. Maybe the Lord is angry with you now; if you are saved but not living right then you should be angry with yourself. Once you realise that your life is not right and you really want to come back into fellowship again with the Lord, He will forgive and restore you. Have you lost your joy? Ask the Lord to restore His joy unto you again. It is a terrible thing to live the life of a Christian without the joy of the Lord.

Have you ever noticed when a father chastises his child and the child cries, moments later the child will run back to their father with love and a smile. This is what it is like with the Lord. We just want to keep running to Him. The more we run to Him, the more we love Him and the more we love Him, the less angry we will make Him when we wander afar off. In everything we do, we should do it for the glory of God. Every day of your life, seek to praise the LORD and call upon his name. Declare his doings among the people and make sure that his name is exalted in every area of your life.

IMPACT *Daily readings*

No wicked thing!

Psalm 101

"I will set no wicked thing before mine eyes." Psalm 101:3

The reason God destroyed the world in the days of Noah was because the world was full of wickedness. The people forgot about God and just did what was right in their own eyes as if God didn't exist. Today in many ways it is really no different than it was in the days of Noah. Many people in many parts of the world have forgotten about God. In many parts of the world it is more vile and wicked than it ever was in the days of Noah.

However the Psalmist here was determined that he would set no wicked thing before his eyes. He was admitting that there were wicked things he could have looked at but was determined in his heart not to look at them. He knew they would affect and harm his relationship with the Lord. It would weaken him as a believer and could possibly steal away his joy in the Lord.

Does it concern you that things you maybe look at could affect your relationship with the Lord? It is often hard to resist temptation but resist it we must. We need power from heaven to fight against the wiles and vices of the evil one. We cannot resist temptation to this degree in our own strength. We need to pray and plead with God for overcoming strength to resist wickedness from whatever source it may come from.

Be like the Psalmist and have that same desire that you will set no wicked thing before your eyes.

IMPACT *Daily readings*

Are you easily offended?

Psalm 119:161-168

"Great peace have they which love Thy law, and nothing shall offend them." Psalm 119:165

Has there ever been a time when just after reading the Bible, you experience a wonderful sense of peace and calm that comes over your soul after meditating on the Word of God? The Psalmist speaks about great peace, that people have, who love the law of God. Many Christians today don't have great peace, in fact many have very little peace, many live their lives constantly worrying about every little detail of their lives. The great peace spoken of here is not their experience, yes they maybe have peace with God in their personal relationship with Him, but as far as the Lord taking the reins in their lives, He does not have them. Sometimes it can be a matter of something or someone coming before the Lord.

The greatest people in the world are those who love to meditate on the law and word of God. The law of God is our guide through life, without it we walk around from day to day aimlessly. The law of God should be our joy and delight. This is what it means to fear God, by being afraid of offending God by breaking His law.

We live in a day when people are so easily annoyed and offended than ever before. This verse is teaching me that the more I love the law of God, the greater peace I will have to such a degree that no matter what comes my way I will not be moved, shaken or offended by anything. This would be a wonderful stage to be at in our Christian lives.

Lost fellowship

2 Samuel 14:28-33

"Absalom dwelt two full years in Jerusalem, and saw not the king's face." 2 Sam 14:28

The story of Absalom is one of great sadness as it ended in tragedy. Have you ever noticed that in scripture and in family life today, it always seems to be the children falling out with their parents? Absalom brought terrible grief and sorrow to the heart of King David, his father. In this portion of the Bible, Absalom had been dwelling for two full years in Jerusalem without seeing the face of King David, his father. David mourned for his son every day. Absalom was still the King's son and had cut himself of from fellowship, from the King's face for two full years.

This is like so many today, wandering far away from the King of Kings. When is the last time you "saw the face of the King" in prayer, adoration and fellowship? It is so easy to go on living the Christian life, yes still a son but living afar off. Maybe even reading and praying, but no longer lingering in His presence. Have you become a stranger to real prayer, real intercession with the Lord? Whatever is the problem in your life, don't distance yourself from the King. Come before Him and seek His face afresh. He is patiently waiting for you to come; you have no idea what the King has in store for His wandering children when they return.

MPACT *Daily readings*

Forgiveness is a wonderful thing

Psalm 32

"Blessed is he whose transgression is forgiven, whose sin is covered." Psalm 32:1

Surely this is the greatest blessing a believer can experience. Many people in the world call themselves Christians yet many have no experience of knowing their sins are forgiven. When I think of my life, I was in absolute turmoil until I was 17 years old. On the 25th June 1989 I sought Christ and realised His precious blood would cover and wash my sin all away. My sin will never be remembered again. My transgressions are forgiven, praise His name!

So many Christians today are living with the pain and agony of their sin. The forgiveness and peace of God is the most wonderful thing anyone can experience. How we need to come with freshness every day to ask the Lord to forgive us for all the sin we commit in thoughts, words and things we do that are wrong every day. Put them under the precious blood of Jesus Christ. Remember that "the blood of Jesus Christ his Son cleanseth us from all sin." (1 John 1:7)

So many people today doubt their salvation. They spend their entire lives in misery and depression but rather they should be the happiest people on earth! God has forgiven them, Christ has saved them, the Spirit of God lives within them but yet they are so miserable. Are you one of these people? My dear friend, you will be blessed when you fully believe with faith that if you have asked Him, then your sins are forgiven, they are covered in His blood and gone forever.

How does it make you feel to know your sins are forgiven?

IMPACT *Daily readings*

I have set before you life and death

Deuteronomy 3:21-27

"I call heaven and earth to record this day against you,
that I have set before you life and death, blessing and cursing:
therefore choose life, that both thou and thy seed may live." Deuteronomy 3:27

Moses is pleading with the children of Israel not to forsake the ways of God. How often we need to be reminded to keep going on. They were about to cross over the River Jordan very soon. Once there, they would begin new lives. This was a very solemn charge put to the people. If they followed God they would have life and be blessed, but if they didn't follow the Lord then they would be cursed and see death.

There was no middle road for the people to choose from, it was life or death. Just like today, either we are saved or not, we are following Christ or not. It is either eternal life or eternal death, no middle ground, no second chance, no excuses. We must decide, 'choose ye this day whom ye will serve,' the scriptures ask us. You will either open or close your home to salvation. If you close it, how will they hear and if you open it, all then can hear.

Don't run from the fight!

Psalm 78:1-9

"...turned back in the day of battle." Psalm 78:9

The challenge in this Psalm is to make God known to all generations. The law of God in the commandments needs to be taught to every generation of children. Verse 6 reminds us 'that the generation to come might know [them, even] the children [which] should be born.' Then the very challenging question follows, who should arise and teach these children?

Why do we want to teach the children? The answer is in verse 7, that they might set their hope in God. If we fail to do this, the Psalmist tells us they will grow up to be like their fathers, a stubborn and rebellious people, a generation whose hearts were not right nor were they stedfast with God. Pray that we would not be like the children of Ephraim who were armed and turned back in the day of battle. We are armed today because we have the truth; we have God's Word in our hands and heart. The children are easy to reach, opportunities abound everywhere, and I see and witness it for myself. Don't quit or give up as many today get discouraged and despondent so easily in the Christian life. God needs an army of human instruments working away for him reaching the rising generation for Christ. Play your part and do what you can to make sure they are reached.

The flowing waters

Proverbs 18:1-24

"The words of a man's mouth are as deep waters, and the wellspring of wisdom as a flowing brook." Proverbs 18:4

One of the most peaceful places to be is by a riverside. I love water, not just water fights or soaking people but actually being beside a river. It is so peaceful and quiet. The world continues to move on and yet the river just flows by. This is a tremdeous lesson for us in the busy world in which we live. A river keeps flowing no matter what is around it. There can be cattle, tractors or people and still the river flows, nothing can stop a river flowing, unless the source itself is dried up.

Many Christians today are drying up, so caught up with the world around them, they cease to flow the way they once did. When a river stops flowing, it becomes stagnant and no good for people, fish or even to be around. This is like the dried up Christian, there is no longer sweet fellowship to be enjoyed. Being around a Christian flowing from God is wonderful. They are so in touch with the source of their Master, the Lord God.

Facing your giants

1 Samuel 17:20-51

"This day will the LORD deliver thee into mine hand;
and I will smite thee, and take thine head from thee...
that all the earth may know that there is a God in Israel." 1 Samuel 17:46

This is probably one of the most popular and favourite of all the Bible stories found in scripture that children enjoy. This is because it has a big bully of a giant and a little boy that stands up to him. Against all the odds of human nature, David takes on the giant Goliath and kills him. From this moment in David's life he became an instant hero.

All of us have giants in our lives and if we are honest they seem to be winning against us all the time. Giants are things in our lives that we think are too big for us to beat or overcome. Examples of these giants can be worry, stress, wrong relationships, peer pressure, bullies, to list but a few. Whatever the giant is in your life, you must defeat it before it defeats you. Notice how David came to fight this giant in the strength of the Lord. We cannot face life's battles on our own strength. Humanly speaking we are not strong enough. Our giants will defeat us and make us weaker and weaker until we find ourselves living in constant fear all the time.

From today whatever the giant is in your life, face it head on and be determined in your heart that you will win, you will have the victory. With God's help, He will give you the victory over your giants.

Growing old!

Psalm 92

"They shall still bring forth fruit in old age." Psalm 92:14

So many people dread growing old. They spend their whole lives afraid of growing old, and in their old age regretting not being young again. Time will not wait for anyone. We have only one opportunity at childhood, youth and then we grow old like those all around us.

Growing old can be a very peaceful and pleasurable experience when one is right with God; otherwise, it can be a time of great fear and dread. The thought of growing old without Christ is a terrible thought. I remember while living in Australia, visiting an old man in hospital. He was dying, so I tried to minister and witness to him as best I could. He was clearly dying and he knew it too. But as I got to sharing Christ with him, he became so angry and told me to 'stop yapping at him.' Can you imagine, at this stage of his life, Christ was his only hope and he yelled with all his might to stop. As I was leaving, very sad and heavy hearted, he called me back, and asked me to tell him some more. His final words I heard him say were "Lord save me". After sharing this story with his wife in her home, I had the joy of seeing her come to Christ as well.

As we grow old we can still bear fruit for Christ, even in our old age. Don't stop living for Christ as you grow old, don't consider retiring in the Christian life, yes make room for and encourage others in service but don't quit serving, there is so much still to do and so much you can do.

IMPACT *Daily readings*

The Lord is my Shepherd

Psalm 23

"The LORD is my shepherd; I shall not want." Psalm 23:1

This is probably the best known portion in the entire Bible. If you randomly ask someone in the street if they can tell you any verse in the Bible, this will no doubt be the most common. It is also known as the funeral Psalm as it is commonly sung at funerals. Sometimes we can miss the simplicity and the personal message God gives to us in His Word in relation to a verse like this.

To fully understand and appreciate what the Psalmist is saying here can easily be missed. He in effect is telling us how the Lord is his shepherd and he has need of nothing. Contrast this to the Christian today, who has so much and at the same time is not really content. There is always something to mumble, grumble and complain about. Even though we know it's wrong we still compare our lives and what we have to others. This is a great lesson in life to take our eyes off others and fix our eyes upon Jesus. When we have the Lord Jesus, then He is our everything. Sometimes the Lord will test us to see how much we love Him, trust Him and rely on Him. To fully test us sometimes we need to lose everything we ever had to appreciate the only thing we ever need.

Who is leading your life?

Genesis 33:1-12

"Let us take our journey, and let us go, and I will go before thee." Genesis 33:12

Are you at the stage in your Christian life right now when everything doesn't seem to be going the way you would like it to? Maybe you are in a rut or in an awkward situation and there doesn't seem to be any way out. Are you studying or working and you don't see any real future where you are at right now?

Then we have a wonderful promise for you. Read Isaiah 45:2 we know that our all-loving, wonder working God does and will go before us. He will prepare the way, provide for the journey and ensure our safety as we go. Jehovah God goes before us making the crooked places straight. Sometimes life can become crooked and we try to straighten the way ourselves. It's tough, it doesn't seem to work and in fact there doesn't even seem to be a possible way. But then the Lord says, "I will go...before you... and I will help you...by making the crooked places and even people in your life straight." Stop trying to straighten things out yourself and getting all frustrated, worried and angry. Learn to let go and let God work in your life.

Look back over your shoulder and see where the Lord has made many a crooked place straight for you in the past. Is He not able to do the same again? Commit your present circumstance to Him and watch with wonder and amazement as God again straightens out everything for you in His own skilful manner.

IMPACT *Daily readings*

God knows your voice

2 Chronicles 18:22-31

"Fight ye not with small or great." 2 Chronicles 18:30

Sometimes we can find ourselves in desperate situations, even to the extent of being in tears over a matter. We don't really know the way out or the way forward. We feel so helpless and even hopeless. No one seems to understand or even really care. Well, this makes your situation special because God cares, loves you and even knows the way forward for you.

In this passage before us Jehoshaphat was in real danger, being surrounded by the enemy, with no real hope or way out. He was in the midst of battle and the pressures and struggles of real life were upon him. Jehoshaphat quickly realised that in his own strength he could not win. Then he humbly cried unto God. He was in the heat of battle and the enemy was too great for him. The Lord immediately responded to the cry of His child and delivered him from his trouble. Sometimes we don't need to fight, the Lord can fight our battles for us.

Jesus is the same yesterday, today and forever. God never changes! He said, "I am the Lord, I change not". If He can help His people in Bible times, then my friend, He can help you today! Right now. Take yourself off alone and cry upon His name for help. Has He ever failed you in the past? He waits to help you! Just come to Him as you are, as a child to a father. He specialises in helping people and bringing them out of troublesome situations.

Remember nothing or no-one is too hard for the Lord...especially your situation.

From morning till night

Psalm 92

"To shew forth thy loving-kindness in the morning
and thy faithfulness every night." Psalm 92:2

There are some things in life we tend to take for granted more than others. One of these are generally giving thanks or being thankful to the Lord for everything. Some people keep a journal throughout their lives of things that happen and places they go to etc. What about keeping a notebook about all the good things that happen to you. Good days you have had, nice people you have met and especially when the Lord blesses you in some form or another.

The Psalmist is referring to the Lord's goodness to him in the morning right throughout the day until His faithfulness to him at night. God is faithful, He is unchangeable, we are the ones who change like the wind, but Christ is the solid Rock who never changes. He says in His Word, "I am the Lord, I change not." Sometimes we need to take the focus of us and away from our problems and fix our focus upon the Lord and all He means to us. The less we are and the more He becomes is a good way to be. You will be greatly encouraged in your own soul as you think of how kind, loving and faithful God really is. Has He ever let you down? Why then do we keep failing Him?

Help me understand!

Psalm 119:33-40
"Give me understanding, and I shall keep thy law;
yea, I shall observe it with my whole heart." Psalm 119:34

One of the great dangers in the Christian life is not growing. Sometimes a year later in our Christian walk we are no further on with God, no closer to Him and have no further or greater knowledge of His Word to our hearts. Whenever we read the Word of God, the Bible, it is always a good thing to ask the Lord to bless His Word to your heart. Ask Him to teach you, to give you understanding as you read.

What is just as important is applying the word to your heart. Putting into practice what you have been reading. Don't just be someone who reads the word of God, but someone who is a doer and does what the scriptures tells you to do. Sometimes we can read a lot and understand only a little of what we have been reading.

It is a good thing to read less and understand more. Pray before you read, while you read and after you read. Ask the Lord to give you understanding, to reveal His Word unto you. Ask Him to speak to you as you read. There is so much to gain in the Christian life that time is too short to lose out with God. Pray against sin and coldness of heart, re-start your reading with greater passion and understanding today. Don't just read half-heartedly but rather with your whole heart.

IMPACT *Daily readings*

Behaving wisely

1 Samuel 18:1-9

"David went out whithersoever Saul sent him,
and behaved himself wisely: and Saul set him over the men of war,
and he was accepted in the sight of all the people." 1 Samuel 18:5

We read in this chapter four times that David behaved himself wisely. His life was now in constant danger from King Saul. God had withdrawn His Spirit from Saul and in fact placed an evil spirit within him. Saul was constantly angry, frustrated and jealous of David.

This is where we can learn so much from David. Saul was David's boss. Whatever Saul told David to do, he did it, wherever he told David to go he went. He never argued or complained. Even though David had a position of huge responsibility, he still "behaved himself wisely" (v 5).

The secret of course of David's success was that the Lord was with him (v4). Due to this, Saul was afraid of David. The people now thought more of David than they did of Saul. They continually praised David for his success. David behaved himself wisely in all his ways (v14) and again in verse 15 he behaved very wisely, so much so that Saul was afraid of him. Saul became David's continual enemy, he sought David's death more than anything, but again we read in v30 how David behaved himself more wisely than all the others.

Maybe there is someone you work or study with and they hate you and are always trying to bring you down, then learn from David. Stay close to the Lord, watch your back, don't react rashly at any time and always behave wisely in everything you do.

MPACT *Daily readings*

Troubles keep mounting!

Psalm 46

"God is our refuge and strength, a very present help in trouble." Psalm 46:1

Is it the same with you that when trouble comes it seldom comes alone, often in three's some say? This forty sixth Psalm has been a tremendous source of encouragement to many over the years. It is one of those Psalms that is worth memorising because it will encourage you so much when your trouble comes. Often trouble comes when we least expect it, that is why it is so important to build up a good supply of God's Word to strengthen and encourage you through these difficult times when trouble comes your way.

Sometimes folk are in very difficult situations, life becomes difficult and everything seems to be going against them. This is why it is so important to keep close to the Lord, He will steer you through to the end. He is a very present help. Therefore it would pay you greatly to bring your troubles to the Lord. On the other hand there are those whose life seems to be a constant struggle when really it is not so bad. They are often very negative in their outlook on life, the glass is always half empty. I would love to take them for a walk through the hospital wards and soon the troubles they think they have will soon disappear and they will soon realise they are not so bad after all compared to some.

IMPACT *Daily readings*

What a wise person does

Proverbs 3:1-7

"Be not wise in thine own eyes: fear the LORD, and depart from evil" Proverbs 3:7

There is a tremendous challenge to parents here in this verse. Many today are so focused on their children having the best education, the best careers and the best weddings and all very well. But what about praying for your child to put all on the altar for Jesus? Praying that your child will have the call of God upon his or her life to serve the Lord in the far ends of the earth. It's good to pray for the salvation of your children and keep praying, but what is the real reason and motivation for this, is it so that they will not go to hell? Is it sinful to stop praying for the Lord to take your child and use them for whatever He pleases to do? Even if it is far away from you, reaching people who are far far away from God.

The scriptures tell us that 'he that winneth souls is wise.' This verse tells us that the wise, turn many unto righteousness. Sometimes we can be wise in this world. People are more educated than ever before and yet the unemployment levels are at an all record high. So education doesn't necessarily make one wise, it may give you brains but no wisdom, there are a lot of smart people out there with no common sense. This surely should be the great goal of every Christian, to turn many to righteousness. How many have you brought to the Lord in your lifetime? Is there anyone who has turned to righteousness because of your righteousness? Seek to turn many to the Lord in your lifetime. That's a challenging thought!

IMPACT *Daily readings*

In times of trouble

Psalm 91

"I will be with him in trouble; I will deliver him and honour him." Psalm 91:15

Away back in the year 1922, in the Western Hebrides, a five year old boy lay, dying of diphtheria. His mother had to turn away in tears, so she could not witness his last breath. Just at that moment, there came a knock at the door. It was her brother-in-law, from the nearby village. "I've just come to tell you that you don't have to worry about the child. He is going to recover, and, one day, God is going to save his soul." "Whatever makes you think that?" exclaimed the distraught mother.

"I've been sitting by the fire tonight reading Psalm 91, and God distinctly spoke to me through the last three verses."

The words of that brother-in-law proved to be prophetic. The boy did recover and was gloriously saved 13 years later. The boy's name was William MacDonald, famous for his Bible commentaries. The word of God was real and came home like a hammer of conviction to that uncle. The Lord hasn't changed; His Word hasn't changed, so why should we not read with expectation expecting God to speak to us with the same clarity, power and conviction.

Whatever trouble you may find yourself in, remember the Lord is there to be with you in the trouble and if it be His will, to bring you out of the trouble as well.

How much do I really care?

Psalm 142

"I looked on my right hand, and beheld, but there was no man
that would know me: refuge failed me; no man cared for my soul." Psalm 142:4

How often do we walk past strangers and we look at them and they look at us and we just keep walking? Maybe they were ripe and ready for the gospel, ripe and ready to be loved, ripe and ready to receive Christ, but we didn't really care. If we are honest before the Lord, most of us have reacted this way many times.

The Psalmist here was that person in need, yet no one seemed to care for his soul. All around us there are people who yearn for someone to care for them to have an interest in them, to talk and take time for them. Yet, we don't bother; maybe we don't have time or is it because we just don't care? What about their soul? Do we really care for their soul, whether it be lost, really lost? The Lord has saved us so that we look out for souls to rescue them from perishing. Do we have a burden for souls, a real burden? When is the last time we shed tears over lost, perishing souls, family, friends, strangers, precious souls dying without Christ?

The next time the Lord presses a soul upon you, go at once and tell them. God is preparing the way so you must go now and go quickly. Maybe you cannot go, call them, text them, email them. Are you ashamed of the gospel, are you ashamed of Christ? After all He has done for you, why not go and tell some poor soul today? It could change you and them forever.

How much do you really care for the souls of strangers?

Head knowledge or heart knowledge

Proverbs 19:1-10

"That the soul be without knowledge it is not good" Proverbs 19:2

The book of Proverbs is so full of wisdom; every little verse has so much truth and wisdom found within it. The old saying goes, "an apple a day keeps the doctor away." we could almost say, "a proverb a day keeps the devil away." Today there is much focus, more than ever before on education. Many children even of primary school age are having private tutoring so that they will become academically brilliant, pass all their exams and end up in the best university possible. This is well and good if that's what you want for your children. I firmly believe that not all children need to go to university. Of course there is a time and place for everything, but when everyone eventually has a university degree of some description, how can one tell who has knowledge and who hasn't.

Sometimes we can be so focused on our heads being full of knowledge, and blind to the starvation of our souls. This is the challenge here, that if our souls be without knowledge it is not good. Someone once told me, as a Bible college student, that the easiest place to backslide is in Bible College. The reason being is that they are so busy cramming their heads full of knowledge to pass exams, that they often can neglect their quiet times with God, therefore starving their souls. I have no formal education at all, never even made it to P7 in primary school, yet I find myself in some of the most intellectual schools in the country, instructing children not to neglect their souls at the expense of their heads. On my way home I often chuckle to myself at the very thought of it.

IMPACT *Daily readings*

The deceitful man

Psalm 101

"He that worketh deceit shall not dwell within my house." Psalm 101:7

Dishonesty and deceit are two terrible things. Some people, including Christians are among the most deceitful people on earth. Within the business world they seem to think they can justify their wrong doings by dressing up and going to church on Sunday morning. Sometimes they can think by telling lies as long as they aren't too big is all right in their eyes. The Lord puts deceitfulness and lying as among the worst crimes we can commit, in fact it goes on to tell us in His Word that such people shall not enter into the kingdom of heaven.

I remember many years ago I asked a friend to tile our new house. It was our first home. I didn't ask around for quotations, he gave me a fair price to tile the walls and floors of the kitchen and bathroom. After he was finished he gave me a massive bill, charging for all the broken tiles, stuff he ordered that he never used and all sorts of extras. When I talked to him about it he said it was normal practice and it was a good price. I then phoned around ten other tilers and asked their opinion; every one said they charge by the square metre. My friend insisted he was right. I paid my bill and told him our friendship was over because I felt he was being deceitful. On another occasion I was working around the garden. Another friend of mine told me he was off work on a public holiday so he came and helped me. At the end of the day I asked him if he wanted any money for helping me. I was shocked when he demanded double what he would normally get for a day's work; he said it was a public holiday. I also paid him his money and told him he had just lost a good friend. By quoting the above Psalm they soon realised my Christian life was a serious matter and they were no longer welcome in my home. Both of these men were professing Christians to their shame might I add.

IMPACT *Daily readings*

Patience in waiting

Exodus 14:13-31

"And Moses said unto the people, Fear ye not, stand still, and see the salvation of the LORD, which he will show to you today: for the Egyptians whom ye have seen today, ye shall see them again no more for ever." Exodus 14:13

Pharaoh in his wrath and anger was pursuing Moses and the children of Israel with his Egyptian army. The tenth plague had just come upon the Egyptians and Pharaoh had shouted at Moses to go. After realising what he had done by letting them go, he gathered the whole army to bring back the children of Israel.

Moses led the people right to the Red Sea and as they looked behind them, there in the dust and the distance was Pharaoh and his powerful Egyptian army. The people were so shocked, annoyed, disappointed and even angry. Then they began to blame Moses by saying he should have let them stay in Egypt to serve the Egyptians. At any moment the army would come upon them with full power. Their only choice was to be drowned in the sea or be killed by the sword! There was absolutely no hope..... or was there?

Just at that moment God stepped in. Moses reassured the people and told them not be afraid, to stand still and watch God work. Just then before their very eyes the sea parted and God made a path for them to walk to their deliverance and safety. Once they were all across, the Egyptian army tried to follow but before they could reach dry land, the walls of water toppled in over them to their destruction.

God does not change. Are you in an impossible situation right now with no hope or no way to turn? Then fear not, stand still and watch God work for you too. He can and He will if you completely trust Him whatever your situation.

IMPACT *Daily readings*

Forgiven

Psalm 103

"He hath not dealt with us after our sins;
nor rewarded us according to our iniquities." Psalm 103:10

Without doubt the Psalms truly are a great tonic for the soul. What a comfort they are to the child of God as they read them. Many Christians are troubled about their past sins, whether they were physical, emotional or other types of sin that happened in their sinful days. The devil has an field day when he makes Christians remember their past. Every time we try to do right in our Christian life, the devil tells us to remember the time when...Or maybe you are in a difficult situation in life and you have been praying about something year upon year and there just doesn't seem to be an answer. Then the devil again says "you remember when"...and off he goes.

Well, my dear friend, we must take scripture at face value and think about what God says in light of His Word. The Lord does not deal with us according to our sins. As far as the east is from the west so far has the Lord removed our sins from us and will remember them no more. This is the power of forgiveness with the Lord, unlike most human beings who seldom forgive and never forget. How thankful we must be today to know and realise that we have been forgiven! When Christ forgives He forgets. When He says He has forgotten all about it once you have genuinely sought forgiveness, then rest assured my friend He will remember it no more! Please stop lingering over regrets in your life. Whatever has happened, bring it to the cross and move on with your life and enjoy the wonderful benefits that Christ has in store for you.

Is there something you regret doing in your life that seems to hinder your walk with God and brings continual sadness to your heart and soul? Then read the above verse over and over again until it sinks in.

Instruction from God

Psalm 32

"I will instruct thee and teach thee in the way which thou shalt go." Psalm 32:8

The Lord makes it clear to the Psalmist that He would give clear instruction to him as in the way he should go with his life. This is what the Lord wants to do with all of His children. He wants to guide every one of us. He knows exactly the way our lives are to go. He has clear instruction for everyone of us. The question is are we willing to listen to the instruction? Even when we are being given it, are we concentrating on what the Lord is telling us? In school, students aren't allowed to use their phones or look at worldly magazines during their lessons. How can we then expect God to instruct us when we have a phone on one hand and a book or magazine on the other?

God doesn't work like that my friend, there needs to be an earnestness to seek God. We have got to cast away everything else that would distract our listening to the voice of God. God does not like laziness, nor the half hearted Christian. Very often to find God's will in your life it will cost you something. The question is are you prepared to pay the price? It may mean rising up early in the morning to hear from God. It may mean giving up your worldly possessions to live somewhere more primitive or it could even mean breaking up with that boy or girl you have recently started dating because you know it's not the will of God. The Lord will instruct you in the way which you should go, if you will just take the time to wait upon Him.

Walking through the fire

Daniel 3:19-30

"He answered and said, Lo, I see four men loose, walking in the midst of the fire, and they have no hurt; and the form of the fourth is like the Son of God." Daniel 3:25

We have here one of the most beautiful illustrations of the presence of Christ in the entire Bible. King Nebuchadnezzar had commanded Daniel's three friends Shadrach, Meshach and Abednego to bow down and worship the golden image that he had set up. But they refused to bow to it. As a result they were thrown into a fiery furnace to be burned alive. King Nebuchadnezzar watched to see them burn but to his amazement they were unharmed. In the furnace stood four people, despite the fact that only three had entered. The fourth figure was different; He was like unto the Son of God. As a result no harm came to the three men.

Jesus Christ, the precious Son of God was with them in the fire. Praise His name He can still walk with us through the fire today. It can be the fire of personal affliction. A situation you are going through that doesn't seem to get any better. It can be the fiery flames of fire of severe temptation. You know that on your own you would have yielded a long time ago. Maybe your trial is from financial pressure or an uncertain future is a fire you thought you would never be in. Christ can be with you in the fire to protect and encourage you, to help and to guide you. Certain dangers can be avoided when Christ is with you in the fires of life that may come your way.

What trials and fires are you passing through right now? Commit them afresh to the Lord.

Make every day count

Psalm 90

"So teach us to number our days, that we may apply our
hearts unto wisdom." Psalm 90:12

Here is a lovely verse to help us take note for a moment. The challenge is to number our days. I have met so many people who look forward to retiring so they can do something for the Lord. The reason they give is that they will have so much more time. This sounds like a really good idea but in reality I don't think it will work. I have known many people who were very active in serving the Lord and when they retire they seem to have even less time as most time is taken up with looking after their grandchildren.

I would suggest that you get into the habit now to do something for the Lord. It doesn't have to be an hour a day, or an hour a week. It can be ten minutes here and ten minutes there. Speak to this one and visit that one, in doing so you will soon find the time to do more and more for the Lord. We are taught to number our days, not one of us is guaranteed to have a long life. If you plan to start serving the Lord when you are sixty-five, all probability is that you will never do anything for Him. Why don't you start to do something today for the Lord? Hold a mission, a Bible Club, do whatever it takes to get unsaved people under the sound of God's Word. The Lord blesses such efforts in His name. From today make every day count for God. Time is quickly running out!

Speak up for God!

Psalm 66

"Come and hear, all ye that fear God,
and I will declare what he hath done for my soul." Psalm 66:16

It is amazing how the Psalmist continues to acknowledge God in his life. No matter what circumstance he seems to find himself in, he continually thinks and talks about the Lord. Wherever he went he sought to witness about the Lord and what He had done for Him. Here we cannot miss the opportunity of wondering when was the last time we spoke up for the Lord? If the Lord really means so much to us, why then do we not speak more about Him to everyone around us?

How easy it is to talk about our holidays, car, job, family, but speaking about the Lord seems to be a little or a big bit different. After church, start to talk with someone about the sermon the preacher preached about, (if you remember what it was, that is.) Don't be surprised if the Christian looks at you strangely and suddenly the moment becomes awkward and the conversation seems to dry up. Rather than be put off by this reality, seek to speak up for the Lord. Give your testimony to everyone you know. Speak with feeling in your heart; use it to win others for Christ. The Apostle Paul testified everywhere he went. It wasn't long before everyone around him knew where he stood with God.

If you were taken to court and tried for being a Christian, would there be enough evidence to prove you guilty?

IMPACT *Daily readings*

The Lord gives counsel

Psalm 16

"I will bless the Lord who hath given me counsel." Psalm 16:7

Whenever we think about guidance and counsel from the Lord, it really does depend on whether we accept it or not. Sometimes we pray to the Lord about a certain situation and if we are honest most of the time we already have our minds made up and we just want the Lord to approve it. The question then is do we want to live in God's will or our own will? Follow God's way or our way?

When you are in doubt about your course in life then you need to urgently seek the Lord in prayer about the matter. Many people have the opinion to sit back and wait until the Lord opens the door. I have a different opinion, I believe there are many open doors, and when you try to open that door, and if it is the wrong one then the Lord will shut it firmly. If you insist upon that closed door, then the Lord may need to slam that door in your face, which is not always pleasant. Pray that the door you come to will be the open door God has for you. God gave us wisdom and brains; I think it pleases him when we use them. Especially things like common sense and discernment, ask the Lord to teach you and help you to use these wisely.

When the Lord does give you counsel and instruction from His Word, don't forget to thank and bless the Lord for helping and guiding you. Keep in the Word for daily direction in life; this is what He is pleased to use to speak to us His children.

Something God does not tolerate

Isaiah 52:7-15

"Be ye clean, that bear the vessels of the LORD." Isaiah 52:11

There is a warning here for all Christians but especially for those involved in any aspect of the Lord's work. God cannot and will not tolerate deliberate sin. God has standards, high standards for His servants. They are high standards of purity and holiness. The challenge to remain separated from this world is more challenging today than ever before. Too many churches and individual Christians are living so close to the world it is almost impossible to tell the difference.

To "bear the vessels of the Lord" is a wonderful privilege. Together with it also comes a tremendous responsibility. God exhorts us to be clean; He will not use a dirty vessel to do His work. The calling of God to an aspect of His work is a wonderful privilege of the highest kind, to serve and represent the Lord of Lords and King of Kings.

May this be a time of soul searching, heart wrenching and flesh culling for all of us. Surely it is time we came clean before the Lord, therefore confessing any continual or known sin is vital. How much more effective can we be to bear the vessels of the Lord after we have cleansed ourselves afresh in the precious blood of Christ.

Am I ready to stand before the Lord on the great judgement day with honesty?

IMPACT *Daily readings*

Not in my own strength!

Psalm 119:110-120

"Hold thou me up, and I shall be safe." Psalm 119:117

One of the greatest lessons I ever learned in the Christian life is that I cannot live for and serve God in my own strength. Every day and especially every time I seek to do something or say something it is important that I realise I need to be filled with the Holy Spirit to do this. Many Christians fall by the wayside here, they tend to live the Christian life in their own strength. Many have made ship wreck in the Christian life, fighting the fight in your own strength will never gain victory. This is a spiritual battle you are engaging in, fighting against the world, flesh and the devil. In our own strength we will never have victory.

However with Christ we will have constant victory, because He cannot be defeated. We need to trust in the Lord every single day for divine protection. We need power to fight and power to live. This power comes from God, ask the Lord today for this power. Ask Him to fill you with His power, ask Him every day for power, Holy Ghost power and you will be a new person. All the downcast, depression and continual failure will soon flee because you are now fully trusting in Christ, this will make all the difference when you stop relying in your own strength and fully rely in God.

He is here to help

Psalm 50:1-15

"Call upon me in the day of trouble: I will deliver thee, and thou shalt glorify me."

Psalm 50:15

Have you ever found yourself in trouble? I'm not really thinking about being in trouble with your parents, school or even the police. I mean trouble in the sense of pressure, like tough decisions having to be made on your part and you find yourself in real trouble. Maybe there is no way out as finances are mounting and all your post seems to be bills or pressure at work, family crisis and the list goes on and on.

Well then, have good cheer as this Psalm is for you! Have you considered the Lord in all this? Are you telling me the God who made this world, Creator of Heaven and earth, Saviour of precious souls cannot steer you back onto the straight and narrow? Well I'm telling you He can and He will. He says "Call upon me and I will deliver you!" Maybe God is speaking personally now to you. Maybe you are in a crisis right now and maybe you have tried all else, friends, family, even the bank can't help you! Your frustration is mounting. What will you do? God says, "Call upon me."

Of course we must take every verse of scripture and read it in its context; the previous verse tells us to offer unto God thanksgiving. It talks about paying your vows, maybe promises you once made when all was well. Have you forgotten? Is this another reminder? Only this time it's more serious. I believe if you call upon the Lord with all your heart and soul like you really mean it then the God of all comfort will bring comfort to your soul and bring you out of your trouble.

In all your trouble, have you seriously considered seeking the Lord for help?

Do you continually worry?

Psalm 27:1-14

"The LORD is my light and my salvation; whom shall I fear?
the LORD is the strength of my life; of whom shall I be afraid?" Psalm 27:1

This is the Christian's secret in life, knowing God in a personal way. The Lord must be the focus of everything we do in life. He not only has become our salvation, but He is our light along the way. When times become dark and the pathway in life unclear, then remember the Lord is our light. He will give you direction along the way to lead and guide you in the way in which you should go.

People today are full of fear and worry about so much, including the child of God. The Psalmist was saying, in reality, because God was with him, why should he or who should he be afraid of. The Lord was his strength, the shoulder he would lean on; the God he would rely on. God was everything to him; he trusted completely in the Lord therefore he was afraid of no one or anything. Even though constant danger was always around him and people sought his life, he still said with confidence because God is with me I am not afraid of you.

Let the Lord take away all your worries, fears and anxieties today. He specialises in helping the fearful. Many times we read in His word, 'fear not, for I am with you.' We have no reason to be weak, fearful or even tearful because our strength comes from God. He is mighty to save and mighty to keep and look after you.

Bring back the tears

Psalm 126

"They that sow in tears shall reap in joy." Psalm 126:5

During great times of revival there clearly was a working of God and many sinners repented of their sin and were gloriously converted. Many of the preachers were maybe not the best of preachers, but many of them wept and yearned over souls, travailing in prayer until God broke through and souls were swept into the kingdom.

When is the last time you saw your minister weep over souls? When is the last time any of us wept over souls to come to Jesus? Today many preachers are very fundamental, clear, concise but yet as cold as steel. Many of them are so unapproachable. They stand so mighty and proud as if they were closer to God than the Christian in the pew. General Booth once received a letter from one of his officers lamenting that he saw very little fruit for all his preaching, and asked the generals advice. The reply came back in two words, "Try Tears!"

How we all need to get a fresh vision of Calvary love today, and see once again what it cost God to send His Son Jesus into this world for us, and what Jesus had to go through to pay for our sin on Calvary's tree. Then on the other hand lift the lid of the road to hell, and see the flames and the screams of loved ones shouting, "Why didn't you tell me about Jesus?" Would that not move you to tears, as we think of countless millions heading downwards and few there be who care?

IMPACT *Daily readings*

The graveyard is the same for all!

Ecclesiastes 12:1-7

"Man goeth to his long home, and the mourners go about the streets." Ecclesiastes 12:5

Isn't it amazing that throughout life we easily fall into the trap of putting people into classes of distinction? We judge people by the way they look, dress, the car they drive, the job they have and even by the house they live in. We can easily be intimidated by such people and yet, on the other hand when we are blessed with fortune we can easily start to look down at people.

Let's fast forward life and go for a drive to the local graveyard and take a walk. Have you ever noticed how quiet a graveyard is? Everyone now seems to be equal, all lying still, in a box below the ground. Is it now so important how they lived, what car they drove, how they dressed and what job they had? Living is important but dying is even more important. How we die is something worth considering. Not physically but spiritually, none of us know the day or the hour when we will die. We must be ready; Christians will give account of their living and serving. On the other hand those who are unsaved will give account of all their missed opportunities of rejecting Christ and His glorious gospel.

Every day we live we are one day closer to death; this is why it is good to make good preparations to meet God. "Prepare to meet thy God," Amos tells us. We will be a long time dead people often say, so enjoy live to the full. This is true in many ways but, since we have only a short life to give to God, why not give Him our very best because He alone is worthy!

The praising Christian is often a powerful Christian

Psalm 107
"Oh, that men would praise the Lord for His goodness." Psalm 107:8

If there is anything that pleases the Lord here on this earth, it is when His people praise Him. Many praise the name of the Lord with their lips, but real praise comes from the heart. The word praise is referred to many times in the Psalms, four times alone in this one Psalm. The Psalmist would often be found praising the Lord, not just when all was going well, but also when things were not going so well with him.

This is very encouraging! Sometimes we can be discouraged and even feel a little bit low. One of the best ways to overcome this is to quietly or loudly praise the Lord. This can take the focus away from our difficulties and place it on the Lord. It pleases the Lord that we can praise Him in the good times and the bad times. Have you ever wondered and pondered how good the Lord is and how good He has been to you? Is He not worthy of our praise? Sometimes we can be embarrassed about worshipping and praising the name of Jesus. The world gladly sings and plays their music, why then are we embarrassed to sing the songs of God and really worship Him? We need to take our eyes off man and focus more on the One we are praising, not on how we sound but rather on who we praise. Don't worry about what others think of you! God is greatly pleased with every effort we make to praise Him. After all, when we consider all He has done for us, how can we do anything else but praise the Lord?

Make good use of your words!

Psalm 79:1-13

"We will shew forth thy praise to all generations" Psalms 79:13

Someone once said of a good sermon, either you will come away greatly strengthened or wake up greatly refreshed. Whenever we think about our conversations, sometimes we spend hours talking a lot of nonsense, idle talk. Try to steer the conversation around to the things of God and see if the excitement and enthusiasm continues.

The Psalmist endeavoured to praise the Lord all day long from morning until evening and through the night too. His conversation was on the righteousness of God, not on some worldly affair. Very often Christians meet up for fellowship which is great, but God sometimes is not even mentioned or spoken to. It is impossible to build yourself up as a Christian without speaking to or about the Lord. You will be greatly encouraged and strengthened in your walk with God if you bring Him into the conversation. Be the one who turns the conversation around, this is a great challenge for you, the next time you meet with Christian friends or even unbelievers, see how long it takes for you to turn the conversation around to the things of God.

Your affliction is for your own good!

Psalm 119:65-72

"It is good for me that I have been afflicted; that I might learn thy statutes." Psalm 119:71

This is a very challenging verse; the Psalmist is telling us that he is glad to have been afflicted because it has brought him back to God. Have you ever thought about that? Maybe God has brought you to where you are at today so that you might realise that you are in fact, or were wandering afar off from the Lord. God makes no mistakes. If you are sick, hurt or going through a bad patch for whatever reason then thank God for it. Maybe the Lord has allowed it to happen so that He may get your attention.

If at the present time you are drifting far away from the Lord and you are not living right before the Lord, then you need to take warning, the Lord could bring you down. Without warning, you might even lose something precious to you, but God needs your attention and He will get it, whatever it takes. You won't be the first; the Bible is full of examples that God has had to deal harshly with to get their attention. Take Jonah for example, running away from God. Even when you are being afflicted, can you say with the Psalmist it has been good for the sole reason of bringing you back to God, that you can once again learn from Him?

Joy comes from God

Psalm 43

"God my exceeding joy: yea, upon the harp will I praise thee, O God my God."
Psalm 43:4

Here the psalmist has many difficulties to deal with. There was an ungodly nation all around him, his enemies seemed to keep raising their ugly heads and deep within himself he seemed to be fighting a depressive spirit. There seemed to be joy missing in his heart. That was until he remembered and thought about God. When he thought on Him and all He meant to him and had done for him, then his heart began to warm as he thought, "God my exceeding joy."

This was not an ordinary joy; it was exceeding joy that can only be found in Christ. It comes with salvation and it comes with seeking after and a longing to know God better. This exceeding joy comes when we meet with God in earnest prayer and meditate upon His precious word. That is why today many of God's children are miserable as they are, just going through the motions of Christian living, starved of God and deep down they are starving for God. Today seek to get back to your first love and get the joy of Christ back in your soul! Remember when you first got saved and you were full of joy, ready to take on the world, ready to witness to anyone and never missed reading your Bible? My friend, if you want joy, real joy, wonderful joy, then not only should you let Jesus come into your heart, but let Him into your life as well.

Would you say you are a joyful Christian?

The lost vision

1 Samuel 3:1-10

"The word of the LORD was precious in those days;
there was no open vision." 1 Samuel 3:1

This is such a short sentence with so much alarming truth contained within its words. Today if there has ever been a day in the history of the Christian church, we have lost the vision. That is the vision for God, the vision for souls and the vision for God to pour out His blessing upon this land. It is no hidden fact that we live in a busy world, therefore there is no point in using that as an excuse, we cannot slow the world down, we have got to accept the fact that this is the way it is.

Many areas are lying spiritually derelict today because even the Christians that live there are so inactive that the local people don't even know they are Christians. Even when there is a gospel mission on where the truth is preached it is only supported by the denomination that is running it. When it is an independent preacher, the denominations don't support it because it is not run by a denomination. Therefore the church is focused on the church and not on Christ and when we take our focus off Christ we therefore have no vision and when we have no vision, the people will perish. What about the souls of men, women and children, dropping into hell everyday because no one seems to care? Do you care? Do you have vision? If you do, don't let your church or denomination stop you from fulfilling your vision and seeing precious souls won for Christ.

The pressure is too much

Psalm 118:1-17

"The LORD is my strength and song, and is become my salvation." Psalm 118:14

I remember as a child growing up on a farm. Every Saturday in the winter the day was spent cleaning out calf and pig houses. The wheel barrow in my opinion is the best invention ever, apart from a toilet. I remember filling the wheel barrow up with dung until no more could fit on it. My dad used to shout and say, "Put less on it and go an extra time." He could see the pressure in my face and the way I would push the wheel barrow wobbling all over the place. Those were good days with lots of fond memories.

However today many are under a lot of pressure from family, finance, relationship, work expectations and the list goes on. Sometimes we can again lose the focus of the Christian and that is Christ the LORD. He takes control of the Christian, we are no longer our own, we are bought with a price, the price of the precious blood of Jesus. Sometimes we find ourselves living beyond our means and much of the pressure is often self inflicted. Whatever the reason for your stress and pressure from whatever form, remember the Lord does give grace and strength to those who ask for it. Go to Him today afresh and bring your worries and pressures before Him. He will hear and answer you, in His own divine way of course.

A natural build up!

Deuteronomy 6:1-9

"And thou shalt love the LORD thy God with all thine heart,
and with all thy soul, and with all thy might." Deuteronomy 6:5

It amazes me how the Lord can speak and challenge us from any part of the Bible. After all, it is His word from beginning to end.

In verse 5 we are challenged to love the Saviour with all our soul, heart and strength. Sometimes we can go through life and only love the Lord half-heartedly. Here we are commanded three times in one verse with the word 'all'; such a small word can make such a big difference.

Then in verse 6, we are encouraged to learn the scriptures. This is how the Lord speaks to us, through reading His Precious Word. Time and time again God emphasises the importance of His truth. His word is final and will never change. If we want to hear from God, then we must search the Scriptures. We don't just want scripture in our head on a Sunday morning, but rather to have it engraved in our hearts.

When we love the Saviour and learn the Scriptures, we will lift up our eyes unto the fields and labour for souls. It is especially important to reach the souls of the children, the rising generation. This surely is the greatest and most important work on earth - to tell children about the Lord Jesus Christ and how He can and will save them from their sin. Grasp every opportunity that comes your way to serve God. Love the Lord, serve Him with all your heart and look forward to the well done of God!

The voice of deceit

Genesis 27:15-22

"The voice *is* Jacob's voice, but the hands *are* the hands of Esau." Genesis 27:22

As we think of children today it is so easy to accuse them of being badly behaved, resentful and not having a care for the things of God. From my experience this is not the case, children generally can behave and have a natural love, respect and care for the things of God. However as they grow older it changes. I believe it is not the children who are at fault but rather the parents.

In this case here with Jacob and Esau it was their mother Rebekah who was the fault to this terrible fall out between Jacob and Esau. She was the one who plotted the plan to have Jacob kill the animal, she would make the meal for Isaac and it was her idea to put the skin around Jacob to make him feel like Esau. The wonderful romantic story of Isaac and Rebekah has now taken a turn. Rebekah has been very deceitful causing bitterness, resentment, anger, lying, and friction between two brothers that led to the thought of murder. Do we ever realise that our scheming, plotting, resentment and hatred to someone can be the actual cause of family members and close friends falling out with and hating each other for the rest of their lives. Jacob and Esau did eventually make up although it was after many years. Rebekah had the power to make or break them when they were young but she favoured one and that is where it all went wrong. Do you have the power and influence to make or break a friendship or relationship? Do it today before it's too late.

Do good to someone today

Psalm 37:1-19

"Trust in the LORD, and do good; so shalt thou dwell in the land,
and verily thou shalt be fed." Psalm 37:3

This is a beautiful Psalm full of instruction for the child of God as are all of the Psalms. Quite often as we grow up we hear all the time about people relying on good works for their salvation, which of course will never save anyone. The Lord talks about our good works without salvation as filthy rags. On the other hand, there are many believers and they hardly ever do a good turn to anyone. In fact if you never saw them dressing up nice on a Sunday to go to church one would hardly even know they are saved. The Bible also talks about how faith without works is dead.

In this Psalm we are encouraged to delight ourselves in the Lord, to wait on the Lord for strength and to completely trust in Him for everything. Many today are often feeling down and depressed. Yes, they have trusted in the Lord for Salvation but have stopped trusting God for His keeping. Christians especially have the whole Bible opened unto them because they can read it and understand; Christians can understand the Bible due to the help given to them by the Holy Spirit. The Word of God is a treasure box of wealth for the child of God, full of promises, instruction and encouragement. We all have a responsibility to build bridges and get over what or who has annoyed us and get on with life and get back to God. Sometimes we continually expect others to do good to us, the Bible tells us to trust and do good, expecting nothing in return.

IMPACT *Daily readings*

The hand of God upon your life

Ecclesiastes 2:24-26

"There is nothing better for a man, ... and that he should make his soul enjoy good in his labour. This also I saw, that it was from the hand of God." Ecc 2:24

How many of us really enjoy our work. Or like so many are we just toiling away, just to get a week's wage. There is probably very little you can do about your job right now as there aren't so many jobs out there. However what can help is, in your job, keep labouring as unto the lord. This is what He would have you to do. The Lord would have you to be content in your labour. He knows all about you and your work. He is with you every minute of every hour of every day. Although maybe there is another reason why you are not happy in your work. Perhaps there is a higher calling; maybe the Lord has you to be miserable for a reason to take you from your work, so you can serve Him. This is when it gets serious, if you are not prepared to give Him your all and answer the call then I suggest you buckle down and be more content with your job.

It is a most wonderful thing when a man is content with his work. To have the full assurance in his heart that that is where the Lord would have him be. To know the hand of the Lord is upon your work and upon your life is surely a most blessed thing and much to be thankful for.

IMPACT *Daily readings*

Never forsaken

Psalm 37:23-31

"Though he fall, he shall not be utterly cast down:
for the LORD upholdeth him with his hand." Psalm 37:24

Over the years and in recent times many a good man and woman have fallen by the way. Once they were going on really well with God, loving His service and walk, but now they have become out of touch with Him and cold at heart! Are you one of these people? I have great news for you today. Even though you may have forsaken the Lord, He has not forsaken you. It is gloriously possible to rise again from your depths of despair, walk again in close fellowship with the Lord and once again do great exploits for Him.

Maybe you are in despair today because of something that is going on in your life or something that has happened. Do not be discouraged. There is forgiveness with God. He will not ignore you, shout at you or fail you in your hour of need. We must come to Him and look to Him afresh! Confess everything, openly and honestly to Him now! It may mean heart searching and heart rending tears, but that's good. All your sin and wrong doing must be brought afresh to Him right now. Your failure will become a victory! Have it all cleansed afresh in the precious blood of Jesus.

Whatever it is that has brought you down and so low, the Lord knows all about it, He holds you in the palm of His hand, protects, cares and provides for you. Don't keep a distance but rather come close to Him again, right here and now. He has not and He will not forsake you.

We can have the victory

Psalm 44:1-8

"Through thee will we push down our enemies:
through thy name will we tread them under that rise up against us." Psalm 44:5

The people of God in the Bible had many enemies. Today the Christian has many enemies and the sooner you realise this the better it will be for you. You cannot and you never will please everyone. If it is your intention to live a life and do something worthwhile for God, then you must expect to make enemies. I have found this to be the case in my life, the more we do for God, then the more enemies we make. Others will be jealous of you, be envious of you and will never understand because it's never been done before and they wonder why you have to be different.

I have found that depending on my own strength is never enough to fight the enemy. Even the psalmist found in the above verse that he could not trust in his bow or sword alone to fight. We must be vigilant at all times, treading carefully, praying and seeking God every day for wisdom and strength. Through Christ we will have the victory and we will push down our enemies! I have found this to be the case many times that the victorious Christian life comes through Christ alone. We may have won today but the battle continues tomorrow! Be constantly watchful as the enemy comes in many forms, shapes and sizes. Be careful who you talk to as they may seem like a friend, but deep down they may be an enemy.

From today watch more carefully for those who may hinder your walk with God.

IMPACT *Daily readings*

Fear of growing old

Psalm 37:23-40

"I have been young, and now am old; yet have I not seen the righteous forsaken, nor his seed begging bread." Psalm 37:25

The Psalmist David enjoyed a long and useful life. The young shepherd boy eventually grew old as is the case with all of us. No-one stays young forever, although we all like to look young and we certainly love to feel young, reality is life's clock continues to tick by. The question is do we accept this or not? I believe it bothers many people; they just don't want to grow old. They seem to think everyone else stays young while they grow old. This is not the case, everyone who was your age in school are the same age as you are today.

As David grew older he relied more and more on the Lord to help, guide and direct him. He trusted in the Lord completely for everything. This is the secret of growing old. Growing old gracefully with the Lord by your side. Every day we live we are one day closer to being with these great saints of old and most of all with the Lord Jesus Himself. Life is too short to continually worry; actual worry will cause you to age faster than you will want to. So instead of worrying about growing old and all the flab and wrinkles that come with it, renew your trust in the Lord completely to guide you along in the later stages of life.

Thanksgiving and praise

Psalm 100

"Enter into his gates with thanksgiving, and into his courts with praise:
be thankful unto him, and bless his name." Psalm 100:4

Sometimes we can have days when we feel particularly down or discouraged. This can be quite common for many people and unfortunate for many people, instead of building a bridge and getting over their problems, they tend to keep lying down and burying themselves in their sorrows. For the child of God, there is an escape route for you when you find yourself down and it is called P & T, praise and thanksgiving. Some people would tell you prayer, well that is well and good, but when you're feeling low, sometimes it's hard to pray. However when you listen to praise and try to recall all the times when God was with you before, then this will lead to thanksgiving and praise which will in turn lead to prayer.

Being thankful is something we tend to forget about sometimes. We tend to ask the Lord for everything instead of being thankful for everything. Especially as things become tough and we find ourselves getting on in life we need to keep thanking God and praising His Name, otherwise we will be all caught up with the cares and woes of this world which are going to be there anyhow. We must focus on the Lord with Thanksgiving and Praise. God is good and He loves it when we praise the name of Jesus.

The birth of Christ

Isaiah 7:14

"Therefore the Lord himself shall give you a sign; Behold, a virgin shall conceive, and bear a son, and shall call his name Immanuel." Isaiah 7:14

It's Christmas morning again for another year! Family, presents and food, lots of food. This is what I remember, this is what I like and this is what I look forward to every year. We like to receive a present to know someone cares for us, we like to see family to know someone loves us and of course we like to see food because well, who doesn't like food. Sometimes we can be so busy and work so hard and be so caught up with everything we can easily miss out on the very reason for Christmas time.

However today is a day we often remember as the incarnation or the birth of Christ. We can often become so caught up with presents and everything that surrounds Christmas that we can miss out on the simple and yet very important reason for Christmas. To celebrate the coming of Jesus Christ into this world, to live and die so that we might live forever with Him. This year take time to reflect on the reason for this beautiful time of year! Love is the greatest gift of all, love comes from God. Remember the reason is because He loved you and gave Himself for you! May your Christmas be even more special for you this year as you think about the gift given to you, the gift of God's dear Son the Lord Jesus Christ! The knowledge of sins forgiven and the assurance of eternal life!

God loves music

Psalm 42

"I went with them to the house of God, with the voice of joy and praise." Psalm 42:4

Have you ever wondered why God mentions praise so much in His Word? Surely the conclusion is that He loves it when we praise Him. It is a good thing to continually sing and praise the Lord. You maybe think you cannot sing, maybe not in the ears of the world, but what about forgetting what others think? From your mouth sing, glorify and worship the Lord! For three months in early 2011, in my busiest year of preaching and ministry, I lost my voice while on a mission trip to Poland. I thought I would never speak again, let alone sing! While we have air in our lungs and sound in our voice, use it to continually praise the name of Jesus.

Have you ever thought about the marvellous construction of the human voice? We may just think that the voice is a very simple part of the body without much detail at all. Well, from reading a little bit about it, I understand that there is more to the sound of our voice than meets the eye? In our throat and lungs there are at least fourteen direct muscles which can make over sixteen thousand different sounds. As well as these there are thirty indirect muscles which can make, it has been estimated, more than one hundred and seventy-three million sounds. When God constructed the human voice, surely He is pleased when we use it for His glory every time we open our mouths to sing.

Learning to leave it with the Lord

Psalm 55

"Cast thy burden upon the LORD, and he shall sustain thee:
he shall never suffer the righteous to be moved." Psalm 55:22

Life today seems to be so busy compared to what it used to be. Although it amazes me that no matter how advanced we become with cars, phones, social net working etc, life seems to be even busier. People don't seem to have the time to talk and visit with each other like they used to, rushing around like headless chickens.

I remember sitting at traffic lights one day being really impatient as I was in such a rush, late for an appointment. Beside me in another car was a man driving with his little boy in the back. How content the child seemed to be, totally trusting in his father with not a care in the world. What a lesson that child taught me, to trust even more, completely in my heavenly Father to look after me no matter where I go. Sometimes life can bring unbelievable pressures upon us, more than we can sometimes bear. This is when we need to learn the valuable lesson of casting our care upon the Lord for He cares for us. Just like the verse for today tells us to do, to cast our burden upon the Lord. He will sustain and look after us. Have you done that today? Try it in prayer right now and enjoy living much more than you have been doing.

Whatever burdens you have, take them to the Lord today, He cares for you!

Cast thy burden upon the Lord

Psalm 55:16-23

"Cast thy burden upon the LORD, and he shall sustain thee." Psalm 55:22

Have you ever been in a position when life seems to be so difficult and all seems to be against you? The burden you have may seem so heavy that you can no longer carry it? There may be something troubling you that maybe nobody knows anything about, an inner struggle, an impossible situation? Then this verse is for you today. Not only are we told to cast our burdens and struggles upon the Lord, but there is a promise that follows this, and that is that the Lord will sustain you. He will help you with your burden, He will not make it impossible for you to bear it, rather He will carry your burden for you.

Christ is the great burden-bearer. Remember burdens are lifted at Calvary where the wonderful work of the cross was completed. He wants you to give your burdens over to Him. God wants us to be direct and honest with Him in prayer. Ask Him now to take your burden from you and if this is not possible then ask the Lord to help you carry your burden. The secret to dealing with all our problems, fears and burdens is to take them to the Lord and leave them there. let God take care of them. So many Christians today are worried, depressed and down in the dumps daily because of the many burdens in their lives. This doesn't have to be the case! Cast your cares, whatever they are upon the Lord and He will help you! He promises to do so, take Him at His word.

From this moment leave your burden with the Lord and see if it makes a difference.

Time to praise the Lord

Psalm 150:1-6
"Let every thing that hath breath praise the LORD. Praise ye the LORD." Psalm 150:6

Sometimes life can go rolling by so quickly, like a child's roundabout, going so fast we can hardly stop it! As a result, our spiritual life and our relationship with God is affected. We find on the Lord's day that it is no different as we rush into church and rush home again to get the spuds and without realising that something has happened! We missed out and forgot to really take time to thank God and to praise His name the way we should have.

As we think of the numerous blessings He has given us, is it selfish of us not to take time to be thankful unto the Lord for absolutely everything we have and are? It is a good habit to thank the Lord every day for something. Even in the difficult times, thank God. No matter how difficult a situation you may find yourself in, give God thanks and work it out together. Look back to see everything He has done for you in the past and look around you to see everything He is doing for you at present. Why then should we worry about the future? Entrust your future entirely into His care and keeping. The more we praise and focus on the Lord, the less we'll worry about ourselves.

Others depend on you

Proverbs 4
"Keep thy heart with all diligence." Proverbs 4:23

There is a saying that the river doesn't rise higher than its source. Without realising it, there are many people in your life who look at you as an example. What you say and do and how you react to a particular situation may have major consequences in other people's lives. With this in mind, it is important that we watch our life and testimony like a hawk. How important it is for us to keep close fellowship with the Lord! If we fail at something, then others may fail too! If we stumble and fall, others who look to us may stumble and fall also.

I remember in November 2011, I went with a team to China to smuggle Bibles from another neighbouring country. It was a really exciting adventure. Would we get stopped at the border or could we pass by without being stopped and searched? We crossed backwards and forwards many times sometimes getting stopped and other times getting through. After being stopped several times it was very discouraging. Stephen, who was the leader of the team, never lost heart once. He was always optimistic! "There's always another time, remember the last time when you did get across" he would say. Even though they would take almost everything, there were always a few Bibles smuggled through. "Focus and be thankful for everyone who makes it," he would say. Others looked to him for leadership and encouragement. If he went down the team would go down. He stayed strong and the whole team was united in their purpose throughout the trip. Others will be watching you today, so be careful and remember the bigger picture all the time.

We are either stepping stones or stumbling blocks.

IMPACT *Daily readings*

Victory in the battle

1 Chronicles 5:18-22

"They cried to God in the battle, and he was entreated of them;
because they put their trust in him." 1 Chronicles 5:20

As we travel through life it can be a constant battle, especially if you don't have many Christian friends to enjoy fellowship with at home, college or work. Therefore it is essential, my friend, that we never leave down our weapons for war. The Word of God must constantly be in our hearts and the praise of God must be forever on our lips.

Take courage today and know that in the battle we can be victorious; the secret in this battle is to know and admit that we cannot fight in our own strength. The enemy is too powerful. The "arm of flesh" will constantly fail us. These valiant men of God of whom we read in our text today "cried to God in the battle." God heard their cry and delivered them

Are you in a battle just now with someone? They appear to be stronger, always having the stronger arm to fight. Take courage from the Psalmist, "This poor man cried, and the Lord heard him, and saved him out of all his troubles" (Psalm 34:6). Another important lesson to learn is that when the battle is at its height, stay close to the Lord. Even though you may be wounded, angry or rejected, stay close to God, the protector of your soul. These men of war of whom we read put their trust in God to help and deliver them and we must do the same.

"The first step on the way to victory is to recognise the enemy"- Corrie Ten Boom.

Other books written by Colin Tinsley

- Bible sword drill
- Bible crossword
- Bible word search
- The story of Creation...for children
- Stepping Stones ... a book to help children grow in their Christian faith
- Helping mum...colouring book
- Helping dad...colouring book
- Jobs...colouring book
- Walking with God...daily devotional for children
- Word search fun
- Crossword fun
- Sport...colouring book
- Tractors and farm machinery...colouring book
- Ways to travel...colouring book
- Cats, dogs and horses...colouring book
- Animals...colouring book
- Impact...daily devotional for adults